P9-CFK-092

Nowhere
Near Normal

Nowhere Near Normal

a memoir of OCD

Traci Foust

GALLERY BOOKS

New York London Toronto Sydney

This work is a memoir. It reflects the author's present recollections of (her) experiences over a period of years. Certain names and identifying characteristics have been changed.

Excerpt from "On the Maypole" from *Blinking with Fists* by Billy Corgan. Copyright © 2004 by Billy Corgan. Reprinted by permission of Faber and Faber, Inc., an affiliate of Farrar, Straus and Giroux, LLC.

Gallery Books
A Division of Simon & Schuster, Inc.
1230 Avenue of the Americas
New York, NY 10020

First Gallery Books hardcover edition April 2011

GALLERY BOOKS and colophon are trademarks of Simon & Schuster, Inc.

For information about special discounts for bulk purchases, please contact Simon & Schuster Special Sales at 1-866-506-1949 or business@simonandschuster.com.

The Simon & Schuster Speakers Bureau can bring authors to your live event. For more information or to book an event contact the Simon & Schuster Speakers Bureau at 1-866-248-3049 or visit our website at www.simonspeakers.com.

Designed by Jaime Putorti

Manufactured in the United States of America

10   9   8   7   6   5   4   3   2   1

Library of Congress Cataloging-in-Publication Data

Foust, Traci.
    Nowhere near normal : a memoir of OCD / Traci Foust.
        p. cm.
1. Foust, Traci—Mental health. 2. Obsessive-compulsive disorder—Patients—California—Biography. I. Title.
    RC533.F86 2011
    362.196'852270092—dc22
    [B]
                                                              2010047289

ISBN 978-1-4391-9250-4
ISBN 978-1-4391-9255-9 (ebook)

To Max

für alles

You do not merely stretch rhino leather over your own fair skin, for that would deflect pleasure as well as pain, and you do not permit your being to turn stinking inside a shell, but what you do is swirl yourself in the toughness of dreams.

—TOM ROBBINS, *EVEN COWGIRLS GET THE BLUES*

part one

I'd rather tell you a story about someone else.

—KURT COBAIN

1

then, us

Mixing blood with rose oil
We are leaving too soon,
To make new friends we shall not remember.
—BILLY CORGAN, "ON THE MAYPOLE"

The day my mother said we were moving out of my father's house and not taking my father with us, I worried about two things: how many people in my family I would poison with the bologna in the refrigerator, and would we still be able to use the pool at our neighborhood swim club if we weren't part of the neighborhood anymore?

But before any of these questions could be answered I needed to get all the way through Queen's "We Will Rock You" while bouncing on my brother's pogo stick without making the record skip, without worrying about contaminating his favorite toy by the filth and neglect of my hands. Bologna sandwiches came from pigs who hung in a line, their innards hollowed and ruined. I'd seen this on the tour of my mom's work. She brought me to the San Jose Meat Company a few times, once to show me file cabinets and typewriters, once to show me how the animals don't feel a thing after the blood is drained from their bodies. I told my mom both outings were equally fun, but what I didn't tell her was that the shoe booties and hair covers I had to put on before I could follow one of the butchers into the slaughterhouse confirmed what I already felt to be true—the air around a dead animal is nothing to fool with. The germs can cause stomach viruses and send people to a watery diarrhea death, like in our *Family Guide to Health and First Aid*, where it said babies who are vomiting should be weighed every half hour and their skin should be pulled to check for signs of dehydration. Plus, there was also the *National Geographic* in my ENT's office with pictures of dry-lipped kids drinking dirty water from tin cups—and the next picture showed the rotting body of a bull or a wildebeest or something—and the next picture was of a butcher slicing meat and smiling at a mom with her baby at his counter. I don't think the mom and the baby knew that they were connected to the decaying carcass.

I knew. Even when I tried so hard not to think about deadly bacteria, I knew it was still out there. If you don't stay on top of all the things that can rip a family apart, it's the same as doing the ripping with your own filthy hands. Along with never missing an episode of *Project UFO* or *60 Minutes*, I read a lot of stuff that other seven-year-olds (unless they were already declaring their ColecoVisions to be outdated) wrinkled their noses at or considered to be super retarded. I went on faith that the words I didn't understand in the article about the bad water would in no way contradict what the pictures were telling me. I paid extra special attention to sentences conveying how *the government was unwilling to open its eyes* and that *it could be anyone, anywhere, at any time.* But with my pogo stick and Freddie Mercury and my mom saying we all had to have a serious talk, I completely forgot to double wrap the lunchmeat after I made myself a sandwich. Maybe I got a little too into pretending I was onstage with Queen to care about my family getting sick. Maybe it wasn't me forgetting.

Is there a difference between careless and selfish? I knew never in a million years would Queen ask me to be onstage with them. I didn't really know how to play an instrument. My last year of piano lessons had been spent sitting around my music teacher's house upset about something, a dull but persistent pressure in my abdomen every time I was asked to demonstrate how I'd been practicing at home. And plus, even if Queen did kind of like my style and said come to Hollywood or wherever they lived, who would get to see me onstage? My family would be under the dirt at the graveyard—white ribs and a little bit of back muscle like the picture in the magazine.

Because I didn't love them enough to check the bologna.

Because my mom said get off the pogo stick and turn that shit on the stereo down. She needed to talk to us about how we would no longer be living with my father.

"What do you mean?" I asked. "Living here?" I pointed to lots of wicker and a gold pleather footstool. "Like living here with Daddy?"

"That's right," she answered, "like living here with Daddy. That isn't going to be us anymore."

My older sister had just started smoking and had developed his scary gag/cough reflex that sometimes made it hard for me to sit next to her without thinking about napkins. "I knew it," she said. Gag/cough. She was also crying. "Oh, I just knew it. I could see the signs." She looked past me and asked my brother, "Didn't you just know it? Oh man, I knew it all along." Of course all of us had seen it coming. Some of us had even wanted it.

My brother shrugged. "I guess. So where will we be?"

"We'll be in our own place." My mom tilted her chin up and blew out the smoke from her cigarette. "We're moving to the Apartments," she said. "The ones by Lucky's."

Everyone knew the Arbol Verde Apartments by Lucky's supermarket. We called them only "the Apartments." South San Jose wasn't big in the seventies for condos and high-rises. New cul-de-sacs and hilly old roads wrapped around mosaics of nuclear family tract houses with Spanish exteriors. Palm trees and rock gardens shared earthquake cracks with giant redwoods. Every corner of every road in our Silicon

Valley neighborhood was a swirl of sacrifice and urgency. The Apartments sounded fine but I did have some recreational concerns. "Can we still swim at the club?" I asked.

My mom said no. "We won't be going there anymore."

"Why? That doesn't sound fair," I said. "Why can't we keep going to the club?"

"Because I just told you why. The Apartments have their own swimming pool. A nice one."

The Rancho Santa Teresa Swim & Racquet Club had nice pools too. It had animal crackers in the vending machines and moms with tan lines whose husbands worked on computers. My older brother, Bryan, said the moms were just begging for it. I knew *it* without an explanation after the word meant having to do with your clothes off, but I didn't care about that right now. I just wanted to make sure we could still go swimming.

"Plus we'll be saving money on those club fees," my mom said, her dark eyes flushed in a pink dew like an almost-sickness. A corner of a penciled eyebrow had been smudged a little. "No, swimming at the Apartments will suit us just fine."

In my head I saw the word *us*—people together. But my mom's *us* made me think of fingers spreading apart, pulling and reaching until everything was unconnected. Would my dad still be an *us* if we got divorced? I imagined myself walking to school and having to pass the Rancho Club when I wasn't allowed in there anymore. The begging-for-it moms looked at me from the sliver of shade below their sun visors. Sorry, Traci, you are no longer welcome here to swim and eat animal crackers in the kiddie pool when you think no one is looking because you have to have a dad to belong here. You guys aren't an *us* anymore. I cracked my knuckles, the grease of open-chested animals still glistening on my fingers.

My sister swung her arms around my mother's neck. "Oh, Mommy! I'm so, so sorry. Mommy, I don't know what to say."

"You don't have to say anything, honey. Good Lord, Kim, watch the cigarette." My mom's arm shot up at my sister's sudden outburst. "Look, everyone. I just want us all to be calm about this." She stroked the head of her oldest child. Seeing my fifteen-year-old sister cry like that gave me a cramping sensation right above my intestines.

My brother asked if we were moving in with Frank Ranaldo, my mom's boyfriend. But we weren't really supposed to know about Frank Ranaldo so he put his head down fast, his smooth black bangs falling into his face.

"We're moving in with Grammie," my mom said.

"That'll be kind of fun," I answered. "We can all be together and never run out of fried chicken." My grandmother was broad shoul-dered and loud and used phrases like a cowboy who is pissed off about whatever cowboys get pissed off about. Heat. Stolen horses, maybe.

"Hold on," Kim said. "Is Grammie going to live with us or are we going to live with Grammie?"

"What difference does that make?" my mom answered. "We're going to move into the Apartments and everything will be good."

"Well, if it's Grammie who's coming to live with us, then fine, what-ever," Kim said. "But if it's us going to live with Grammie . . ."

Then no more pot smoking in the house and no more boyfriend spending the night for you, sister. But it also meant soap operas for me and Spam sandwiches for me and games of Scrabble for me, which I won the last time because I did not overlook the silent *P* in *pneumonia*. There would be no more of my dad in a tizzy if I wanted to spray the doorknobs with Lysol and no more of him saying I wasn't talking like a person who is right should be talking just because I tried to educate him on lurking microbes when I told him about a movie we watched in health class on the importance of hand washing and hygenic food storage, and how bathroom germs can sometimes turn into a squiggly cartoon man in a derby hat and walk with a briefcase right into your nose, where he will later decide to move into your lungs, where he will later laugh heartily and give a thumbs-up while you lie in a hospital bed with an expression that is also squiggly to indicate you are feverish/confused/guilty about not wrapping up the bologna.

We heard my dad come in through the garage door.

"He doesn't know I'm telling you guys," my mom whispered. She grabbed my hand and kissed my fingers hard. "Shush it, okay?"

I couldn't stop myself from smiling and nodding like we were playing a fun and secret game.

One of the first things my father did when he came home from working his printing press was to take a bar of Lava soap and try not to get ink poisoning. "If you don't take care of those cuts on your hands," my mom would tell him, "that ink's going to kill you."

Sometimes when I sat with my dad during his Mutual of Omaha nature shows I would look at his hands for a long time, the blue paper cuts in his skin like cartoon veins.

"Hi, everyone," he said. He took off his glasses and rubbed the bridge of his nose. "Oh boy, what are we all doing sitting on the couch without the television on? Did it break?" My father set his lunch box on the kitchen table. The clank of the metal on Formica made me think of him at work, smiling while he ate his hard salami sandwich, proud of his good life. "So what's going on here?"

"What do you mean?" my mom answered. "Aren't we allowed to just sit around?"

Sometimes on those nature-show afternoons with my father's paper cuts and the stupid salmon leaping right to their death in a bear's mouth, I would close my eyes and dream of little fountain pens swimming through my dad's blood. The pens were fat, with rubber finger grips, like from my Calligraphy in Twenty Easy Lessons kit. I imagined the pens puncturing his hairy arms like grizzly teeth: *here comes the danger you've been warned about but chose to ignore.* When the ink reached his heart it made a stream of words.

You

Are

Now

Killed.

"Why does there have to be something going on?" my mom said. "We're just taking a break here. Catching our breaths." She stood and wiped a cube of ash from her blue polyester pants. "Just sitting and chatting. No law against that, right, Ted?"

I wasn't really sure what could be causing the burning sensations around my heart, but I definitely understood that nothing good ever comes from hearing your name at the end of a sentence.

———

In my sister's new metallic gold Camaro, I rode down the street with Bryan and Kim. We listened to Aerosmith and I tried to feel the fun in being treated by my big sister to ice cream at Thrifty's. I knew we were supposed to be giving my mom and dad time to talk and yell and say *asshole* and *selfish bitch* because I carefully watched my sister's face in the rearview mirror. When you're taking someone to get ice cream just for fun you don't keep mumbling and shaking your head like you're asking yourself a question and telling yourself no.

"What do you think is going to happen now?" I asked.

Bryan looked out the window. From my spot in the backseat I watched the bar-code shadows of giant cypress bushes speed past the reflection of his face. "Yeah, what do you think we should do?" he asked.

Our sister had an answer that involved all of us watching our step and not acting up.

Bryan said he didn't do anything wrong, and while I picked at an interesting scab on my elbow, he turned to me and said it was probably my fault.

"What do you mean?" I asked, but kind of knowing. "What's my fault?"

"You're the one who's always throwing big fits about everything," he said. "You're the one who made a thing about the orange juice this morning and made Mom say she needed to go for a calm-down walk."

"Well, I just didn't want paper floating around in my drink," I said.

"Orange juice pulp is not what paper is made from."

"It still looks kind of dangerous." I lifted the scab slowly and liked the way the pink string of skin was still a part of me but wouldn't be for long. "I could've choked. Stuff floating around in my breakfast. I don't want that."

"Yeah, but I told you, juice pulp and paper pulp are two different things," Bryan said. "I told you that. But you had to cry and spaz around anyway." To my sister he said, "She saw on *Mr. Rogers* how paper is made and now she thinks someone is putting paper pulp in her juice." He leaned back. "See, it's not me, it's her."

The teenage girl with the driver's permit who still called our mom Mommy and had just finished getting her head stroked because our family was breaking up asked me, didn't I think I was too big to be watching *Mr. Rogers*?

"I'm so sure. It wasn't *Mr. Rogers*," I said. Although I could recite the lines to almost any medical show, new or syndicated, my science programs were pretty much limited to *Lost in Space*. "It was that one show with that guy," I said, "and there's this big thing."

Bryan crinkled up his nose. "You mean Doctor Bunsen Burner?"

"Yeah, I think—yeah, Doctor Bunsman or whatever."

"Oh my God! I totally just caught you right now!" Bryan clapped his hands. Hooray for Bryan. "I just made that up. I seriously just made that up right now. There is no Doctor Bunsen Burner. Ha-ha. Are you retarded?"

Kim laughed too.

"See. Do you see what I mean?" Bryan said. "It's because she lies and makes things up all the time."

I pulled at my scab until I felt nothing. "Not all the time," I said. I could've told my brother I was actually (maybe a little bit) positive it wasn't paper floating around in my breakfast—even though it could have been—and that I was sorry about my mom needing to go out-side because she said she couldn't handle me starting in with her this morning, and I saw how the blue veins in her hands were so close to the surface like they always were when I couldn't get my head to calm down. I couldn't say to anyone, "Something's telling me I'm going to choke." If I told my brother the voice in my mind said, *Drink that juice and see how you stop breathing,* he would have looked at me the same way everyone did when I wasn't making any sense, like when you have no idea what someone is trying to say but you know it has to do with you messing up.

Before you could get to Thrifty's you had to pass the sago palm walkway of the main entrance to the Apartments—the place that would soon be our new home without our dad. The car slowed. Our heads turned at the same time like we'd been rehearsing this move for show. I thought about what I could do to help the situation—to at least not make it any worse. What if I didn't get my favorite Mint 'N Chip double scoop in a sugar cone? Maybe I could do that while watch-ing Kim and Bryan eat their ice creams and I wouldn't say anything about how hungry I was or how my throat burned, and if my stomach started growling I could wrap my arms around my abdomen and apply a sufficient amount of pressure, then maybe cough a little to help them understand I was trying.

Except that somehow my ice cream appeared in my hand, melty green and needing me. I wiped the rim of the cone with a napkin, then tried to toss the napkin directly into the trash without missing. If I got it on the first try it would mean no one in my family would get a fever or be too sad and experience acute stages of anxiety or depression over moving out. But the lid was one of those swingy lids, so the weight of my pitiful girly throw wasn't enough to make it move. And now look, I couldn't pick up the napkin from the floor due to Thrifty's being a public place, which meant the floor was also public.

"I have to be outside," I said, because there just wasn't a time when I could remember not being upset over dirt and germs and the possibility that death can arise from these things. At some point, the faces of those around you will let you know regular people don't worry about stuff like this. You see your brother's open mouth and the way his eyebrows arch down hard when you start crying in the middle of *Cheech and Chong: Up in Smoke* and you have to leave the movie theater because you just overheard the man behind you telling his wife he hopes the blood tests come out okay and when you turned around to look at the sick and inconsiderate man he was so obviously full of fever you could almost see in your mind how fatal those blood tests were going to be. You hear your sister sighing about having to run out of Thrifty's because even though you can never let anyone know about the voices in your head that tell you to wash and scrub or there will be hospital consequences, you realize you'll have to find a secret yet thorough way to calm yourself down. People may die because of you. There is no way to *not* do something about that. *Get away from the tightness, say something funny so it looks like you're not crazy. Run away. Stay.*

"Hey, I know what," I said. "We could go to the Apartments and walk around like we already live there. We'll pretend like we just bought the swimming pool and if we see someone standing around by it we can say, 'Oh no you don't. We own this pool now. Sorry, you'll have to go to the club.'"

"That's gay and stupid," Bryan said. "How come you always like to do stupid things?"

———————

Is it evil and are you a terrible person if you're kind of excited to pack up your stuff and move into a place where your dad won't be? Kim said not really. "But it's nothing to be dancing around about either."

"I wasn't dancing," I told her. "I have sharp and persistent pains in my back from bending down to label all my boxes."

"Why do you have to play music when it's not a good time? You're not even supposed to be getting into the records without asking."

"Everyone's busy." Plus, was I really going to bother my parents with the Captain and Tenille when their fifteen-year marriage had been reduced to a rented flatbed truck with my piss-stained mattress in the back?

"Well, turn it off," Kim said. She sat on her bed with her knees pulled up to her chest, clutching her old Raggedy Ann doll in a way that made me think of a show I watched about a brain-damaged foster child whose real mother tried to kill her by putting fabric softener in her bottle. "It's not the thing to do right now. Not like we're having a party or something."

So I did. And then I wondered what was the matter with me because I had fibbed. I had in fact been doing bad stuff in my room. I was a liar because I was supposed to be sad but instead I was pretending to dance with Andy Costa, the fourth-grade boy who came to my class once a week to help kids who were *struggling horribly in mathematics and should be tested for special academic programs (thank you, Mrs. Foust, I look forward to our meeting).* I thought about how he held his pencil the wrong way and how he looked liked Will from *Land of the Lost* and the way he said, "See, you know what you're doing, silly" while my hands shook through an addition problem with two rows of nervous and uneven numbers.

Beautiful Andy had come into my room to help me through this sad and horrible time. Even though the real Andy Costa didn't resemble the crown molding on my door frame, I went ahead and let him kiss me on the mouth and agreed that, yes, maybe it would make me feel better if we danced and moved in a very romantic way like Sandy and Danny did on *Grease*. But now I was disgusting and sweaty because I had been in my room begging for *it* with my wall while my poor sister turned to Raggedy Ann for comfort.

I climbed onto her bed and sat next to her. I hugged my knees like she did. When she breathed hard and said, "What a weird day," I said that too. From the doorway we could see everything that was going on in the hall and clear into the living room. We could even see into part of the kitchen. In a California ranch house, if you want to be in every room you only have to be in one room. To know the secrets of a home, you only have to live there.

I tried to remind Kim how much fun it was going to be sharing a room with me in the new place. "Like a slumber party," I said.

"Uh-huh." She put her chin on Raggedy Ann. "Weird how Mom and Dad are saying please and thank you so much to each other today."

In the hall our parents passed each other like friends at school. My mother said, "Oh, don't worry about it, that's fine." She carried a laundry basket with the giant abalone ashtray. The cord from the Mr. Coffee dangled over the side, trailing behind her like the arm of a skeleton baby who needed something.

I went on: "Plus, in our new room we can pretend like we're at camp. We can build a fort and we'll—"

"You know what?" Kim closed her eyes. "You're going to have to get real, Little Miss. I mean, you just have no clue, huh?"

I shrugged.

"So, okay, you know that Mom and Dad aren't going to be living together anymore, right?"

I nodded. "That's why the boxes and stuff. That's what divorce means. Sometimes it's also called a trial separation," I said.

She squinted her eyes and tilted her head in a way that made me go back and say my last sentence in my head, just to make sure I hadn't said something completely different than what I wanted to say. That sort of thing happened a lot.

"Uh, right. But you don't seem like you're really understanding. You're like dancing around and stuff. Mom was crying this morning. Did you know that?"

Nope. "Of course I know that." But hadn't we watched our mother cry for a while now? We all knew it was because of something our dad did. She always said it was because of something our dad did. Were kids supposed to do something when their moms cried? Some people have empathy. Some people make out with their door frame and pretend it's a beautiful boy.

And something else: I couldn't tell my sister, but I often dreamed of a world where my dad wasn't. Where no one told my mom to shut it about what a great president Kennedy was and why didn't she move to San Francisco with her Jewish best friend, who of course was a lesbian with that haircut; then they could do a lesbian march and say it was not against God to kill babies. I wanted to jump on my sister's bed like I always did while she played her Kiss records and remind her that we would never have to go through another Christmas Eve watching our parents throw giant Styrofoam candy canes at each other on account of women who were not Italian like my dad's mom couldn't really make spinach manicotti the way it's supposed to be made and my dad should just spend Christmas at his parents' since he was such a sonofabitch mama's boy. I just couldn't see a whole lot wrong with keeping my dad in a handy spot of my life for when I needed rides to the library and ice-cream-man money, but with enough separate time so I could call the Kaiser help nurse whenever I needed to ask if she thought the air conditioner in my Brownie troop leader's home was a possible cause for my constant ear infections.

I guess I was supposed to be feeling as awful as Kim and her shaky voice, but the Apartments were only around the corner from our little green house on Camino Verde. My dad would still be living there until the house sold. My uncle Tony would still come over to spend the night and he and my father would still marinate artichoke hearts and go deer hunting and tease me, saying they caught Bambi while I laughed and laughed, thinking how disgustingly funny it would be to see stupid Bambi lying in my uncle's pickup truck all gutted and lame with a look on his face like he totally wasn't expecting that. All of my cousins would still come over and we'd watch *Saturday Night Live* and I would still do my Gilda Radner impersonation and me and my best cousin, Theresa, would lip-synch "Bennie and the Jets" into the vacuum handle for one of our shows.

But Kim didn't look like any of that stuff was going to happen. Maybe she already knew how much time and money would be involved in a grown-up getting his life back on track and the right he has to be happy and the women and the discos that were going to help him get to that point.

"Go finish your boxes," my sister said, "and don't do anything bad for the rest of the day."

Andy Costa wasn't in my room when I returned. My father was. He was ready to yell. "I thought we had an agreement?"

When I breathed in something felt hot and undone.

"I told you, three by three," he said. "Three boxes completely finished by three o'clock."

This was the easiest way to give me directions: write them down in my ledger book and make sure I read it back to you. If five math problems need to be done by five, be very specific about it. Seven bites of tuna casserole by seven? Is that seven in the morning or seven in the evening—better make that clear. If there are going to be numbers, put them as close as you can to the left-hand column of the paper. Are the numbers even? Do they have an even amount of straight lines and circles? I'll have a better chance of getting things done if the numbers are even. Or three. Three was always even, to me. My special made-up even number. Just the way nine would later be, dominant with its perfect fat head and straight spine. You ask nine first. If nine doesn't know, there's always three.

Two boxes of Legos to be picked up by 2 P.M. One chance to shut my smart-ass mouth.

One spanking.

I looked at the ledger. *3 P.M.: Three boxes of toys packed and labeled.*

"So you've pretty much done nothing all morning but dance around." My dad started throwing things in boxes. Unorganized things: dominos and Barbies were placed next to my Spirograph artwork. My Flintstones Colorforms just thrown in with my Weeble Wobbles. Word-search magazines in the same box as all of my Beverly Cleary books. Socks. My Holly Hobbie nightgown smooshed in between my *Jesus Christ Superstar* album and my jar of Noxzema that I was only allowed to sniff and not use because most creams gave me a rash. A different box, *a completely separate box* for my Barbies' clothes—totally different from the box where I carefully stacked all my Barbies. Was he drunk?

"Wait, that's not right." I cracked my knuckles, tried to exhale. My cat Sprinkles hightailed it out of a milk crate when a bag of Lite Brite pegs landed on him. "Where's my Weeble Wobble tree house? It was here in this corner. Where did it go?"

"Goddammit, Traci, I got way more important things to do than worry about a damn tree house." A Lucky Strike dangled from the corner of my father's mouth, his big hazel eyes pinched against the smoke. "We have that truck rented for two hours. This is goddamn bullshit in here. Twenty-five-dollar deposit and here you are with nothing. Get some pants on, for Christ's sake."

"I have pants on."

He yanked up my nightgown. "Then why the hell are you still in your pajamas? Can't you even get dressed without a big production? Hand me that pen." He wrote on my boxes, in the places where I had already listed my item. In a matter of seconds, *Very Breakable Perfume Bottles* and *Books You Can't Read Unless You Ask Me First* were reduced to *T's Bedroom*. From my doorway my mom asked if I had a fever. "Come here," she said to me. "Get your hair out of your mouth and come here. Why do you look so red?"

"Carole, for Christ's sake," my dad said. "She's been fiddling around all morning. Not a damn thing done in here."

My mom bent down to feel my forehead. "Are you warm? You feel warm."

"Kind of," I said. "I didn't make my three by three. I think I do have a fever." I clutched my mom's blouse and crumpled some of it into my mouth. Through the fabric I mumbled, "Maybe I should take a baby aspirin." This was kind of our little thing, her letting me talk into her clothes when we didn't want my dad to hear what we were saying.

"Well, let's just wait and see. Get yourself out of your nightie and then we'll see how you feel."

Among the chaos and disgrace of Carly Simon mixed in with old crayons that I only used to pretend like I was smoking, my ears rang. The glands on the sides of my neck felt swollen. Where was my goddamn Weeble Wobble tree house? I sat on the floor and pulled my nightgown over my knees. I stuck my head into the neck opening. Everything was mismatched, disconnected. My peripheral vision shrank until it felt like I was looking down at my white belly through one of those telescopes on the pier in San Francisco where you can put a quarter in to see light gray and regular gray.

My brother asked which boxes he was supposed to take to the truck.

"All of them, I guess," I answered into my nightie. "I sure wish I knew where that tree house was."

As Bryan lifted and stacked without me helping, I watched my dad's writing bounce in the air and into the hallway. *T's Bedroom*. In the beautiful penmanship of someone who wasn't me. His printing was perfect, each letter a dance in a long gown. The leg of his *R's* curled up at the right foot, his *T's* looped on top like a sewing needle for a princess with a secret. I would spend the better part of my paper-trail life trying to emulate the way a pen in his left hand was certainly just an extension of other things he was meant to do.

"Are you going to help?" Bryan asked. "Or are you just going to spaz around and be in the way?"

For me, cursive would always be a series of stuck and anxious letters, my ambidextrous hands never making up their mind. Place this here. No, place this here. That's not right. One unsteady grip after the other.

"I don't know," I said. "I'll probably just be in the way."

2

almost skipping generations

You don't hate their evil. You hate the good in them you can't
understand. You hate the good in them you can't get at.
—JOHN STEINBECK, *EAST OF EDEN*

In our new small apartment, I was big. There was hardly any space and I took up most of it. I played Blondie and Gary Newman loud on Kim's stereo and memorized every lyric to every song that made my grandmother say, "That don't make a lick of sense."

I danced around the linoleum of our tiny kitchen with boys in my mind and a stuffed-animal audience who never got up to check on the roast. I bumped into the pieces of furniture Grammie had brought with her from her trailer in the desert, from her apartment in the city—from all the places where she had loved the men and the scenery.

My mom held up a monkey made from dried cactus leaves and said, "This just screams class, doesn't it?"

Grammie pointed to a birdcage with a fern trying to get out of it and said she didn't understand why tree huggers liked this sort of thing. "You're either inside or you're outside," she said. "Everyone wants everything all at once, don't they?"

Though it had been almost a full year since we moved without my father, my mom used the phrase *temporary situation* a lot.

The swamp of each other gave me some sort of counterbalance against myself. Aggravation and exhaustion is what I understood: when you're nervous all the time, you want deep breaths in places where no one can breathe.

On Saturday mornings I pirouetted in my rainbow kneesocks and waited for my father to pick me up, the ink smearing under the sweaty grip of my latest spelling test—my 100 percent, all correct, even I-S-T-H-M-U-S, spelling test. Maybe I couldn't add without using my fingers, but getting into kindergarten just before I turned four and zooming through everything Shel Silverstein by age five fueled me with a super-hero confidence I could only find in words. No matter how many times I washed my hands, or how I fixated on numbers equaling the power of evil or the intent of redemption, time and again it would be books that eased me away from myself. The clean sound of a typewriter bell at the end of a perfect sentence, the soft electricity of a blank page—all of it meant you could rearrange things how you wanted them, invent a place where everything was in order. And if you screwed everything up, all you had to do was rip out the page and start over.

"Your father's here," my mother said, but I had already heard our truck—*his* truck, the sound of the engine like someone calling my name.

"Hi, Ted," my mom said. She handed him pillows and duffel bags. "Everyone's ready."

"Good deal. Let's hit the road."

My parents talked in clean and weird sentences now, orders being given without screaming, taken without cussing.

"Make sure she keeps her jacket on, Ted. Watch that she uses her Kleenex or she'll be wanting to wash her sleeves later."

"Sure, Carole. See you Sunday."

"I stuck the baby aspirin in her pillowcase. She's got tons of math homework to catch up on. Make sure Bryan gets to Little League practice on time."

"Yep. We'll get it finished. See you. Have a good weekend." Porch. Car. Front door. Truck. The routine in those steps made it easier not to get a stomachache. I liked it when my dad parked his truck with the passenger-side door facing the curb. Just before I walked outside I said in my mind, *If the car is parked the way I like it, I won't feel sick tonight when it's time to go to bed.* This one time, after he'd bought a new Cadillac and called to say he was just going to honk, so we'd better be ready, I told my mom I wasn't going to his house if he didn't park right.

"Park right?" she asked. "What's that supposed to mean?"

But there was no way I was going to tell her how right-side curb parking made me relax. Though there was no explanation, and I could actually feel my brain moving when I tried to figure out the reason why it calmed me to see my dad's car parked the way I liked it, I knew the whole idea of even caring about curbs was totally off. Plus, she was putting on her makeup, getting ready to see Frank Ranaldo.

"Park right or park left," she said. "I don't give a damn how he parks; just make sure you've got everything."

I watched as she dabbed concealer under the thin skin around her eyes. She winked at me from the bathroom mirror. On Friday nights my mother looked as if the week had mashed her up just enough so she'd have to put a little effort into getting excited about me and Bryan leaving for our dad's house. When she looked at me I could almost feel the weight of her false lashes. "I got everything," I answered, then nothing else. Weekends with my father would have to start in whichever direction I was told to get into the car.

On Halloween my dad took us all, no matter if my sister's new boyfriend was almost exactly like Peter Frampton or not, to the pumpkin patch behind the 76 gas station. In a yellow field surrounded by foothills and freeways, we acted up, wanted to be there, didn't want to be there. We chose pumpkins that helped us to understand our father wasn't made of money, then took them back to our old house so he could carve them.

Now Dad had roommates. Our old rooms filled with other people's things.

"What do you want your pumpkin to look like?" he asked me. I stood at the doorway to the bedroom I used to have all to myself. Smells of menthol cigarettes and Nair. Smells that weren't mine. My yellow paisley curtains pulled open with ugly green rope things. "Mean," I said. "Make mine really mean and scary looking. Make it evil."

At night, back at our apartment without my father, I looked at my pumpkin on the bedside table. A sad nervousness crept through me, telling me to do stuff.

Stay quiet. Count.

Be loud. Check.

Some nights I got up and walked around in the blue light of television coming from almost every room. When we lived with my dad he always said, "A house is like a ship. You open one door, you automatically close it behind you. A light goes on to enter—a light goes off to leave." But my mother was determined to no longer be sealed up in a sonofabitch cave, and left everything on if she damn well pleased because goddammit, who was going to stop her?

Maybe me. I sneaked out of bed to check outlets and appliances. I wasn't exactly sure how electrical currents worked—the working part having to do with what I guessed was electricity coming through the walls, the not-knowing-for-sure part having to do with being placed in an after-school science and math tutoring program where the kids chewed the strings of their sweatshirts and one boyish girl went out of her way to explain in detail to me what a cunt was and what she could do to mine if I would just raise my hand and say I had to go to the bathroom—but what I pretty much got out of those afternoons of fleece suckling and trembling was that electrical things were dangerous.

Unplugged electrical things, not so much.

Yes, alarm clocks will not go off and automatic coffeemakers will not start whatever it is they do to make coffee, but you just have to not worry about the tears in your mom's eyes when she tries to explain that she will be fired from her job if she's late one more time, and yeah, the spanking may sting a little or the way she calls you a smart-ass know-it-all when you suggest she buy an alarm clock that uses batteries, but you have to think about everyone's safety—about getting your brain to authorize some sleep.

In the winter months the battleship lungs of the San Francisco Bay exhaled over our city and my job got a little harder. Electric floor heaters were left on all night, which made my cheeks red, but because my mother had a bad morning cough and was susceptible to chest colds—two packs a day of Merit 100's having nothing to do with this—we had turned into a family without limits. No one again would tell us how wasteful we were.

"It's hotter than hell in here," Grammie said.

"I know," was my mother's answer. "I like it this way."

If I didn't get up and unplug appliances/check all the outlets/check around the outlets for debris igniting material, I would lie in my bed and watch the whole what-if scene unfold: my mother screaming, reaching over the fireman's shoulder while he held her back from her world gone up in flames, the stupid and lazy daughter fleeing the scene in a dirty nightgown.

The first time my mom caught me trying out these new safety measures was the night of a small earthquake. Only a four point something—the usual lamp swing and odd angle of fingerprints on a door frame—but I went to bed with the idea that the San Andreas fault had pushed up our carpet just enough so that the tip of each fiber was certainly touching all the floor heaters.

She came into the living room for her *Cosmopolitan* and her lighter. I was halfway under the sofa with the magnifying glass from my Nancy Drew detective kit. "What are you doing down there?" she asked. Her hair was rolled in pink curlers. One fell to the ground when she bent to an angle to look at my face.

"Kim said she lost the back to an earring somewhere around here,"
I lied.

"And you're helping her find it?"

"Yeah. Trying to."

"I see."

That, combined with her not offering to help, meant I'd been caught.
I stood up from my spot on the floor and straightened out my nightgown. "I don't know. I was just fooling around or whatever because
I couldn't sleep." A lie that wasn't one entirely. My mom was used to
catching me prowling around the apartment when I was supposed to
be dreaming about pancakes or unicorns or whatever regular eight-
year-old girls dream about. My excuses ranged from seeing the face of
a robber in my window to if sunlight really did kill the influenza virus
did that mean it was waiting for us to go to bed so we could breathe it
in and give it life?

Whatever story I came up with to cover my inabilities to ignore
the voices of *check this, check that* in my head, I made sure each clever
anecdote ended in the fail-safe harmony of a stomachache.

"It feels like butterflies, but worse. Like throw-up butterflies."

My mom pressed her hand against both our foreheads (mine was
to check for a fever, hers to sigh and smooth away the deep lines of her
brow so I would not forget that single moms have to work so much
overtime and it's worse if they have a lot of backaches and female problems and children who won't stay in bed).

But every now and again—and if I held my stomach enough,
brought my knees up to my chest and made gagging noises like any
minute I would let loose all over my Strawberry Shortcake comforter,
if I could show a legitimate physical illness, she would pull my blanket
up to my chin and wrap it around me and munch-kiss my neck and
call me her sack of sweet potatoes. I learned early on that tummy aches
worked well for the times I needed my mother to hold me without telling me how tired she was or how tired I was making her. People tend
to love you more if they can see you hurting on the outside because

you're afraid you may vomit instead of screaming on the inside because you're afraid you may have just contracted polio from a doorknob. Mom sighed; she was tired, she was used to me not sleeping. But I couldn't bring myself to let her in on what was so hard for her to see since single moms have to work so much overtime, and they have lots of backaches and female problems. It was the same strategy I used with the kids in my new apartment complex: say nothing about the crazy things you are thinking and they'll hear you thinking nothing. If that doesn't work, avoid everyone. Actually, I sometimes thought it very clever on my part, kind of Jodie Foster in *The Little Girl Who Lived Down the Lane*, that I had lived in my new place for a over a year and still managed to completely avoid talking to children who I knew didn't want to talk to me—who I almost didn't want to talk to either. I had my books, my ledgers with poems and new words and directions. I had hard crushes on the lyrics of David Bowie and thought I'd like to run away with the boy who answered my mom's ad on the laundry room bulletin board for a math tutor. He wore Le Tigre shirts in colors that made me taste spumoni and got paid three bucks an hour to drill multiplication facts into my head.

"Let me borrow your calculator watch," I said.

"No, I can't. My dad will get mad."

"Hey, you want to see this dance I made up to 'Fly Robin Fly'? It's cool because in the dance you don't know if I'm a ballerina or a bird."

"Not really. Let's look at this quiz I made for you."

"Did you know when you can't have children the word is *barren*, but not like the kind that flies a plane?"

It only took two weeks for my mom to go back to sitting at the kitchen table with me and a pack of flash cards. She waved her cigarette smoke from my face and said to stop crying because she had things to do and wouldn't it be nice if just this one night she could watch her shows?

Friday afternoons I went to my cousin Theresa's house to work on long division. Here was an adult-free zone where grandmothers didn't live and brothers did things after school and it was plain to see that absolutely no math would be taking place. In the safety of minimal supervision I talked my cousin into making me garlic-and-grilled-cheese sandwiches while I prank called as many teachers as I could find in the Santa Clara County white pages. One afternoon Theresa was supposed to be boiling pigs' feet to start my uncle Tony's special marinara sauce, while I was to work on correcting red-check-marked problems from the morning's math quiz. But we spotted *The Exorcist* on top of the VCR.

"I don't think we're supposed to," Theresa said quickly. She twirled her hair with her finger and read the back cover. "Yeah, see—no, I definitely don't want to." My cousin was almost two years older than me, but it seemed as if I was always waiting for her to get around to my corruption. Instead, she minded her parents, finished all her homework, and when her older brothers said, "Hey, Moose, looks like you're putting the laundry away," she walked down the hall with the towels folded in threes.

"No one's here to stop us," I said, "and no one's going to tell, either."

When we were about halfway into Linda's Blair's vaginal Jesus, Theresa ran into the bathroom and made sounds from her throat like a harbor seal. She lifted her head up from the toilet and said we should call someone because she had a bad feeling.

"Call who?" I asked. "What's the matter with you? We're not doing anything wrong." I know I should've helped my cousin with her pretty blond hair and her dry heaves, but there was a spinning head on the television. A horrible, wonderful spinning head. "It's just a movie," I said, but it would be only a few hours later, alone in my evening bath with the memory of rising beds and backward sentences that the truth would become so clear. It wasn't just a movie. It was a sign. And I was a sign seeker. If I had a stomachache and saw the number 10, say on a receipt or a piece of mail, and if the 1 was written too close to the 0 it made the number look sort of like a person with a disgusting growth or fetus in their abdomen, and if I kept seeing the number it meant my stomachache would turn into a viral intestinal flu and I would wake up from red nausea dreams, crying for my mother to please come and rub my back.

"Tell God not to make me throw up," I would say, frantically rubbing the collar of her nightgown between my thumb and forefinger, her cigarette and hair spray smells softening the droning metal in my head.

There in the too-hot bathwater, I decided the similarities between me and the *Exorcist* girl were an eerie but definite match: Linda Blair's character, Regan, pissed on the floor in front of a bunch of her mother's friends. One of the friends was a priest. I wet my bed at least twice a week. Not in front of clergy, but there was a framed picture of the Virgin Mary in our hallway. Plus, in the movie, Regan's room was always freezing because I guess when you have a lot of demons inside you and they're trying to come out, it's supposed to make you feverish and you need the window open all night. I always kicked my covers off and so many nights awoke in sweat to the point of having to change my clothes.

I climbed out of the bathtub and watched my reflection in the mirror as I dried and dressed myself. Dark, snaggly hair. Pale skin. Crusty, chapped lips. Did I look like a girl who had bad spirits in her body? Pretty much. But was there really something so horrible about trying to accept my fate?

"I'm telling Mom," Bryan said. "You can't go around saying things like that. You can't tell people the devil whispers things into your ear. Plus, who said you could watch that movie?"

"*I* said could," I answered. "And you're stupid because it's not that bad, really. It's not like I've got a rare but contagious case of leprosy. It's just . . . powers."

I brushed my bangs down over my too-big forehead and watched my older brother in the mirror behind me. He wasn't smiling. I should've chosen different words to explain the strength of honest sin, but so what if I wanted to snarl and show my teeth? Didn't he realize, like I was beginning to, that something had always been wrong? Even if I was so good at keeping it all hidden: *"Because I've been on the monkey bars all day, that's why my fingers are all sore and bloody."* Even if no one ever questioned why I was always worried about us not having enough Ajax, then maybe it was okay that I started to accept the darker side of things. Maybe I had always been the winged dog on the roof of a haunted house. Why should my brother be surprised? I wasn't.

For the past year or so I'd been getting drunk on Stevie Nicks and long flowing skirts. I read *Lois the Witch* and *Sleeping Beauty* until I completely sided with Maleficent and thought Aurora to be a bumbling idiot with her stupid tiptoes and handbaskets. Under the influence of bad I felt good. And pretty. Instead of dirty and tangled, my hair was bewitching. Where the cadaver lines of my spine stuck out under my T-shirt, where my knees protracted and my knuckles ached to be cracked—that's where I sprang up like a cat and crawled down like a spider.

In *The Exorcist*, Linda Blair made her furniture move and smacked her mom until her nose bled. I walked around at night preventing fires. If I didn't prevent them, wasn't that kind of the same as having the evil required to make them?

"But I don't really think you're evil," my brother said. "Who thinks you're evil? Not me. I just think you're a little bit stupid."

I was quiet for a minute then thought, *If I hit him in the face with my brush, he would probably show me all he knows about half nelsons.*

"I've never thought you were like the devil or bad spirits or whatever," he said. "Mostly you act like someone who's been in a bad car accident or like this movie we watched in Family Ed about people who do a lot of angel dust and stuff; they're like—you know, they're not really stupid. They're just not . . . all the way there. Like you."

I ran to my room and cried into my pillow.

What an ass my brother was. *Someone who's been in a car accident?* Why had I even bothered telling him anything that required a thought outside of *Gomer Pyle* reruns? We're talking about a fourteen-year-old boy who didn't even bother to hide the fact that he was playing with his privates the whole time we were watching *The Blue Lagoon*.

I sobbed as quietly as I could until Sean Cassidy came to rub my back and tell me he was going to make Bryan apologize. "But Sean, if it's not the devil," I whispered, "then what is it?" He promised we would figure it all out later. But even after Sean was done touching my face and kissing me seductively, I just couldn't stop thinking about all those stupid things Bryan said. An hour ago I had an answer. I came home from Theresa's with a certainty like the moment before fitting the last piece of a jigsaw puzzle. Okay, so green puke and feeding tubes meant that being possessed wasn't going to be elegant, but it didn't seem fatal either, not like if you had a brain tumor or something. I had watched the movie until the end, even when Theresa went into her room to fiddle around with her rosary beads. I wanted to see what would happen because I just knew— I *knew* Regan would be all right. With holy words and church water, the priests helped her through her ordeal. They died at the end, yeah, but still—I wanted to be a part of that, of a manifestation bigger than the mixed-up words in my head. The gripping fear of knowing something is wrong with you, but having to stay put in the safety of silence, feels like the whole world with furious hands pressed against your throat. A sky without air. Nothing good ever came from me; why did it have to be so bad if I was willing to accept that? I sometimes wished I could get possessed so that someone would look at the way my nervous pulse ran into my ears and made my hands shake when I couldn't keep my mind quiet.

"Well, no wonder," they would say. "Why didn't we see this all along?"

The week I turned nine I decided to go ahead with the screenplay I'd been working on. Sitting tight on presenting myself as a demon debutante seemed like a good idea until I could know for sure. I wrote little poems about *girls who could fly and boys who would cry and all the lights would flicker whenever I walked by*, but when my mother read them, the best she could come up with was "Sounds very Irish."

"It's about witches."

"I know that," she answered. "It's really spooky." But the way she said *spooky*, with her eyebrows all raised, then combining that with Ireland, made me think of a smiley-face ghost in a Crayola graveyard and the Lucky Charms guy.

I went through my ledgers and ripped out poems about unicorns or anything that had my favored and repeated line: *Heaven above / The one I love.* Nine-year-olds shouldn't be thinking about crap this gay. I felt ashamed and silly and flushed a whole bunch of ripped paper down the toilet, making a whirlpool of baby talk in blue water. Nine was too big to be acting like an idiot, and if I wanted certain things out of my almost-double-digit life, I would have to do the required work. From Woody Allen movies and Andy Warhol books I began to realize that marrying the most famous playwright in New York City—who that was, I had no idea—required I learn the proper techniques on black turtlenecks and French kissing. Just as securing a spot in *Parade* magazine as the Bay Area's Freshest Young Writer probably involved good writing. And a great story. It was time to buckle down and get myself a really good disease.

"You need what?" my grandmother asked. "A disease? What the hell for?" She made a part down the middle of my head with her ratting comb and sighed and reminded me for the love of Pete not to speak in riddles. She was just too worn out today.

"It's for the movie I'm writing," I said. "I'm going to send it to ABC Television." I waited for her to say something. "The offices for ABC are in Hollywood."

She used the hard pointy end of her comb to trek through my knots. "What the hell is this? It sure don't look like you washed a lick of your hair this morning."

I shrugged. "Hmm. I'm pretty sure I did." I was positive I didn't. There had been the promise of my favorite French braids, which I was supposed to prepare for this morning with a good slather of crème rinse. But I ran into a little problem with the alphabet. See, last night there were six bottles of hair care products in the one shower we all shared. Gee Your Hair Smells Terrific had to be the first in line—obviously, the *G* in *Gee* coming before the *W* in *Wella*. I made sure of this myself last night before I went to bed so I could make my shower a fun and safe thing to do right away when I got up.

But someone came along and erased everything I did. The crème rinse had been thrown away, right there in the yellow wicker trash basket with a balled-up maxi pad and a wad of my mom's black hair. I was left with five bottles. Five.

I didn't like five. Five was uneven with a weird square head and an unfinished body.

"I need the disease for my screenplay," I said, then told my grandmother all about my idea for a made-for-television movie dealing with issues concerning young people today. "I'm calling it *Debbie Is Pregnant and Not Married.*"

"Yeah, that sounds about right," Grammie said.

"See, the main character—that would be Debbie—she's going to have something really bad happen to her after she has the baby. I want a disease that's totally disgusting. Something with pus, maybe even seizures. Seizures would be cool."

She pulled my head back hard. "What the hell is going on here with your hair?" She yanked up my elbow and sniffed the air around my armpit. "What is this shit? You didn't even take a shower at all this morning, did you? I heard the water running and saw you—what the hell were you doing in there?"

"I, uh, well—I was going to tell you . . ." that the only thing I could do after I discovered all that chaos with the bottles and the uneven five was just stand around in the bathroom. I ran the water. I got naked. I splashed a little Mr. Bubble on the top of my head, but I was all alone in there with five and the messed-up alphabet. "I don't know. I'm sorry. I guess I was just singing or whatever and forgot to wash."

What else was there? I certainly wasn't going to tell my grandmother that if I got into the shower with all that unrest someone in my family would get sick or hurt. Maybe something bad would even happen to me, like I'd come down with a mysterious skin disease, rocks and knobs popping out all over my body like in the Elephant Man because just the idea of surrounding myself with that kind of craziness gave me fluttering chest pains and numbness in my lower extremities.

Or what about this: let's just say you get into that shower, washing and smiling, and maybe Rick Springfield is in there with you and the shower is actually a waterfall that you and Rick spotted on your honeymoon in Hawaii, but you have to push your new husband's hands away from your privates because your brain is reminding you to be careful, pay attention, or you'll stop breathing and faint in the steam. No one would even start to look for you until after *The Phil Donahue Show*, so your lungs would pretty much be filled up with water, and cardiopulmonary resuscitation at that point? Completely useless. Plus, isn't that kind of like suicide? Since your brain already cautioned you about your carelessness and you totally chose to ignore the warnings? How would your mom go to work and be responsible for almost everything since your dad seems to be backing out on a lot of his promises, and how would she ever get a parking space with her name on it, because they just don't do things like that for secretaries, no matter how sexy they are, plus the sexiness of your mom would probably wear off from so much crying because her daughter had problems that weren't dealt with. Also, how would you finish *Debbie Is Pregnant and Not Married* if you're dead and full of water?

I had to make a decision and I made it: a bright and shiny scalp was not necessary for a future of the same dynamics. What I really needed was a good disease.

"Why not just let poor Debbie be?" Grammie said. "If you're writing a story about a teenage kid having a kid, then I think that's enough all by itself. You don't got to throw something terminal in there."

"Oh, oh, wait a second." *Terminal.* Did I know that word? I did. I traced out the letters in the palm of my hand: T-E-R-M-I-N-A-L. I liked how the *nal* at the end sounded like *null.* Null and void, life over. Plus, eight letters. Nice and even.

Man, did my grandmother know her med talk. She was a diabetic with high blood pressure and asthma. Every day I watched her and saw all the remedies she needed just to stay alive. Things you *have* to have or you won't live. Can you imagine? Oh, those little cans of mist to inhale, syringes with real needles and their vials of fluid like caught and perfect raindrops. There were creams that smelled like chewed gum and cloth patches with little rulers on them that had to be worn under her left boob. There was a pee-pee strip with a fun assortment of colored boxes to dip in your urine so you could get an idea of how many good years you had left in your kidneys, something like that. My diabetic grandmother used them to get an idea of how many Ding Dongs she could have before bed.

"All right then," she said, "if you're just a-hell-bent on this disease, give me a minute to think here." She worked my braids too hard, stretching all the way to my temples with the strength she maybe forgot about with all that medicine. "So this disease, guess it can't be nothing like the flu or nothing, right? Got to be way worse than that?"

"You got it," I answered. "Way, *way* worse." Surely someone who lived through the Great Depression and the dust bowl deaths of the Southern Plains knew a thing or two about hardship. So that she could better grasp my devotion to the project, I said, "I've been at this screenplay for more than three hours now. I feel really committed."

Three hours. It was the longest I'd given my attention to any one project without a Kleenex. "Come on, Grammie," I said. "Something bad—I mean, real bad, something you almost never recover from."

She lit up a Salem and misted my head with No More Tangles. Then she told me to choose cancer.

"No, that's retarded," I said. "Cancer's not really not all that pretty." This I knew from my mother's tumory friend from Oakland who came to our house and brought us all Rainbow Club T-shirts. She insisted on celebrating the end of herself by refusing to wear bandanas over her scary poisoned head and said the removal of her uterus was the most liberating thing she had ever experienced.

No, cancer would never do. I needed something life threatening for sure but that could still give a terminally ill girl plenty of room to look into the camera, kind of glistening with death sweat while her father, who happened to be feeling very guilty over so many things he couldn't even separate them all, sat next to her hospital bed and wept.

"Well, hell, then, I don't know what it is you want," Grammie said. "You make my brain hurt."

I said, "Tell me a story about when you were growing up. You know, when Hoover took the country to hell in a handbasket. Tell me—then I can get some ideas."

She laughed. Her laughs were wet. "Well, one thing's for sure, ain't nothing could've been a more terrible disease than the Hoover administration. Never thought we was going to pull ourselves out of that one."

"And the dust storms," I reminded her. "The dust storms too."

"Sweet God in heaven, never thought them would end neither." And what came next was the familiar tale of when my grandmother was little, before her neon-flowered muumuus and *The Price Is Right*, when she was Fannie May Yandall and had a pretty sister named Violet who all the boys liked, but Fannie May didn't care because she wore overalls and had fast feet and threw left hooks better than any boy even though she was right-handed.

When I asked my grammie if she hated her mother, she flat-out always told me no.

"But didn't Grandma Ruby gamble away a bunch of your money and crush up poppies so she could smoke them with the Indians?"

"It was some kind of illness," Grammie always said, "just something not wired right in her brain. But now, Daddy, he was a real easygoing fellow. He was a land surveyor and he rode all over the plains on a horse. He had a pistol in one hand and a Swiss Army knife strapped to his leg."

Daddy and his easygoingness and Swiss Army knife strapped to his leg showed up in just about every story my grammie told. Neat enough, I guess, but I really wanted to hear more about "the time when your daddy had to leave on a long trip and you and Auntie Violet were all alone with your mom and she ran off to stay at an Indian reservation and you guys were little and all alone."

"Yeah," Grammie said. "She pulled stunts like that all the time."

"And then you told your daddy when he got home and your mom was acting like nothing happened and your dad was all, 'Oh, my girls are silly.'"

"Mmm-huh, he said that."

"And then your mom said if you guys told any more lies she would sell you to the Gypsies." Though I saw very little threat in getting to roam the countryside with monkeys and sparkly scarves, I felt sorry for my grammie just the same. "Then what about that time she dropped you facedown on a hot griddle? You were, like, five or something."

"Hell. That was—yeah, I was five."

I wanted to, but I never asked my grandmother if she was pushed onto that griddle.

"And then didn't your daddy spread Crisco over your burns and tell you not to cry and tell you to be thankful for all that you had?"

"He was always telling us to be thankful."

I tried to drawl a twang like my grammie's when I imitated her father: "'Now lookie here, Fannie May, you oughtta be on your knees just a-thankin' Jesus for everything, 'cause some people, they got nothing.' Didn't he say it like that all the time?"

Grammie shook her head. Sometimes it was hard to tell if she was doing that because she couldn't believe how funny I was or how hard everything else was. "You got it. That's what he said all the time. Be thankful for all that you have."

But when all they had was covered in a billow of dust, my grammie and her family would have to move away from the iron maiden skies of Oklahoma and practice being thankful in St. Louis. There my great-grandmother Ruby would trade in her Indian chiefs for jazz musicians and her peace pipes for syringes of heroin.

Just before Ruby Yandall died she wrote a letter to the FBI and put it in an envelope without an address. The letter said she was ready to give up.

"Well, it was a cryin' shame, is what it was," Grammie said, and when she starts talking about her mom being all paranoid about the cops and the FBI, I can hear the sudden shadow of her voice, like that one second just before the BART train glides into the tunnel through the bay and everything gets dark, just before you realize you are under the cold Pacific and the train is a filthy sea monster holding its breath. "She was in her basement," Grammie continued, "living in there, didn't never want to come out of that damn basement. She took her radio apart and threw her television off a two-story balcony. I'd just bought her that damn TV too. Big one. I don't know how she carried that damn thing up the stairs all by herself. She was little, like you, little bones and stuff, but she done it, carried that TV, just a-screaming that the law was after her."

"God, how scary," I said. How almost gorgeous.

"We was all set to make her go to the hospital, but by the time we got there—"

"She was already dead by then, huh?"

Grammie paused before answering, "Just a-worn out from all that craziness, I guess."

Then I got a little dizzy from the thought that my great-grandmother tried to light her own eyeballs on fire before she died.

Grammie said, "Yeah, she took matches to them, pupils all scarred, eyelashes all singed."

How? How does someone hold their eyelids down on a flame long enough to ignite their corneas?

My grandmother was quiet, which normally I didn't like, but it was okay for just a second so I could think about this woman—this tired and sick woman who I had never met and had only seen one picture of. In a creased and musty photograph she's maybe forty or so, with thick hair piled in a big loose bun, messy, like how I wore my buns. The old picture shows her in a doorway of what looks like a tiny log cabin, porch all shabby with a bunch of empty and cracked flowerpots. She's in a sleeveless dress and an apron. Her body has strict angles. She's got her arms folded in front of her and you can see where the lines tighten next to her muscles. She's looking off to the side of an ugly porch, like someone just called her name. *Ruby!*

Grammie said she never smiled for pictures on account of her teeth were bad. In the photo there's no way to tell what color her eyes were before the lit matches.

"All right. I'm through now," Grammie said about my hair. "Go busy yourself."

I ran my hands over the tightness of the braids. I liked it when they felt like ropes. "But hold on. I still don't have a good disease for Debbie."

Grammie didn't answer. She straightened out her tenty muumuu and walked into the living room. On the television I could hear the opening song to *The Courtship of Eddie's Father: People, let me tell you 'bout my best friend: / He's a warmhearted person who'll love me till the end.*

In the mirror over the dresser I saw my big head and my own bad teeth. I wasn't a best friend. If I truly was anyone other than me, I would tell my grammie how sorry I was that she had to grow up the way she did. I would've told her that maybe people can't always help it when they do crazy things like spray their clothes with Lysol because they're afraid the coughing toddler who was in line next to them at Kmart may have had tonsilitis. Now, I would've never thrown a perfectly good television out of a window, but I could kind of see myself having a kid who gets burned on a hot griddle.

Just before my grammie's rear reached her favorite spot on the gold and green sofa, she yelled down the hallway: "If you really want something interesting, why not make the baby be born with some awful disease and let poor Debbie have a rest? She's already gonna be in for a lifetime of hardship being a teenage mom and all."

I heard my breath get caught in my throat. "Yeah, uh, I'll try that out. Sounds not too bad." I didn't actually say the word *brilliant*, but I could almost see it on the wall above her head. As I walked back to my bedroom my peripheral vision showed me glitter.

I sat down at my grandmother's sewing table, which doubled as my writing desk. Outside the bedroom window I watched the first solid signs of autumn. My season. Giant sequoias spread their fairy gold shadows across the cracks in the sidewalks—this is how I felt even and grounded: between muted light and sea clouds smearing up the foothills with their criminal thumbprints. I thought about what Grammie said as I stared into the keys of my IBM daisy wheel, my birthday present. I pictured myself in the important offices of ABC Television. The ones in Hollywood. I sat in a leather chair in front of a desk without a sewing machine in it, not a single stitch of macramé in the whole place. The men who present me with money for my script and the women who whisper in the hallway, "Is that her?" have never accepted Sloppy Joes wrapped in tortillas as a suitable lunch.

Give the baby a disease.

I'd seen *It's Alive* about a half dozen times, and *Rosemary's Baby* was one of the films I'd quoted when I practiced auditions in the bathroom. I was pretty versed on the shame and heartache of a labor and delivery gone wrong.

DEBBIE
(*Closes eyes, head falls back on pillow*)
Doctor, is it okay? Is it a boy or a girl? Why isn't it crying?

NURSE ONE
(*Gasps in horror, eyes wide*)

NURSE TWO
(*Runs out of the delivery room screaming*)

DEBBIE
Will someone please tell me what's going on? What's wrong with my baby?

DOCTOR
(*Pulls off surgical mask. Scared look on face, raises head*)
Dear God in heaven, please tell me it isn't true. Please tell me that this child is not the son of S————

But I couldn't type that word. The S word. I mean, of course I could spell it, punch the typewriter keys, semantics, whatever. I just couldn't put that word on paper—I couldn't look at it.

This is what was supposed to be living inside of me, making me do and say things like a girl in a movie about possession or someone who'd been in a bad car accident. I turned in my chair, feeling like someone was standing behind me. *Type it. See what happens. See who gets sick and who dies.*

I paced the room and cracked my knuckles. I thought about that night after I watched *The Exorcist* and how I was so ready to affirm myself as bad, how tall I was in the mirror, explaining to my worried brother my plan about accepting my wicked affliction. And now, when I truly needed to not be scared, when I needed the art of just enough evil to finish my screenplay, to follow through, I couldn't summon it. I was back to being the paranoid, stupid girl Bryan called "not all the way there."

"Fuck this," I said, loud enough to give my spine a tingle and raise tears in my eyes. I pulled hard on my braids, then ripped the paper from my typewriter. I'd have to go back to my original plan for making Debbie sick after she has the baby. I would just have to will myself to stay seated.

Type.

Stop crying.

You're not a baby!

I leaned back in my chair and closed my eyes. "Please God," I whispered. "Please, please just let me finish this. I've made such a stupid big deal about this play: please make me think of some good ideas. Please, please, give me a really good disease."

3

killing misty

The correct spelling of nuisance is n-u-i-s-a-n-c-e.
—SPEAK & SPELL

For three days in a row I've been hanging out at the playground of our apartment complex, scanning the scene for potential friends, rocking back and forth on a metal pigeon with a fat spring where his penis should have been. When I got tired of the pigeon, and didn't see anyone who looked interested in being my friend, I pressed my stomach into a rubber swing seat and flew myself until I almost threw up my Chef Boyardee. Each time I caught sight of a skateboard or a faded sneaker by the chain-link fence I said, "Hey there."

Some kids stopped.

Most didn't.

At the end of the day I left the playground, sweaty and annoyed. I sniffed my fingers. They smelled like bathroom pipes.

Of course this new fascination with strangers and seeing if I could get someone to hang out with me wasn't entirely my own idea. I mean yeah, okay, over the last year I had experienced some thoughts about trying to be a nicer person, but more along the lines of writing poems to my mom's sponsor kid about how I understood life must be terrible for her, and that living in America with access to Pepsi and clean towels whenever I wanted wasn't really as great as it seemed. Shoving me out into the world for friends was kind of everyone's doing but mine.

"When someone comes to the door and asks if you can play," Grammie said, "I don't care if they do have a runny nose. You're a-gonna do something else besides having the TV and that typewriter a-goin' all day."

Sure, Theresa played with me, but the relative thing made that kind of by default, so she didn't really count as a friend. Plus, she had chronic bronchitis and was always coughing all over my stuff. When I asked her to rinse out her mouth with a little peroxide or help me spray my Judy Blume books with Lysol, she wouldn't do it. Even when I explained very nicely and slowly about the definition of the word *airborne* she didn't seem to care. Instead she threatened to walk home and take back her Fleetwood Mac album if I didn't stop talking about tuberculosis.

Sometimes I wondered what she would say if I told her I couldn't stop. What if I told her that I knew it was stupid to think about bits of lung lining getting caught in between the pages of *Blubber*, even though I guess letting her hold one of my books would not get me sick, but still, what if it did? Even though I knew it wouldn't.

But what if it did?

I had no idea that making friends would involve so much actual interaction with other people. But it was explained to me that my grandma needed a little time away from kids—away from me—during the day: snapping green beans without someone who needed to wipe their hands after each bean. There just had to be an easier way for all meat and starches to occur right at six o'clock. The way my dad liked it when my parents were married—the way my mom still had to have it.

"And try not to come back until you've spent some time playing with someone nice."

That was the easier way.

I spun around on the swings and pretended the split ends of my dull brown hair were the just-born baby spiders from *Charlotte's Web* who flew away laughing before they even realized their mother had died. I could see my ugly fingers bent around the chains. My cuticles looked diseased from so much hand washing. Scrubbing with nail brushes, with toothbrushes and scouring pads, made them blister and bubble. *I'm an old lady*, I said in my mind. *I'm a witch with baby spiders in my hair and my hands are creepy.* That's when I saw her. I got off the swing and walked toward the legs sticking out from under the slide. She was playing with a Barbie and eating a slice of bread.

"Hey," I asked, "who are you?"

"Misty," she said. She had a brown shiny face. "Who are you?"

By the unidentified stains on her My Little Pony T-shirt and her two missing front teeth, she was clearly a few years younger than me—making her seven or eight, and therefore not worthy of a proper introduction. But within three or so minutes I knew these things: Misty Salvano lived in apartment H-3; she was not allowed to watch *The Wizard of Oz* on cable the previous night on account of God; and her mother made homemade bread from scratch because American women were lazy when it came to caring for their families.

I put my hand on my hip and didn't even flinch when she asked if I could move so she could get to the seesaw. I just couldn't walk away. I'd never seen anyone eat a slice of bread for a snack before.

When I was four I squeezed a kitten so hard I almost killed it. The one thing I can tell you about that incident is I'm pretty certain I was not trying to crunch the kitten's ribs or pop her little heart. But I never ever forgot how the might of all that helplessness felt in my palm.

Misty looked nothing like a kitten. Though she was younger than me, she was taller, with smooth black hair and an accent that demanded the tip of her tongue stick out between her teeth on words that began with *th*. Her long toes hung over her pink flip-flops and she had something like a warm sofa smell to her, like what I imagined her apartment to smell like—with all those baked goods from her mother's un-American oven.

The first day Misty came over we played Kitchen. We mixed water and grass blades and tanbark in my miniature Corningware. She didn't even raise an eyebrow when I asked if she would use a fingernail brush before she touched my Easy-Bake oven. When my mom came in and pretended to smell something delectable, Misty told me I was so lucky to have a mom who looked like Cher. "I wish my mom was that pretty," she said.

The next time Misty came over we played Hospital. I taped safety pins and strings of yarn to her scrawny arms and told her there was no hope. "Try and make yourself cry," I said.

But she didn't want to. She said she wanted to go home. Maybe she wanted some bread.

There were days of beauty parlor and *Charlie's Angels*. Some afternoons we waited until my grammie had enough of her game shows—when her sleepy head bobbled back against the sofa, we'd prop up pillows at the kitchen table and play Boyfriends at the Bar. Sometimes we loved and kissed the pillows. Once I saw Misty stick out her tongue so that the salamander tip of it touched deep into the fibers of my pink pillowcase, the one with the mushrooms and the little frogs that looked like they were dreaming about something. I saw her tongue press into a frog. It touched places where saliva could stay, where if you had, say, the influenza germ in your spit, (or the kissing disease like Kyle Gaines gave to my sister), it would stick there. When I asked Misty to please take that pillowcase home to wash she said fine, no problem. She even waved 'bye to me, her silky black hair bouncing like the name of a fairy-tale pony above the jasmine-lined walkway in front of our building.

Sometimes when Misty left I got this knotty feeling in my stomach, kind of like hunger but without wanting food. The time between dinner and being sent to bed was filled with the chance of things going wrong. Maybe my mom would check the mail and see that my dad hadn't sent the child support yet, or my brother might want to watch reruns of *Hogan's Heroes* instead of doing my math homework for me, or what if everyone was exhausted on account of my being up all night again licking the window locks so that no one would break into the apartment and kill my whole family?

Once, after telling Misty 'bye, my mom asked if I knew when eight o'clock was.

"Yeah," I said. "It's when *Happy Days* starts."

"Happy days for me maybe," she said. "Because you will be in bed by eight and you will stay in your bed." My mom had a way of saying things that I would normally find super funny if someone else were saying them.

Sometimes my grammie added: "And don't ask for any of my M&M's—there ain't gonna be none if you get up and an' prance around the whole damn place. You're gonna do what you're being told. You're to stay in your bed. No reason we got to put up with your horseshit all night."

What a dumb thing to say. So what if I had to get up and lick all the locks? Big deal. Besides, no one knew I was actually *licking* the stupid things; they all thought I just liked to check them. And plus, it didn't take all night to run my tongue over what, the five window locks in our tiny apartment. Of course I never expected my mom or my grandmother—anyone, really—to understand that what I was doing could help save their lives. *Sort of* save their lives, I guess. I mean, you have to lick the locks before you go to bed, otherwise how can you send out the message to God, or whoever it is that's in charge of stuff, that you're paying attention? Somebody or something in your head told you to lick those locks, said if you didn't do it robbers would come in and murder your whole family. So you do what you're told to do, to shut up those clicks in your brain. *Click, click* behind your eyes. You do it to make those clicks softer—until the edges float away from you. You do it because no matter what anyone says, you love your family, you love your mom, and you're sorry about her having to work a bunch of overtime as a secretary for a company that doesn't appreciate her. You do it because nothing for you will ever quiet down if you don't do it, and then for sure you're never getting to bed. You do it *or else.*

When the days started to get hotter, Misty and I stayed inside with *The Brady Bunch* and air-conditioning. We got into my sister's Rod Stewart albums, sang "Maggie May" and played guitar with tennis rackets. Then this happened: Misty looked under my bed and discovered my Speak & Spell, and my mom saw that the girl had a knack for words and made a comment about her being advanced for her age.

That's about the time I remembered the kitten.

The things I excelled at in school were stomachaches and spelling. I was pretty good at dodgeball—it felt so right to get points for aggression—but spelling was my thing. My life changed the day my mom brought home Speak & Spell, a purse-size computer game that knew words I didn't, but which it was willing to teach me through a series of questions and buttons.

He was beautiful. Polished orange, with a dark display window similar to the glasses Eric Estrada wore in *CHiPs*. I named him Ram, after Sara Crewe's Hindu gentleman from *A Little Princess.* I wrapped my fingers around his handle and turned him on. He asked me to spell *astronaut.* He asked me to spell *comfortable.* After each word he said, "You are correct!" in a voice that sounded like an android who knew all about feelings. Each time I heard his praises a hot surge of completion hit me in the heart.

Ram and I walked around like lovers. I took him to the dinner table, to the bathroom, propped him up in my bed at night. In the dark of the room I shared with my sister, surrounded by posters of John Travolta and Avon perfume figurines, I'd lie with him. The pretty glow of his display screen lit up my face. He would ask me to spell out a word and just before I pressed the Enter button I asked a question about myself: "Ram, I'm the best speller in the whole world, huh?"

"You are correct!"

"Ram, lots of people think I'm the smartest, prettiest girl ever, right?"

"You are correct."

"Ram, don't you think I should marry Scott Baio?"

But isn't it funny how easy it is to get all caught up in our silly triumphs? Maybe I had become too comfortable with my life, with Misty and how good I felt when we were together, how I could go for days without checking that the dish towels weren't too close to the stove burners or asking my mother for my just-in-case baby aspirin. I grew settled under the influence of playing with my new friend all day, then retreating to the comfort of a strong vocabulary in the evening.

See that? I wasn't watching. And when you're smiling at the butterflies above your head there's a set of white knuckles clutching very close by—a tiny tug and *wham*! Your mom is giggling with some yeasty little girl, telling her how smart she is, and the machine you thought you knew is telling someone else that they *are correct*!

"That's good, Misty," my mother said. "V-o-l-c-a-n-o. You're right. And *volcano* is a pretty tough word." She was on the sofa. She had her arm around that girl.

"I should try a harder word," Misty said, "like *daffodil*. I missed that on a spelling test once."

I tugged on my pigtails and turned to Grammie, who was in the kitchen with her onions and Hamburger Helper. "Volcano? Daffodil?" I whispered. "Is she kidding? Those are like the easiest words on the face of the planet."

But Grammie didn't have much to say. My chest felt funny. I said Misty was making it hard for me to breathe. I was offered some mentholated rub and a Spam sandwich.

The next time Misty came over I told her my Speak & Spell had been taken away by the FBI because someone tried to spell out the words *humping* and *butthole* and those words were against the law and shouldn't be on a kids' toy.

She pressed her skinny hand against her chest. "Well, I know *I* didn't try to spell words like that," she said. Then she suggested we play Kitchen again. "I can show you how to make homemade noodles."

I thought about the possibilities of noodles for a minute. "Let's go outside," I said. I took my grammie's duplicate car key from under her Wayne Newton ashtray. "I know something we can play."

As I pushed Misty on my skateboard toward the back parking lot of our building she kept saying, "It's so hot! Hot, hot, hot like a boiling pot, pot, pot."

"Hey, that's pretty good. You should write that one down for Ram."

But she didn't ask who Ram was. The wind was in her eyes. Maybe she smelled how the eucalyptus trees heated up the back walkway and turned the asphalt into good medicine. When we stopped, her face was all scrunched up. "I'm not allowed back here."

"Why?" I asked. "Nothing's wrong with back here." In fact, "back here" was kind of a handy place. Tucked away against the brown stucco of the A through F buildings, it was perfect for teenagers—especially my sister—who were always on the lookout for make-out and marijuana places. Boys peed in the ivy and sage clumps, and I sometimes dumped my mom's disgusting watercress sandwiches in there before school.

As Misty wondered aloud if she should go back home I made a few mental check notes: Keys? Check. Electric locks that could only be controlled from the driver's-side lock panel made more impossible to figure out by the combination of panic and a sweltering day—no matter how many times my mom said, "She's so advanced"?

Check.

I opened the door to my grammie's white Monte Carlo. A swell of jellied heat smacked us in the face when we got into the car. Misty didn't even ask why we were doing this.

I gripped the steering wheel and asked her if she'd ever been to Disneyland. "Because that's where we're going. I'm the mom and you're the daughter who just got all A's on her report card so I'm taking you someplace special. Somewhere you've always wanted to go."

"Beep! Beep!" Misty said and pushed her palm against the dashboard. "Never been to Disneyland. No sirree. Never been to Disneyland, no, not me." She giggled at her cleverness and shrugged her shoulders. "It's a rhyming day today."

My stomach unknotted.

"Well, then, strap yourself in and let's take a spin! Mickey Mouse, here we come."

But Misty didn't want to see Mickey Mouse. "I sorta like Goofy," she said. "I've always wanted to see Goofy."

"Goofy, really?"

I tried to hide my disgust and confusion. Had she never heard of Cinderella or Snow White? Goofy wasn't fun.

Misty wiped her sweaty face with the apron of her sundress and mentioned again about the heat. "How hot do you suppose it is? Let's roll down these windows."

She touched buttons.

"They don't work unless the car is on," I said.

"Whew. Then let's get going." She said it weird, like she totally believed we were taking a real trip.

"Misty?"

"Huh?"

"We're not really going to Disneyland. You know that, right? We're just making believe." I guess I forgot she was younger than me. What with her height and v-o-l-c-a-n-o.

"I know we're pretending," she said. Her cheeks were red. I bet she didn't know. That can happen sometimes. You think you're so sure of what's going on, but you have no idea how many things in this world *should* be pretended. Like when you're extra happy because the sixth-grade boy at school that you've been liking for a long time asks you to come sit with him at lunch and says he wants to share his Lik-a-

Stix with you, and even though no one has ever come right out and asked if they could sit with specifically you, and though you very much understand sharing food can spread trench mouth, you do it anyway because no one that cute has ever even glanced in your direction, and sometimes your entire body aches for something that wonderful. But instead of the candy he throws a handful of dirt in your mouth and says he's just pissed in that dirt.

I looked again at Misty's face. Her stupid smile. I knew I must have looked like that just before I tasted the disillusion of that boy's urine.

"Oh crap, you know what?" I said. "I totally forgot the Cheez-Its and Pepsi." I opened the door a crack. "We can't take such a long drive without some snacks."

Misty opened her mouth to say something, but instead just nodded.

Before I could change my mind, before I could think that what I was about to do was probably the worst thing I could ever do to someone—I just went ahead and did it. I pressed the lock button, slammed the car door, and took off. I ran back toward the trees and the ivy and the sidewalk, glancing only once at the parking lot to see the girl's fists banging against the window. On my skateboard, I pushed myself as fast as I could go. Over Misty's screams I heard the blood graze of cicadas and the chains of the playground swings unraveling themselves. My plan was to get as far away from my apartment complex as I could, which meant the strip mall two blocks away. Maybe the warm fry-oil air of McDonald's could hold me safe until—I don't know—until my mother came and got me and maybe made me apologize or whatever. But I ended up in the laundry room right next to my building.

Just as I opened the door I threw up on my shirt—big chunks of raviolis and neon Pixy Stix foam. A teenage girl sat on a dryer smoking a cigarette and listening to Led Zeppelin on a transistor radio. She got up and stood next to me while I bent over a trash can and covered hunks of lint with my vomit. It was the first time I ever threw up without my mom rubbing my back.

"Shit, kid, you okay?" the girl asked. She had a heart-shaped patch sewn onto the crotch of her jeans. "What apartment do you live in? You want me to get someone?"

"Just shut up," I said. "Shut up and leave me alone." Sour strings of mucus dripped from my nostrils. The girl with the heart crotch stood there for a moment, called me a little fucker, then left before I could tell her I had just killed someone.

I knew Misty would be dead. I would walk out of that laundry room with my skateboard, and my nostrils stinging like the bleach I sometimes scrubbed my hands with, and there'd be a dead body waiting for me in my grandmother's car. The car with the electric locks that Misty couldn't work. The car that played the eight-tracks my grammie and I sang along to while we drove down Monterrey Highway to the Pink Elephant for fresh cilantro: *Hang down your head, Tom Dooley / Poor boy, you're bound to die.*

There would be a smell in the car. Would she be a skeleton by the time I got there?

My whole body leaked sweat as the sunlight across the cement floor slowly changed places. I hugged my knees and tried to cry but couldn't. Something like fingernails and hot water blocked my throat. Maybe that heart-crotch girl would come back. Behind my eyes I heard the familiar clicks. In the distance I heard sirens. *Click*—a light switch on—*click*—a light switch off. *Click*—light—*click*—dark. I said, "God," then snapped my fingers just after the *da* sound of the *d* in *God*. Hard *da*—soft *da*. Softer *da*—softer. Fade to nothing. Little bit more.

Off.

The timing was exact. Had to be exact. If you snap your fingers at just the right moment, between syllables and sounds, it's easier to align yourself. If the word *God* floats in front of your face because you had to push it into the air so that it could become a real thing and not just a voice, it's better to break it down by letters when you need it to disappear.

No. She wouldn't be a skeleton by the time I got there. Nothing that bad happens that fast.

There was a voice at the doorway. "Traci, come on out of there now." It was my mom. She walked to me, then eased me up by my shoulders. "It's time to go home." I looked past her. The air outside had fogged and hardened like a crusted sore.

"Hi," I said. "What happened to the sunlight?"

Next to my mom was a police officer, Misty Salvano's mom, and Misty. She was crying. She wasn't a skeleton. When we all walked back to my apartment I felt the cold of urine in between my legs and I asked if I could change my pants. The police officer talked into his shoulder, then told me to wait. "We need to figure out what went on here."

"Where's Grammie?" I asked.

My mom said she was out by her car giving a statement. I didn't know what that meant. I just knew the kitchen didn't smell like anyone had been cooking.

Misty's mother wore a crucifix around her neck and her fingers kept fluttering toward it. She wiped Misty's face and touched her hair.

"You just left me there," Misty said. She looked right at me. "You left me."

"Hold on now," my mom said. She crouched to get to my eye level. "Traci, we just need to know why you didn't come back for your friend, honey."

I rubbed a lock of my mom's dark hair in between my fingers.

"You need to be very clear about why you never came back," the police officer said.

I told him I didn't understand what he was asking. "I was just getting some snacks. We were pretending Disneyland."

"No, that's not how it happened," Misty said. She shook her head hard. "You just left me there."

"Misty, are you kidding me? You're my friend." That part didn't feel like a lie.

"But I saw you. You were laughing at me. You made a face and did this—" She rubbed the air around her eyes with her fists. "You were never going to come back!" She practically exploded into a crying burst and buried her face in her mother's side.

For a few seconds nobody spoke. All I could hear were police radio mumbles and the *sscchhkk* sound at the end of police sentences. I counted four *sscchhkk*'s and liked that it was four. Then Misty's mom spoke: "We need to do something about this."

"We are," my mother said. Kind of loud, too. "We're figuring out what happened between the girls." I was half hoping my mom would finish with something like, *and your daughter is always at our house, which I think is pretty irresponsible of you, especially when we have to eat dinner at six and I have to work so much overtime as a secretary and what's the reason why she plays outside all day?* My mom was good at voicing her belief (mostly in line at Lucky's or during an open house at my school) that children who acted up did so because their parents ignored them and were probably off at the bars—and that's why they were latchkey kids.

Misty's mom said yes to pressing charges of assault. My mom said, "Jesus Christ," and put her hands over her face. I guess everyone saw how bad her hands were shaking and that's probably the reason Misty's mom ended up changing her mind about the charges. The police officer handed my mom a phone number to the Santa Clara County children's crisis hotline before he left and advised her to keep it near.

I didn't get arrested that night. Somehow, I knew I wouldn't. I knew little kids didn't get taken away by the authorities. I'd thought about this a lot, mostly at Mervyns before I shoved lip gloss and hair ribbons down my underwear. Little kids don't know what they're doing, so you just have to look like you don't know, or you can make yourself cry and say you're so, so sorry, but you don't have any money because your dad is never on time with the child support. My mom threatened me a lot with Bad Kid Jail. Apparently this was where the naughty children were sent if they accidentally threw away a note from a teacher requesting an *emergency phone conference* or if they wouldn't stop talking in the movie theater about how the guy in back of them is laughing a pneumonia-chunky kind of laugh without covering his mouth. In Bad Kid Jail I was supposed to believe you're only allowed to watch the news and there definitely isn't any beef jerky to eat or baby wipes to clean your hands with every five minutes.

The police officer left and I went to my room to change my wet pants. My legs felt cold and heavy, like the weight of an unmeant apology. When my grammie figured out I still had her car keys, she told me to stick my hands in the pockets of my pants and give the damn keys back to her. I did what she said but I couldn't turn my pockets right side in to get at the keys. They were soggy and stuck together.

"I'm a-gonna tell you to get those damn things out now!" She did this kind of whisper-yell thing, real close to my face, then cupped her big hands over mine and pressed my skin into the grooves of the keys. One of my blisters opened up and started bleeding.

"Look at that," I said, holding up my hand. "Look what you just did."

She grabbed my wrist. "Someone oughta skin you," she said. "You know what they had to do? They had to break my window with a club."

My kneecaps got all fluttery and the skin on my face felt like it was sunburned. I almost started crying—in front of my grammie, who said all the time that crying was for babies in their cribs. I probably would've done it too, but I couldn't stop thinking of police clubs and shattered glass. Behind my eyes I saw *smash!* and *crash!* like in a comic book.

––––––––––––––

About a week after I didn't kill Misty, my mom and I were at Bob's Big Boy waiting for our food. "I'm taking you to talk to someone," she said.

I knew exactly what she meant.

With my favorite egg/bacon/pancake stacker sitting in front of me, I tried to feel hungry but I kept thinking about "talking to someone" and could only make a hole in the middle of my pancake with my finger. A counselor. A psychiatrist. Once on a rerun of *I Love Lucy*, Ricky used the phrase *head shrinker*. I knew that was just to be funny, but still.

"You're not eating your food," my mom said. "Are you sick?"

I shrugged. Maybe. "I was thinking about what I'm supposed to tell the person I'm going to talk to."

She looked up at me from her coffee cup. "Well, you might want to tell the truth, but who knows if you're even capable of that."

"Capable of what?"

"Of telling the truth," she answered. "You know what that means, right? The truth?"

Was she being funny?

"You know, the complete opposite of what you usually tell me," she said.

"Why are you talking all backwards?" I asked. "Of course I can tell the truth. I know what the truth is."

She hit a pack of Marlboros against her palm, then pulled up a cigarette with her teeth. "You sure?"

"Sure I'm sure," I said. "I tell the truth all the time."

My mom made a noise like when you take the lid off a soda bottle. "Oh, okay. Well, in that case, you should do just fine. All you have to do is tell the counselor the truth."

I was finished now. Finished talking, answering, whatever it was that I was supposed to be doing, because it was obvious I wasn't doing it right. I let everything get real quiet and watched my mom blow her little ghost trails of smoke into the blinds of the window. At some point she asked me again why I wasn't eating, but I just shrugged. And when she said, "Well, I guess that means you're sick," I nodded, real forceful and exaggerated, because I wanted her to see that I could also be funny in that annoying way that was supposed to be intimidating but wasn't. Plus, most likely she was right. I probably was sick.

The woman I went to see wasn't a real counselor. I know this because when I was telling her something she said, "I'm a student, so I really don't know much about that," which made me not want to speak at all, because what was I doing talking to someone who didn't know much about anything, while my mom sat in the waiting room like she was pissed off about something—not even cracking a smile when I made up a funny little question about head shrinkers and asked do they make necks smaller too, or do they just shrink heads?

The counselor/student woman was nice enough, I guess. She had fake blond hair, really dry. You could tell she used a lot of peroxide. I could even see the bubbles of hair spray in the parts by her ears where her hair was feathered. There was also this big gap between her two front teeth like what you would see on a Halloween mask. A piece of her gum or something hung down a little bit between that space. At first I thought it was a wad of food. Maybe a chunk of salami or something. I had a lot of spaces where my teeth bucked out or just refused to grow in, and lunch meat was always a problem so I wasn't trying to be testy by staring into her mouth when she asked me questions. Actually, there weren't many questions to answer, because she spent most of our hour talking to her boyfriend in the hallway while I colored pictures of Rainbow Brite. She did ask me if I had bad feelings toward my parents and if anyone ever touched me in places that were private.

"Of course I have bad feelings toward my parents," I said. Then I told her no way on the touching part. I added that if those private places were touched, they wouldn't be private anymore. "Probably they'd be shared places." *Ha-ha.*

But she didn't laugh. She just looked at me with that gummy spot in her mouth. She said there was no need to make fun of the situation— that what I did to Misty was serious and that kids all over the world were hurting. Just like me.

"I know," I said, trying to understand what the hell she was talking about. *Hurting kids in the world.* "Wait. What kids do you mean?"

Just before she got up to see why her boyfriend was in the hall with his arms crossed and an expression like how my mom looked in the car the whole time we were driving to the counselor's office, she said, "Kids like you."

Huh? Kids like me? Kids who couldn't sleep if the microwave door wasn't open a crack because the thing could magically turn itself on and start a fire in the middle of the night and when the fireman walked through the piles of charred bodies to ask the Kid Like Me: "If you knew there was a possibility of fire, why didn't you do something to stop it?" Is that what she was trying to say?

"Okay," I said, and went back to coloring my picture.

Misty never returned to my apartment. We never played Kitchen or *Charlie's Angels* again. I went back to Mike and Carol Brady all by myself and watched their children who were very concerned about one another. I always wondered if Misty was watching the same episode as me at the same time. I missed how she would make fun of Jan because Jan barely had any eyebrows, and how weird it was that I didn't think Jan's missing eyebrows were all that funny if Misty wasn't in the room watching me think it was funny.

When I sat up in bed with my Speak & Spell, knowing that the next day and the day after, I could have Ram all to myself if I wanted to, I didn't feel like I had hot sparkles rushing into my hands. Ram did things because I asked him to. Because he was a machine and because I pressed buttons.

One night, not long after Misty and Disneyland and the counselor who wasn't a real counselor, I heard my mother in her bed. She was praying. I heard my name in her prayers and then I heard my name turn into *that child*. I put my pink pillow with the dreaming frogs over Ram's face and listened. When she got to the part where it's time to make the cross she finished with the words her Portuguese father taught her before he died: *pai filho, espírito, santo*. Amen. And when she said *amen* it sounded fuzzy, watery. The same as when you're trying to suck in air instead of crying because you've done something that you're pretty sure is very wrong, but don't want anyone else to know how much you kind of liked squeezing that kitten, and how you know that if you could just press all that warmth, all that innocence—if you could just get all those things down into your own skin, down deep enough, maybe you would be different. Maybe you wouldn't be the kind of person who almost doesn't stop herself from pressing that kitten all the way.

4

blood of the mantis

The third-year man delivering the baby kept saying, "I'm going
to drop it, I'm going to drop it"—in sort of a biblical chant.
—SYLVIA PLATH, "SWEETIE PIE AND THE GUTTER MEN"

When my dad came back from his father's funeral, he handed me a box of miniature Catholic saint figurines. "Your grandfather wanted you to have these," he said. I could only bet that wasn't the case. I hardly knew the man. I'd heard stories of his meanness and things that I chose not to believe because no one wants to imagine their father as a little boy with his hands blocking his face. My lack of memories for my grandfather had made him a faraway man with a microphone voice who forced my dad to hang his wet and yellow stained sheets out to dry on the front porch. When the neighborhood kids walked by they called out to my dad's bedroom window, "Hey, Pee the Bed! Pee the Bed Ted!"

My dad gave me the statues because he didn't want them either.

"Lord, I'm so glad I didn't let you go to that damn funeral." My mom was in her room rolling her pantyhose back into their egg while I lined up my statues on an antique dresser and tried to put God in order. "The way those Sicilians handle death," she said, "it's nuts. Falling all over the place, crying, clutching at their clothes. What a production."

Grandpa Foust was not from the black-haired version of my father's family. He was tall and German, and now he was dead, with Mediterranean women making the sign of the cross where their short necks and large breasts met.

Now I had his dolls, and the dolls were like church. "Hey, Mom, what did Saint Christopher do?" She was on the phone to her boyfriend. I heard the click of a cigarette lighter, my nostrils accepting the peppery tentacles of the first exhale. "Mom! Saint Christopher! What did he do again?"

She told Frank to hold on, then stood at my door with a tight jaw. "How many times have I asked you not to scream when I'm on the phone?"

"Yeah, but I'm trying to—"

"When do I ever get to talk to Frank? What's the matter with you?"

How was I supposed to know how many times she got on the phone with Frank? Frank from her work who was married and everyone knew he had a wife. "I'm organizing my statues," I said. "Look, this one says 'Santo Christoforo.' I need to know what the heck he did."

She secured her cigarette in her lips and inspected the heinous thing. "God, these are tacky, aren't they? But that was nice, I guess, nice of your father to do that. Not as nice as paying for your ballet lessons would've been, but still. I wonder if they're worth anything?"

"I thought I should alphabetize them," I said. "Or maybe line them up in accordion to the importance of what they did."

She pulled her cigarette out slowly, the smoke purling from her nostrils as she spoke. "You mean in *accordance* with what they did, not *accordion*," she said. "You shouldn't use words in a sentence unless you're sure they're the right ones. Cute, though." She touched my face with Chris's backside. "You're funny."

When I finished organizing my dead grandfather's statues I stood back and felt nauseated. I knew I wouldn't be able to handle it—all that God.

By midnight they were already accusing me.

"Stop getting out of bed," Kim said. She paced the floor of our room, trying to make a song for Kyle Gaines because he was going to take off and travel around San Francisco with his band, and this time he was really going to do it, so she might never see him again. "You're supposed to be sleeping. I'm going to get into trouble if you keep fooling around."

But I had to turn those things. They had to face north. Where hell wasn't. "So if the sun sets in the west," I said, "then north would be this way, right?" I pointed to the wall where a very large John Travolta posed seductively.

"I guess that's north," Kim answered. "What are you doing with those stupid things?"

"Making them not point south because the devil—"

She held up her hand. "Okay, whoa—that's fine, just do whatever and then get into bed."

Maybe if my sister would've let me explain, I mean, if she wanted to hear, I could've told her I didn't really, truly believe the devil lived underground, didn't believe that evil dwelled southerly. I just thought it was safer not to take the chance of having God and his friends point that way, in the same direction of my closet crawl space where I hid a *Oui* magazine I'd found behind our building, where I kept my mom's book about Charles Manson (which maybe wasn't all that bad except for the parts about group sex) and the fortune-telling book I borrowed from the library without my library card.

Kim sang a song to herself. The song didn't rhyme. She swayed in her baseball jersey nightgown. I watched the way she watched herself in the mirror. Everyone said my sister looked like Mackenzie Phillips. She did, kind of, with her cool Kork-Ease shoes and big, straight teeth. I sometimes wished she acted more like Julie from *One Day at a Time*. When she and my mom fought I sometimes wanted to hear her say things like she didn't have to take that shit, grab my arm and say, "Come on, we're going." But she never did. Instead she was a spectral girl in turn-of-the-century clothing, her finger over her see-through mouth.

Only once did I ever ask her why she just didn't say no, stick up for herself more.

She laid into me hard. "You have no respect for anything, huh? You're the one who can never act right and upsets everyone all the time. You don't even care how you make our mother feel."

In so many ways I wanted to be like my big sister; in just as many ways—hell no. Where she had hips and grown-up motion, I had bruises from the monkey bars. When she said, "Okay, I will," everyone felt better. When I said, "Okay, I will," no one believed me anyway. I wasn't right enough to make anyone feel anything but upset.

"Wait, what are you doing?" Kim said. She grabbed my wrist and stopped me from keeping the Virgin Mary away from the secret filth of my closet. "Don't put those creepy dolls so close to my stuff." She made something like a karate chop on the dresser with the side of her straight hand. "This is my collection, this is your collection." She pushed the mother of God away from her Avon perfumes.

"Don't!" I yelled. "Who do you think you are? I had them the way they're supposed to be."

"Hey, keep your voice down," she said. "Don't you remember what mom told you about respecting my privacy?" She bent forward and squinted at the work I had done to the dresser earlier that day. "What is this? What's this crap all over here?" She scratched the wood with her fingernail, then pushed all my stuff to one side. Now nothing, absolutely nothing on that dresser was three inches apart like I had made sure of with the masking tape. "It's just tape," I answered. "I tried to make it all even so you wouldn't have to worry."

Kim left the room and came back with our mother.

"Oh, for Christ's sake," my mom said. She padded toward the dresser with Kim on her elbow. "Ok, what tape? Where? Let me look."

My sister coughed a cough that was tears and cigarettes. "She stuck it all over," she said. "It's just everywhere. And I know if that would've been me putting tape all over and moving *her* stuff, she'd be getting a stomachache and I'd have to go get Tylenol."

"Kim, for chrissake, calm down." The theme from *M*A*S*H* drifted from my mom's room as she looked closer at what I had done. "I don't believe this shit here," she said. "Why would you do something like this? To an antique dresser?"

Kim decided to answer for me. "She's going on about hell and everything being all even and stuff. . . ."

"No, no. Just stop." My mom put her hand up. "I'm going to lose it here in a second. This is nuts, I have to be up at five A.M."

I quickly let her know that Kim had been up too, with a song for Kyle, and how hard it is to relax when someone's trying out words that don't even fit together.

"I'm telling you right now, Traci, goddammit." Mom grabbed my arm, then let it go, her eyes darting back between me and my sister. "There's crap all over the furniture—this is Grammie's antique dresser, and you better pray she doesn't wake up and see this. When I come back in this room in the morning, every stitch of this shit tape had better be gone. Kim, I'm going to put you in charge to make sure this is done." Meaning Kim would remove the tape all by herself while I sweated out my sudden stomachache under the covers of our bed.

That's about all I could do—convince myself I was only trying to help; it was the easiest way to make sense of why I could only touch the middle of the sheets as I got into bed, why I wasn't allowed to face the right side of the wall when I slept, why I had to turn my grandpa's saints so that my mom's car wouldn't go over the Bay Bridge because those statues knew they lived with me—disgusting me— they knew that they now resided in a house where people sometimes talked about going to church but went to see psychics instead, where it was okay to hold séances with just paper and a glass but not a Ouija board, because even though everyone in my family said goddammit, a Ouija board was evil and against Christ. Plus, it was pretty obvious that something with the power to stop a car from falling over a bridge most likely didn't want to be touching my sister's perfume bottle filled with a liquid called Midnight Temptress, due to there's something very sexual involved in that.

So I moved them. I made them righter than I could make myself.

It doesn't matter if you're not sure about God; you still need to ask forgiveness that his friends who perform miracles are all out of order because those statues and their creepy painted-on eyes with sometimes no pupils, well, they can see you and they know all about your counting and they saw you kissing your pillow and touching in between your legs like those girls in that filthy magazine you keep in your closet crawl space, and they know how hard you cried the other day because they were staring at you when you could not concentrate long enough to finish your new short story on the subject of teen runaways who turn to drugs and stripping.

I tried to pretend I was asleep while Kim scraped off the tape and wiped the dresser down with Pledge. Tomorrow, I thought, I would really help with her song, and then she'd see how I wasn't trying to destroy her life like she said I was just before she hit me hard in the back of the head with a Snoopy pillow. Tomorrow I would help her understand how much better songs are if they rhyme.

The letter from my fourth-grade teacher, Mrs. Kashiro, said I was spending too much time pulling on my teeth and she was going to have a serious talk with me about always having my fingers in my mouth. It had been almost five months since Misty and the counselor. I was trying hard not to do ridiculous things in front of adults. I knew I was too big to be putting my hands in my mouth. I wouldn't have brought the letter home at all but there are some teachers who think they're funny and smart and stick your 98 percent worksheet from the Vocabulary Builders Club into the same take-home envelope as a letter that basically says you're just a little less disruptive than if someone brought their pet orangutan to show-and-tell.

My mother said she was very impressed, because a lot of grown-ups didn't even know the meaning of *delusive*. "But what I don't understand is why you would purposely try and give yourself trench mouth." She folded up my 98 percent without telling me to put it on the refrigerator. "I thought we had already talked about sticking your fingers in your mouth and pulling on your teeth?"

"You're so gross," my brother said. He was rubbing Jergens lotion on my mom's feet while they watched *Vegas* on her little black-and-white TV. No way was I about to confess how pulling on my teeth was because of the nightmares I'd been having about blood all over my gums while my brother sat there making a face like he was smelling a fart.

"You realize what that can do to your smile?" my mom asked. "And how filthy it is to be sticking your hands in your mouth? You let the cat scratch your hands all up and you're putting those things in the same place where you put food?"

Bryan said, "Sick."

"Fine, then, I won't do it." Lie.

She asked if I thought my dad was going to pay for braces.

I shook my head and said again I would stop. But of course I wouldn't stop, because last week my sister got caught on the back of some guy's motorcycle, and I saw my father hit her closed-fist in the mouth. When I shut my eyes at night I watched the pink meat of her bottom lip and how her chin was so quickly covered in blood when she ran crying into the living room.

In my dreams it was me being smacked, red lines blooming across my shirt like flowers from a stop-motion nightmare. I didn't know it yet, I didn't feel it was on its way or even predict it from my fortune-telling book, but I was coming up close to a hospital bed and an almost lethal infection in my veins because of blood.

Blood was my new thing.

"I'm going to make you a deal," my mom said. "Since you've done such a good job of not telling your dad about that Misty and the car thing, and if you promise that you'll stop sticking your hands in your mouth and leave your teeth alone, I'll show you another letter that came in the mail today."

After I crossed my heart and swore to God, my mom showed me a card like an invitation from the YMCA on Santa Teresa Boulevard. It said that girls between the ages of eight and thirteen should come to a meeting and learn about a father/daughter group that celebrates Native Americans and how fathers and daughters could be best friends.

"Indian Princesses?" I asked, liking the princess part for sure. But as I read on, my hands began to tingle with the familiar onset of worry. "Hold on. *Camping*?" The muscles around my stomach spazzed as I thought of sleeping bags on the ground and poisonous centipedes. Hepatitis in outhouses. Coughing. Jason Voorhees.

"But you'll have to ask him yourself," my mom said. "There's a fee and weeknight meetings and stuff, so you know how that usually goes."

That night I sat up in bed thinking of how I could tell my father he needed more me in his life. I pulled and rubbed hard on Sprinkles's fur. He kneaded the vicious symmetry of his claws into the skin of my thigh. Some of me opened and spilled: red for wet and stepping out of yourself, brown for drying on the sheets and realizing you could do it again if you liked how it calmed you down. Eight more times, eight drops like perfect pills and I would be less afraid to ask my father for money to make me an Indian Princess.

I took out my ledger and wrote, *Indians will happen.*

Kim said all the time that if you want to get a guy interested in the things you like, then you have to be really, *really* interested in the stuff he does. Even if you don't like it. Just lie and say you do. I could do the lying part for sure, but the thing was, when it came to weekends with my dad, I wouldn't have to pretend I liked anything. Just the opposite. Mostly I had to defend how much fun I had on my weekends with my father. I almost always found myself saying, "Well, it was okay, I guess," so that my mom wouldn't bend to my eye level and touch my hair and ask if I was still her Honey Bunny. And since saying nothing didn't work with my mother—"So you sat around and just stared at the walls all night?"—I just lied.

Lied and lied.

A Saturday at Splash Town after my mom lectured me about the dangers of waterslides turned into how hard it was to watch Bryan having so much fun on the inner tubes while I sat with my book in the eating area. Swimming after hours at the Rancho Club in our clothes with no lifeguard on duty so my dad could have a sort of date with the girls' water polo instructor became a very detailed story of how much fun I didn't have playing miniature golf.

Most of the women my father dated were super nice (oh God no, *never* say this to Mom), and because I knew I could not go home and tell her about my good time with Dad and So-and-so, it made me feel sorry for his girlfriends in a mysterious way I didn't understand.

Sure, Nice Lady, you can buy me a hundred dollars' worth of Bonne Bell cosmetics and let me play my Bow Wow Wow tape extra loud in your car while you listen to me explain the lyrics at each red light, but you can only hold my hand or hug me when my dad is looking. Otherwise you'll need to see my dirty looks to remember you are *not* my mother.

They weren't in his life for long, though—these women with their feathered hair and anxious trying. Usually it was just me and dad and Bryan, riding down the street singing to his War or Peaches and Herb tapes, making bacon-and-garlic sandwiches while we watched Creature Features and made fun of the bad B-movie acting.

"My butt could do a better job as a mad scientist," I said.

"My butt with crap in my BVDs could do a better job," was Bryan's response.

And my dad always finished with something that topped us all. Laughing so hard I'd hold my sides: "How disgusting, Daddy—corn."

If our father fell asleep early, Bryan and I would run up and down the street in our pajamas. Once he gave me seventy-five cents to ask a bus driver on a smoke break if he could sniff my armpits and tell me if I needed deodorant. We'd play Disco Lounge and turn on my brother's strobe light and mix Tang and 7Up in brandy glasses. Bryan would say, "Here's your drink, doll face. My, my, you lookin' fine tonight," then do his pointing "outta sight" thing like Isaac the bartender did in the opening credits of *Love Boat*. Sometimes the weekends were books and Stratego and *National Geographic* and rain with the windows open because my dad said getting sick from chilly weather was a myth.

Of all my dad's girlfriends, Michelle was the one he dated the longest. She had red hair and pinkish skin and only wore green eye shadow. When I showed her my poems she pointed out that the words were like Irish limericks, which made me study her movements around the room and not know how to feel.

When she spent the night at the Camino Verde house, Bryan and I got to stay up so late I had to constantly look out the window and remind myself it was morning. The early dawn potions of garlic grass and eucalyptus laced into the window screens until the 2 A.M. words *sleepy, dreamy,* and *hungry* all meant the same thing.

Some Saturday nights my dad and Michelle turned up the Commodores while Bryan and I pushed the sofa and coffee table against the wall in the living room to do the hustle. A few times we drove to the craft shop Michelle owned in Los Gatos to watch old rich people pay a hundred dollars for puzzles of bridges and chimpanzees in hammocks. She showed us the dolphin dream catchers she made herself and little owls glued together from shells. I got to pick out an owl for my room, but it looked at me and said, *So you love Michelle more than your own poor mother now*, and I had to smash it with a flashlight.

One Friday we were all to meet Michelle for dinner after my dad took us to the dollar show to see a movie that had already been on cable for a year. When we were sure he had fallen asleep and it was coming to the part in the movie where the house starts to bleed and the family is seriously getting the hell out of there, Bryan and I fooled around in the lobby making calls to the operator on the pay phone. "But I need help," I said while Bryan pressed his ear to the receiver and stifled a laugh. "I'm having my first period. I need to know how to change a tampon."

When an usher eyed us suspiciously we dashed outside and fooled around in the parking lot. Pretty soon that same usher came out and asked if we were Traci and Bryan?

"Why?" I asked.

"Some black guy is in there looking for you, says he's your dad."

We burst out laughing. "Okay, thanks a mil," I said. "We'll go back to our black daddy."

This mistake had been made before. My father, with his thick, frizzy hair blow-dried up into an Afro, his Lionel Richie mustache and typical large Sicilian facial features, could easily pass for a man of color. Plus, he pretty much only listened to Motown and disco, so it was only natural to think that somewhere inside Theodore Foust was a George Jefferson trying to come out and move on up.

It was late when we pulled into the Bold Knight to meet Michelle. For South San Jose this was as classy as it got. Red velvet seats, cheese fondue, limousine parking, and my dad saying, "Sharp," to just about every Cadillac we spotted in the parking lot. Whenever women were involved in our weekends of fine dining, the rule was no places with laminated menus and no pouring ketchup on everything. On the nights he only buttoned the lower half of his polyester printed shirt and did up his 'fro, we knew Denny's and Sambo's were out of the question. Bryan and I were threatened with spankings if either one of us cut one, and we'd all have to pretend we were the kind of people who didn't pick their ear wax with car keys.

As we usually did so Michelle and my dad could have some grown-up time, Bryan and I sat at the bar and ordered Shirley Temples. I pretended the bartender had been trying all night to ask me for a date while my brother watched the women with their low-cut dresses and xylophone chests. Depending on how many Harvey Wallbangers my dad had before we got to the restaurant, I was sometimes allowed to wear a little blush and lip gloss. I twirled my ice with a plastic glittered drink mixer and pretended a straw was my cigarette. I took out my compact and applied powder to my nose.

"That's so slutty," Bryan said. He tapped the back of my hand hard enough for my little mirror to fall and said girls who did stuff like that in public get themselves raped. I knew what rape meant. I wrote stories about it because it was easier to make the girls so sad and you could feel sorry for a rape victim easier than, say, if someone just got beat by their boyfriend or whatever.

When we joined Dad and Michelle at the table, I asked her if it was okay to put on lip gloss while you're sitting at a bar.

"I don't see why not," she answered.

Dad crushed out his cigarette and shook his head. "Uh, well, makeup should really be applied in a bathroom. That looks a little—I mean, for a young lady, that's pretty seductive." If Michelle hadn't been there, *pretty seductive* would've been *whorish*.

Bryan gave me a told-you-so elbow nudge, and I would wonder about this mysterious decree all through my stuffed mushrooms. This was how men thought? My brother and my father agreed on something without even discussing it. So then this was like a rule? Same as when my sister said you have to act interested in what men like to get them to do what you want. So if I had come to dinner with my Indian Princess agenda was I supposed to pretend I agreed with my brother and father that putting on lip gloss at the bar was trampy? Maybe right now while I had Michelle on my side I could bring up the idea of head-dresses and tom-toms.

But something was crawling out of my father's head.

"Bryan," I whispered from the side of my mouth. "Bryan, oh my God, look."

We weren't allowed to point when dad's girlfriends were around, so when I finally got my brother's attention I guided him with strategic voice visuals: "Okay, look straight in the center of dad's glasses," I whispered. "Okay, now go up a little to the middle of his 'fro."

"Yeah, so? What's—"

"Wait, just look. Right there. That green leg sticking out of his hair. Is that an antenna? What is that?"

Our heads pressed together. Dad saw us squinting. "What?" he asked, then he felt it. He shook his head, made a noise, and we all watched as a baby praying mantis scampered down my dad's shoulder.

"Oh, that's gross!" I yelled. I tried to jump up but I was wedged in the velvet booth against my brother and a cork wall. I wrapped my arms around Bryan's neck and put my head down. "Oh God, I can't look." His body trembled with the laugh he held inside.

"What the hell is that?" My dad stood and shook out his shirt.

Michelle let out a squeaky little scream then tried to compose herself and examine the mantis that was now perched atop a French roll. "Babe, that's a big bug," she said. "How could you not feel that in your hair?"

"Because it's so puffy," I blurted out, though for no other reason than that being startled was a green light for the exit of my pretend manners.

A waiter stopped at our table. "Something wrong here?"

"Yeah, look." I pointed. I snapped. The whole bit. "A baby praying mantis just crawled out of my dad's Afro."

"Not an Afro," my dad said, almost yelling. "And that's not a praying mantis, either." He made a cutthroat signal to me, which meant *shut it*.

Bryan practically stuffed his whole napkin in his face to gag his laughter.

"No, babe, that's definitely a praying mantis," Michelle said.

The mantis didn't say anything. It was perfectly content on the French roll, grateful, I guess, to be out of my dad's head.

Bryan and I were still laughing about the bug the next morning over cold spaghetti and buttermilk biscuits (my dad still insisting that in no goddamn way did his hair resemble an Afro). I knew I only had until the end of the month for late registration into Indian Princesses, so with Kim's man advice buzzing in my ears, I took out the sign-up sheet from my duffel bag. While my father read it I leaned over his shoulders and said, "Wouldn't that be stupid? Like I'm so sure the prize huntsman would totally want to take stupid me camping."

On the phone that night, back in the apartment, I heard my mom tell Dad how great it was that we were spending all this time together, and wasn't it nice that he didn't have to come over and threaten me with spankings as much as he used to? She winked at me while I stood in the hall and cracked my knuckles. Two weeks later my father and I sat in a circle with ten other girls making matching headdresses.

"I'm going to call you Morning Dew," my dad said during the father/daughter naming ceremony, "because your skin is so soft and beautiful." He said this in front of grown men, in front of girls from my school who were always watching me, waiting for me to mess up. *Your skin is so soft and beautiful.* People were in the room, in a circle, they all heard what my dad said about me. I wasn't sure what to do with that.

Once when my father and I were looking at old pictures I pointed to one of me when I was two and asked if he liked that I had his crazy hair. "But I brushed mine when I was a kid," he had said, "and it didn't smell." We laughed and laughed because that's what we did. That's how I didn't cry.

I named my father Thunder Cloud.

Morning Dew and Thunder Cloud did end up going camping. During the drive through the Santa Cruz Mountains I threw up in the front seat while Meagan Thatcher from my class said from the back, "I knew that was going to happen."

When we stopped to get me some crackers and baby wipes my dad told Meagan maybe she would like to ride with her own father.

Our tribe was called the Kiowas, and the first order of tribal business was a contest to see who could make the best tribal banner. In the craft hall with girls and their dads from all over Santa Clara County—

there must have been two hundred of us packed into a musty cabin with the portable heaters full blast—I had an extremely hard time focusing and had to keep going back to our cabin to pull on my teeth and look at the Tylenol my mother packed in my suitcase. On a piece of tape she wrote, *Only one every four hours.* She'd composed a symptoms checklist and said each question must have a clear answer before I could take a pill.

Did I have a headache? Yes.

Did I have a stomachache? Kind of.

Was my body feeling this way because I was excited about something? Excited? Well, I made it here, I guess.

I took my one tablet, but it was never enough to completely stop me from not feeling right. Tylenol helped with a cough due to cold or minor body aches from fever. It wouldn't make me a different person.

At night, the minutes just before bedtime were the roughest. There was a bleakness inside me, a devastation that made the mossy redwoods and spearmint ground a place I could belong in. If I could just calm myself down. I wrote in my ledger and read my tape with my medicine instructions just so I could see my mother's writing. The other girls talked about how scary the woods looked outside the window but I felt more like the scariness was inside. There was no eleven o'clock news, no theme from *The Streets of San Francisco* blaring from the living room where my grandmother had fallen asleep, no touching my tongue to the window locks of our cabin or checking the Dixie cups in the bathroom to make sure there was an even amount.

I did manage to pull myself together enough to pretend I saw a big spider so I could look under everyone's bed for unsafe plug outlets, but at the beginning of lights out I became nervously chatty and cracked one stupid joke after another: "Hey, you guys, did you see that weird woman cleaning up our dinner trays in the mess hall? God, wasn't she ugly, face all squishy like a doughnut with a mouth?" Ha-ha.

Only low grumbles and a hissing *sshhtt* . . . From a bunk in the far right someone said, "She's got Down syndrome."

"Yeah?" I said. "Well, she's totally bringing me down with her ugliness."

Someone clapped, but, slow and obvious, and followed it up with, "What a retard."

I stayed awake most of the night making lists of things I hated, nervous, thinking of ways not to be.

On our last day of camp my dad was acting weird. He kept trying to get rid of me. He told me to go on a hike with the tribe or to stay in the cabin with my book while he went to a fathers' special lunch.

"What special lunch?" Meagan Thatcher's dad asked when I asked him where my father was. "I didn't hear about any special lunch."

I searched for my dad in the mess hall, in the day lounge, and, because I knew this man who took his blow dryer and hair care products on our trip, I checked the girls' counselor's office. Nothing.

There was a final dress rehearsal just before dinner for the skit our tribe was putting on for Forest Follies Night. We had chosen to act out a poem about the seasons from our camper's welcome booklet, but it was pretty stupid because none of the girls cared anything about the seriousness of acting. "Remember the part in *Tommy* where his mom takes him to the church of Marilyn Monroe?" I asked. "We should copy that dance, with the hands lifting and swaying; that's the kind of energy we should use." Eyes rolled. Tongues clicked. Meagan Thatcher pushed her hair behind her ear and said, "I'm totally sure . . ."

An hour before it was time to go onstage I still couldn't find my dad. On the phone in the park director's office I told my brother that our father was missing.

"So what do you want me to do?" he asked. In the background I heard the start of *Gomer Pyle USMC*. It emptied my chest to think he still watched his shows even when I wasn't there.

"You need to ask Mom what I should do," I said. "He's been gone for like, all day."

"Oh, creepy. That's the same as in *Friday the Thirteenth*," my brother answered. "Do you see any blood anywhere?"

A girl who was standing behind a file cabinet waved her arms, motioning for me to listen to her. "Who's your dad, honey?" she asked.

"Ted Foust. We're in the Kiowas from South San Jose. I can't find him. I guess he's been killed by a bear so I'm not sure what to do next." I thought the words *head trauma*.

Bryan said, "Are you kidding me? What bear? What are you talking about? Put Dad on the phone right now."

The girl asked for the phone and told Bryan she knew where Dad was and that everything was fine. I could still hear *Gomer Pyle* when she hung up.

"I know where your dad is, sweetie," she said. "There wasn't any bear." She came around the front of the desk and put her arm over my shoulder. She smelled like Love's Baby Soft and firewood. "There's a surprise," she said. "I can't really say anything because it's for the show tonight."

Together we walked all the way to the huge amphitheater. She said she sure hoped my brother didn't say anything to worry or scare my mom. I reassured her, no, that would never happen because my brother is not a secretary and doesn't give phone messages. "Plus, my parents stopped worrying about each other a long time ago," I said.

Pretty much every tribe sucked with their skits, including ours. Little Owl Flying forgot to gently place my sun mask sunny-face-up on the bench where we kept our costumes for when it was time to change into our respective seasons. I was summer, but on account of my mask lying facedown in the springtime mud of the Santa Cruz Mountains, I was the only one who went out there sans a seasonal face.

"You forgot to smile," Little Owl Flying observed when the skit was over. But I didn't answer and didn't care because I was sure me onstage with my corpsey pale skin and the big cold sore on my lip certainly didn't convince anyone of June, July, and August.

But when I heard a booming voice over the stage sound system announcing the arrival of Thunder Cloud from the Kiowas, my pissy attitude changed immediately. I couldn't believe it. There was my father in a spotlight. In his too-tight jeans and leather fringed vest, my father walked across the stage to a stampede of cheering. He was the star of the whole show. The entire fathers' skit of something like a hundred dads, and mine was the one they picked to lead them all. He opened with a rain dance while the other fathers snuck up behind him and threw buckets of water over his head. Everyone roared with laughter. After that he read a passage out of our handbook. He was clear and loud and articulate when he spoke about the unity of friendship and the blessings of fatherhood. When the play ended with my father leading a group of headdressed men in an extremely sharp dance to "YMCA," with the alphabet arm movements and everything, the audience went nuts.

"Holy cow, Morning Dew, your dad can get down!"

I was so excited, for a second I almost forgot where I was.

In the first grade I asked my dad to come to school for What My Parents Do day and tell everyone about how a printing press works and how to make books and stuff. He didn't want to. Standing on the benches of the amphitheater while everyone shuffled out—some of them patting me on the back, asking me if I liked my surprise—I remembered my dad's response that day I asked him to talk about his job.

"You know what," he had said, "I think I would've made a pretty good singer. Or maybe someone on television who does a little bit of everything, like Donny and Marie."

When we got back to San Jose I tried to think of the funniest way I could tell everyone at home about how Dad was almost Donny Osmond, but I couldn't get myself to walk straight or even see clearly. Something was wrong. I had woken up that morning feeling tight and hot. A prickly rash covered the sides of my cheeks and under arms. My tongue felt swollen and when I pressed on my glands I could've sworn I had Hodgkin's Lymphoma.

"I feel like I can't breathe very well," I said. But I said that a lot.

By the time we got to the apartment I was dizzy in a way I had never felt or pretended. "Pick me up, Daddy," I said. "I feel so wobbly."

I heard my father tell my mother we needed to call someone.

Not long after, the emergency room doctor said these things—We're not really sure. Admit her. Maybe blood poisoning—every muscle in my body started to twitch and burn and shake. Even the skin under my eyes moved. I screamed all through my mother filling out the admittance papers for my hospital stay.

"There's no goddamn way I'm staying here!" I yelled. "This is a fucking hospital, people here are very sick and contagious and some are dead. No way am I staying here! I'll kill myself first!"

My mom tried to hold my wrists and told me to calm down. I scratched her arms with my nails until I saw her blood.

"We're going to give her something to calm her down," a nurse said.

I screamed at the top of my lungs, I cussed out words only boys were allowed to say. I cried and said, "Holy Mary, mother of God." I told the candy striper to go to hell when she tried to show me my nice room and how fun it was to press the up and down buttons on the bed. I wailed and sobbed into my hands, "Please, Jesus Christ, son of Mary!" I closed my eyes and saw my grandfather's statues.

My dad said he'd go back to the apartment to pack some clothes and what books did I want? Did I want magazines too? My mother stood in the doorway facing the wall, holding onto the frame like she was on a ship. There was a sting in my hip and all at once my muscles were warm Play-Doh. I took up a heavy breath and let out an ugly animal sound.

"There we go now." A doctor I thought I knew from television pushed an IV into my forearm and said I was being very brave.

"I really want to know the truth," I said to him. "Am I going to die an untimely death?" The words were whipped cream in my mouth.

"Oh, Traci," my mom said, "really." She smiled at the doctor. "The theatrics."

Everything turned a bluish color. My sister appeared at the door, breathless and swirly. I held out my arms and told her to give me a hug. "I'm sick," I said. "Your little sister is very sick. I think you should pray for me."

Toxoplasmosis. It was a long word. Not the longest I knew, but still, the longest I'd ever been afflicted with. I wrote *tonsillitis* and *toxoplasmosis* in the back of the crossword books Grammie brought to the hospital.

"Toxoplasmosis definitely sounds dangerous," I said to the stuffed panda that had been sitting on the edge of my up-and-down bed for the past week. Poison from Sprinkles's fecal matter under his claws had run into my blood and plugged up my drainage system so that my body swelled up with toxins in every direction.

We're talking about cat shit.

All the times I had imagined myself in the soft scenario of humming lights and concerned expressions, every story I had put myself in as the main character of people who would feel so guilty over everything they had ever said or done to me—this is what it all came down to. Some of Sprinkles's litter box floated in my body, and the only thing I really had to show for it was being able to correctly pronounce the medications on my IV drip. That and I could now hear the softest bass guitar or drum coming from a barely audible radio at the nurses' station all the way down the hall. Actually, I could feel the sound waves behind my eyes like a crackle of electricity. I had purposely made my cat injure me for a weird enjoyment I didn't understand, all so I could turn into a sick dolphin with faulty wires in her echolocation.

My father set up camp in my hospital room, slept in the bed next to me for two weeks. Over hot dogs from the cafeteria and Kentucky Fried chicken he and my mom sneaked in special just for me, I said, "The sickness improved my hearing."

"Neat," he answered into his corn on the cob. "Oh boy. I can't stand

Fantasy Island, that Mexican midget. Turn the channel, okay, is *Dance Fever* on tonight?"

My mom smoked in the waiting room and compared sick children with the other moms. She was filled with nerves to the point where I couldn't take the way she looked at me like there was certainly something more than just bad blood. At night before they gave me a little something for sleep, before Mom and Dad changed shifts, she read me way-too-babyish books and I wondered if I would wake up the next morning. During *The Little Engine That Could*, I told her I was magic.

"You hear sounds coming from where?" she asked.

"Wherever," I said. "Drumbeats or bass guitar. I can hear them from like twenty thousand feet away."

"How long has it been since they gave you a pain pill?" It was the first I'd seen her smile since I was admitted. "I think you're having bionic dreams," she said.

I liked that. *Bionic dreams.* Maybe I could do things like Lindsay Wagner now or Wonder Woman. Or maybe this was just another part of how I couldn't deal with math, of how I barely had any friends and had a hard time loving people the way a normal person is supposed to. Still, there was such an excitement about hearing/doing/being something I actually wanted to share, where I didn't have to keep myself a secret for fear someone would say, *It's just a doorknob, calm down.*

I had a three day vomity stomach flu once and heard my mom arguing on the phone with the pharmacist because an ER doctor had prescribed a weaker strength of Phenegran suppositories than what I was used to. "I am well aware of what strength you would give a child but you have no idea how my daughter gets sick," she said. When she slammed down the phone and told my grandmother that the pharmacist had accused her of trying to dose out enough narcotics to kill a horse, I felt big and illuminated, like I'd been colored in without stepping out of the lines. For all the things my brain couldn't handle, it made me proud to think my body took on the extra burden.

My poor mommy while I was in the hospital. We sat together in the pediatric ward playroom, in a what-do-you-think-of-me silence, like how you act when you first meet someone.

"Mom, do you like Candyland?"

I watched her sit, then get up, sit, then get up, rub her forehead, wonder aloud about her cigarettes. I looked at her veiny hands. If Frank Ranaldo was on the phone right now, he would just have to wait.

There was a boy in the hospital too. Robert. Skinny Robert with blue crescents under his eyes. He had blood poisoning same as me, but his was from a group of junior high kids assaulting him with ballpoint pens. He lifted his gown past his knees and showed me the spot on his calf where they had poked him to the point of twenty-eight stitches. "Like if you were getting stabbed with a knife," he said. "They were all suspended. I was suspended too but that's total crap because I didn't even do anything."

I imagined Robert in handcuffs. White and tired, full of poems: *Fuck off, every single one of you!* One day he would show them all. Maybe I would help him with that. Me and Robert and the sickness in our veins.

When I returned home there were balloons and a declawed Sprinkles with gauze around his paws in the colors of a scary movie. "Oh, Sprinkles," I said, trying to hold his squirming body. "My pretty tiddle tat." I whispered that I was sorry for all those times I purposely riled him, held his feet to my skin, and pressed down. "It's not your fault," I told him. Because, really, it was me who had got me what I wanted: to be the girl on propped-up pillows.

See, I told you there was something.

Now my kitty had his lion taken away and I had nothing to show for myself except a part of my brain that heard things no one else wanted to hear.

Same as before.

At home in my nightgown all day, I picked at the sausage pizza Kim brought from Round Table, and had a hard time feeling like I wanted to color or write stories or watch *Ryan's Hope* with my grandmother and eat her special potato soup with extra onions.

Bryan said, "I'll sneak you outside and we'll doorbell ditch." But my lungs felt funny and I was just too tired for much of anything. A sadness ebbed over me like the compression of low clouds before rain. This wasn't nerves or my usual inside itchiness. This was me watching me in slow motion, trying to hold myself steady. At night I longed for the people of the hospital. The nurses who hovered with their fat arms and bored smiles. The one who played crazy eights with me and told me all about her fourteen-year-old daughter going to live with her ex-husband in Arkansas, how she laughed when I said, "Hicks."

I looked around at the couch bed I'd been sleeping on, my crumpled sheets and the glass of juice my dad had fetched for me earlier that morning when he came to visit. I wanted him to come back. I wanted a little something for sleep. I wanted Robert and the way he tilted his head when I told him someone in the parking lot was listening to "Jamie's Crying" and I knew this on account of my bionic hearing. I wanted the excitement of being discharged tomorrow, the hope of maybe not.

When I went back to my own bed in the room I shared with my sister, when I could finally stand looking at the life I had before the hospital, I cried. And cried and cried. I didn't know why I couldn't stop with the tears. I only knew I had never been this sad. I cried when my mom said let's go for a walk on such a sunny day. I cried when Theresa didn't call and when she did call to see how I was feeling. I put the Catholic statues away in a shoe box and cried because I didn't have enough of my grandfather in my heart to even want those ugly things. My mom called my aunt Pat, a nurse at Oakland's Children's Hospital and asked if this was normal? "All this weeping," she said, "it's not like her." *All this sadness.*

When the sun came just right through the blinds I spotted the tape markings on Grammie's antique dresser where I had made such a thing about Kim's perfume bottles not touching my idea of good and evil. I felt stupid. I had done all that damage and never bothered to apologize or say anything while someone else fixed what came out of my scrambly mind.

You're an idiot. Selfish.

Who was I trying to fool now with the steely hospital smell still in my hair and the paper pill cups I kept hidden in my backpack? I had returned home with my ribs closer to my skin, with chest pains for a boy who would have never spoken to me outside of an 8 P.M. med round.

And I was still me. Always me. Me with my lies and shit for blood.

There wasn't a fever high enough to kill that infection.

5

garage tale theater

Henry looked up and saw more non-kids inside, with faceless
burlap bags for heads.
—JACK PENDARVIS, "YOUR BODY IS CHANGING"

Here is an easy way to remove your fingernails: first, before you check out of your two-week hospital stay from forcing cat claws into your skin, make sure you have a doctor who stresses the importance of hand washing and uses the phrase *could've been fatal* right in front of you so that you hear this over and over in your head and can't even concentrate enough to make it through two chapters of *Are You There God? It's Me, Margaret*. Once you've established the fact that even though you've always been pretty diligent about germs—though it wasn't enough to keep your mom from fighting on the phone with the insurance company on account of your dad can't do a goddamn thing that involves paperwork—make sure to become completely enchanted by Ajax cleanser. Think that the glassy smell and little lines of blue demon hairs may carry a power more potent than disinfecting. You don't know this for sure, it's just a thought, so you start washing your hands with it, and while you're at it you may as well try putting a little on your toothbrush and do this about four times a day (which will eventually turn into fourteen because you've started really liking that number), and when the skin on your hands becomes so dry and disgusting that the guy who sells hot dogs at Golfland makes a scrunchy face when you hand him your money, make sure you stay up all night thinking about this.

Cry.

Hate the pain of your skin and the sores in your mouth.

Just don't hate it enough to stop.

When you drop your book between the wall and your bed and feel kind of panicky about putting your hand in there on account of you're pretty sure there's still a *Juggs* magazine you stole from Thrifty's even though you made a promise to God in the hospital that you were going to stop stealing and touching yourself all the time, except that your promises are like everything else you cannot follow through with so you kind of just have to deal with this, close your eyes and shove your hand behind your bed. Now when you pull your book back up, notice that your pinky nail is almost completely off and two other nails have been peeled so that your fingertips look like white moons over a bleeding horizon.

Also notice how this should really bother you but doesn't.

"My hands are so hot," I said to just about everyone. My little setup, saying something first so that no one would say anything to me. "Why are they so hot? I don't know. And dry too. Probably from the bars in gymnastics."

My brother sniggered and said maybe I was one of those psychic healers like we'd seen on *That's Incredible*. "Call Dad and see if you can heal his hemorrhoids," he said.

I tried gloves but that didn't last long due to the itching. I tried not touching stuff, then only touching stuff with my sleeve folded over my palm. That worked for a while but the weather was getting too warm for long sleeves. On the last day of fourth grade Kim and Grammie took me out for grilled cheese sandwiches at Newberry's and bought me two new pairs of Ditto pants and my very own tube of Neosporin. That didn't do anything. On sweaty days with summer school math tutoring, the burning crept up my arms and into my shoulders. "I have a sunburn," I said, to no one, really, because in a million years that would never happen. I was barely allowed to go to the mailbox without an SPF of 8 or higher.

"I just read some startling statistics on skin cancer," my mom said every summer.

One morning I was in the bathroom watching my mother smoke her cigarettes and put her makeup on. When I laughed about something she caught sight of the inside of my mouth and the sores. "Now what the hell's going on in there?" With a Merit 100 and a tissue over the receiver so as not to rub off her finished face, she called my aunt at Children's. "Well, they're just disgusting," she said as she motioned me to tilt my head back. "I don't know. Definitely not thrush, lesions of some kind."

Together they came to the conclusion that the toxoplasmosis (the "toxo," as we were now calling it) combined with the heavy-duty antibiotics I'd be on for another month had zapped me of everything I needed to have a good pH balance.

"What does pH mean?" I asked. It sounded interesting, like something to do with being smart, but when I learned the definition I made a face. "Now, when you say *body acid*, what does that mean exactly?" And for a second I forgot it was all about my love of bleach.

I tried to relax a little when it was time to take our summer trip to Santa Cruz. I turned up Rush's "Tom Sawyer," snuggled under my Strawberry Shortcake comforter, and forced myself to think about the musty little apartment we rented every year just a block from the wharf. I took deep breaths and did the tighten-and-release muscle exercises my mom showed me for when I felt uppity. "Pick a place," she told me. "A place you see in your mind when you want to relax." I chose that gray-blue hippie beach town. Behind my closed eyes I drew up cold fish wind from the rugged cliffs and the way you could almost taste the corn dog batter in your teeth when the air stood still on the boardwalk. I put myself in the redwoods of the mountains, under the twist of the cypress trees and the terra-cotta bluffs they rebelliously thrived on.

In Santa Cruz I was someone else. Someone not shackled to her brain and body. A sorceress in the mist. A bendable decoration girl waiting in line for the big rides—the bumper cars and the roller coasters—where I watched older boys with sunny hair touch the tanned backs of girls I would never be. But in the pictures I made in my mind, I was allowed the same pieces of summer as everyone else. I wasn't barely over four feet tall, all box corners and sweat.

This was also the summer of our new house—new to us. A four-bedroom rental in a big-tree neighborhood of South San Jose where nobody rented. No apartments, no checks to be taken to the manager with a signed rent receipt in my ugly hands saying yes, despite so much, Traci managed to find the office. Our new neighborhood was polychrome foothills and kids whose parents drove them everywhere.

Our new pink carpet was called *coral*.

There was an upstairs and a downstairs and a swimming pool. I had my own bathroom, which my mom let me decorate in all pink and yellow. I spent hours alone in that bathroom, making kiss lips on the mirror, scrubbing my hands with SOS pads. I locked the door and ran the hot water until I barely existed in the steam. Outside the door I heard the sounds of my family doing things without me. Televisions blared reruns and commercials, Yahtzee cups clanked and rattled out their die on the orange Formica tabletop. Rarely did anyone ask where Traci had run off to. They knew I was in my bathroom, probably with my books and candles and a new lip gloss. Some of that was true. But the bloody soap on my fingers and the cleaning products that scoured away the scabs on my knuckles were the truer parts. As I sanitized my hands by taking off my skin, as I poured peroxide and Ajax onto my toothbrush, as I squeezed shut my watering eyes and clenched my fists at the beautiful sting of chemicals on my gums and tongue, the people on the outside thought I was in there with stories and makeup. I licked the sores on my lips. The sores tasted like somebody screaming.

"You okay in there, honey? Traci?"

I opened the medicine cabinet mirror and tried to see myself sideways.

Across the street, there was a boy. Peter Veneko. He strutted up my driveway in a bright green off-the-shoulder net shirt. "You like Irene Cara?" His face was round and chubby and didn't match the rest of his body. His blond crew cut was an obvious home job—from someone in a hurry. On his thumbnails were streaks of Wite-Out.

"Who doesn't?" I answered.

Practically all summer I had been watching him across the street just sitting on his porch making friendship bracelets with safety pins fastened to his jeaned thigh. When my telepathy of willing him over finally worked, I invited him in to play Atari and listened while he explained his life over Space Invaders: almost fourteen, staying with his aunt and cousins, only here for the summer from Novato, forced to go to a Lutheran day camp "because of my high voice and having a thing for leg warmers." He laughed and made a motion with his fingers like ringing a little bell. "Do you see? They're trying to church it right out of me."

He was the only person I told about the Ajax.

Peter and I spent a lot of time in the bathroom with the door closed. I liked it in there. I liked it in there with Peter. It was dark and cool with no windows. A scary cave for scary me. Peter and I lit candles and chanted Bloody Mary until we both believed so hard he grabbed my ponytail and screamed. We ate peanuts and smoked bubble gum cigarettes while discussing the philosophy of Henry Thomas, who played the little boy in *E.T. the Extra-Terrestrial.*

"There just has to be life on other planets."

"I wonder if Elliot works out?"

When we were neck high in my pool spitting water at each other Peter said, "You sorta remind me of Brooke Shields." Then he made a face like he wanted to take it back. "You know, if you get braces and leave them on long enough, your gums will start to grow down. That would help to make your teeth smaller."

I showed him my books on reincarnation and how to read tarot cards. Together we found out that I was going to have long stretches of unfulfilled relationships and that we were both very famous in our past lives. "Well, I always kind of thought that," he said. "I just wish I didn't have to come back to this life with diabetes."

We were getting ready to do a séance to see if my grandpa Foust was upset about me storing away his statues in my closet when I told him the plans had changed. "Check these babies out," I said and handed him three issues of the *Journal of Pediatric Neurology*. The doctor who had diagnosed the toxo gave the magazines to my mother on a day she was too nervous to do anything but ask a hundred questions and smoke. He told her she would find some good articles on the lasting effects of blood poisoning in children. I would only have to wait a few days for something else to catch my mother's attention before the magazines were mine.

In the candlelight of my yellow bathroom Peter listened while I read about temporal lobe contusions and petit mal seizures. Then, midparagraph I had a question. "Wait. If you're a diabetic do you give yourself shots of insulin?"

He said yes.

"With a needle?"

He said, "How else can you give yourself a shot?"

"How far do you have to stick it in your skin?"

"I don't know. Like, about—" He pinched my arm. I thought I might die from love.

One white-hot afternoon we sat on my driveway waiting around for something to happen. I peeled the skin from my fingertips like outdated fabric on a garage sale chair. We talked about Los Angeles.

"Then one of us could go on auditions for a few months while the other works," Peter said. "That way we won't have a super hard time paying bills and stuff."

"Yeah, I can kind of see how that would work out," I answered. "So what do you think a two-bedroom apartment would run us? Fifty, sixty a month?"

Then our sunlight changed because people were suddenly standing in it. Scott Smalls from down the street and another guy, Dave something. Guys from my brother's school.

"Where's Bryan?" one of them asked. "Is he at work? Go get him."

"I don't know." I had to shield my eyes from their ugly hair halos. "I guess he's at work."

Peter popped in the sound track from *Fame* on my boom box. "Do we look like her brother's keepers?" We both laughed.

"Did we ask you, faggot?" It was the fat one. Scott Smalls. He sometimes cleaned our pool for five dollars. My mom always had to tell me not to look out the window and giggle at him on account of he was a little bit slow.

I thought he was a lot slow.

"I'm looking for her brother, okay," Scott said to Peter. "I wasn't talking to you, Man Girl."

Peter pretended to fiddle with the cassette player. My cheeks burned as the blood rushed into them. I stood. "Look, Scott," I said, "Bryan isn't here. Why don't you call him later or come by or whatever."

The other one, Dave, said, "You suck cock, huh, Pecker?"

"It's Peter," I said, then instantly realized the joke. "Just get out of here, okay?"

"Hey, Horse Teeth," Scott said, laughing. "Why don't you shut your mouth, fucking Black Beauty. You need to tell your brother he shouldn't be fucking other people's girlfriends."

"I'm sure." I nudged Peter's thigh with my toe. My heart made thumps I could feel in my ear canal. "Go get Kim."

Peter got up and walked across the grass. Thank God he didn't prance. Two other kids from around the corner stopped their bikes at the end of my driveway to be nosy.

"Yeah, cocksucker!" Scott yelled to Peter. "Go inside and pack some fudge."

I was embarrassed of the music that was playing: *I'm gonna live forever. / Baby remember my name.* How would I fight these guys if they started something with my new friend?

But I would if I had to.

At the Apartments there was a girl who wouldn't leave me alone, saying all the time my hair was dirty and I smelled like a diaper. When Grammie was plumb fed up with me crying she said, "Then you get yourself out there and whip her ass all over the playground."

So on one of those days when I was forced outside to give everyone some space, I walked onto the playground, made a fist, and slammed it into the neck of a girl who was taller than me, bigger than me, and had a smarter mouth than I did.

But she was not faster. When I ran through the ivy pathways in the back of the complex, the sting of a two-week bruise rising to the surface of my knuckles, I felt as if I had done something wonderful. Impossible. I knew I probably hadn't done much in the way of causing great pain, but I hadn't backed down either. I had been living with voices in my head that told me to lick the window locks or everyone in my family would be murdered by an intruder—clicks in my brain that made it impossible for me to add or subtract a column of uneven numbers. I listened to them all and did whatever they said. When my tired eyes burned for sleep I succumbed to the itch in my brain that whispered. *Check the outlets and the plugs or you'll be sorry.* But the day I hauled off and smacked that girl on the playground, I found something out: even if my mind seemed to be totally separate from the girl attached to it, I still had control over my body. And if I put it in motion fast enough, gave in to the physical impulse without stopping to think, I could make something happen that I could control. If Scott Smalls threatened to hurt my new friend, no amount of hand washing could stop me from helping him.

"You know what, Scott," I said, "you're a fat cow, and if I was your girlfriend I'd be fucking someone else too." That was the first time I ever used *fuck* to reference sex. It wasn't *motherfucker*, like when me and Bryan watched Richard Pryor. It wasn't *fuck this*, as in Kim's Maybelline eyebrow pencil and the lighter she always held over it for too long. It was *fuck* for nasty talk. I stood there in front of those boys unfitting in my small frame. Disgusted with myself. Liking it a little.

My sister came out in her nightgown with a cigarette and a knife. "What the hell's going on here?"

Peter stayed on the porch. Irene Cara sang about making it big.

"I really want Bryan," Scott said. "What the fuck, man, are you serious? A knife? Your brother's been harassing my girlfriend."

Somehow I knew the pretty Filipino girl who came to dinner the other night was the girlfriend Scott was talking about.

"I don't think my brother's been harassing anyone," Kim said. She scratched her chin with the tip of the knife blade.

Scott flinched back. "What the fuck ever, man, you need to go back inside your house and tell your brother to stay the fuck away from my girlfriend."

"I don't know anything about your girlfriend," Kim said, her back straight, her eyes not moving from Scott's ugly face. "But I do know one thing. You come around here saying those hateful things to my little sister and her friends and there's going to be big trouble."

Now four kids looked on from the sidewalk. It was weird to have so many people staring in my general direction but actually watching something else besides my little massacres of normal. It almost made me not even care that Scott and Dave lit up cigarettes and flung matches onto our lawn as they walked away.

"That's right, stay on the porch, faggot," Dave said, but only loud enough for me and a cute boy who followed behind him to hear. I laughed a little. The cute boy nodded at me, his tilted chin saying, *What's up?* For a moment I let myself wish Peter wasn't there.

That night I had a dream about Peter and Scott Smalls. In it we were in my driveway under a red sky with weird blinking lights. Peter messed around with my boom box, pretending to hear something other than that terrible boy and his switchblade words. I called out to Peter to lift his head up and look at the lights. But he wouldn't move. I shouted and demanded. He wouldn't. A faceless girl stood behind him. She took up all of our air and didn't feel like me. I kept yelling at Peter to look at those lights, but he just stood there. The sky pulled itself over us like the skin under a peeled away scab. The girl told me the lights were mine. Not his. I still couldn't see her face.

Just before dawn I opened my eyes. Wide awake, sweaty about the dream. I took out my ledgers and my *Journal of Pediatric Neurology* and would not close my eyes until I wrote it all down in the form of a play that would make Peter and me more than just his flair for head-bands and my craziness. People would know us the way I knew us. The neighborhood would see the way we dreamed.

"But the main theme here is health issues," I said as I handed Theresa and Peter their parts for my production. "This whole show is about preventative medicine."

We drank Pepsi out of coffee mugs and discussed the scenes for Garage Tale Theater's first annual feature-length play.

"If it's annual, doesn't that mean we already did the play last year?" Theresa asked.

"Um, okay," Peter interrupted. He squinted at his paper. "I see what you're trying to do here, and it's cool that you made a part about safe blood sugar levels, but I cannot purposely go into insulin shock."

I rolled my eyes. "Look, you guys, if it's going to be good, we need to get really serious." I rubbed the bridge of my nose even though nothing felt wrong in my head. "This isn't fixing problems on a thirty-minute television show."

I didn't want to start getting all nervous and fight with everyone, but I worried about authenticity. I already had two school plays under my belt and a whole slew of skits I'd put on for my mom's bunco crowd. Onstage, in a character that wasn't me, I wasn't so jagged. I could be an orphan in *Oliver Twist* or Pretty Kitty to Tom Jones's "What's New Pussycat," and if I got nervous it was for real and true reasons and not because I was afraid that yellow fever was making a comeback. Sitting with Theresa and Peter that day, smoking bubble gum cigarettes, I created and decided. Nothing in the back of my brain told me this was wrong or that I would cause something bad to happen if I didn't follow the instruction of rinse, lather, repeat.

Repeat.

Repeat.

Finally, after some debate over how dangerous it would be for Peter to have a real insulin-induced seizure, we decided he would pretend his way into unconsciousness for "The Boy Who Went into Insulin Shock," then end the scene with a jazzy bit to Elton John's "I'm Still Standing." I put Theresa in charge of set design and gave her the part of the teenage mom addicted to cigarettes in "What Smoking Does to a Fetus."

Though Kim was hardly home these days because Gil Johnston was ten years older than her and had his own apartment, I still hoped/expected she would be enthusiastic about helping us with the play. She sprayed glitter paint on an old shower curtain and told us to have fun.

My grandmother had taken a part-time job dealing blackjack at Sutter's Card House, and since it was my brother's job to watch me when Kim was with Gil, we told Bryan he could be our stagehand. Mostly he just stretched the phone cord into the garage when we rehearsed and sat dripping into the receiver to Scott Small's girlfriend. "What am

I doing now?" he said, purposely loud. "Nothing, really. Watching a bunch of dipshits dance."

With my scene revisions and my dictionary I stayed up all night with a reason. I drank Sanka extra hot and almost turned into a regular girl. I even stopped with the Ajax for a while. I was so in place that one night I pretended the tile wall in the shower was Peter and his mouth, even though I knew—you know, I just wanted to.

The afternoon of the show Theresa and I passed out flyers. We walked barefoot in the shade of eucalyptus trees, talking about boys and last-minute changes to the skits. When we leaned against the hot stucco walls of someone's porch we said, "You can pay the fifty cents now or at the door."

My lungs stretched for big air. I imagined how our fold-out chairs would look all lined up on my driveway, how smart it was that I had so carefully chosen Devo's "Beautiful World" as our opening song because the lyrics talked about the universe being so great and people combing their hair all fancy, but the video showed things like a woman on fire and students getting beat in riots, and that's really what the play was about—keeping your eyes open to the dangers in your body or wherever, because most everything seems beautiful. Especially when it isn't.

On purpose, we saved Kitty Thurman's house for last. No one really knew Kitty except for her creepiness. The most interaction I'd ever had with her was when I stood around in the street while some boys asked if she really once lived in a tree house in Oregon and ate wild fox.

She answered by saying that sounded like fun.

Another time I saw her at RadioShack with her dad buying wires.

One afternoon I pedaled my bike alongside the kids that knew me only from my swimming pool. We stopped on top of a high street and watched Kitty stomp around like Frankenstein in the canyon below. She threw a Frisbee to a gray-and-white husky that was a lot like her in a way none of us could place. We waited for the first one to start, then we all took turns: "Of course she's homeschooled. That's what they do with retards."

"There's no way she's only twelve. Look at the size of her."

"Where's the mom? Did they like, stuff and mount her on the wall?"

And when I was sure I could jump into the swirls of laughter, like how you put your hands up to the air and move them with the rhythm of the big jump rope, when I had waited and synchronized, I grabbed my mark. "Look at those kneecaps!" I said. "Holy fuck, they're like turtle shells. Oh, mama, you are sexy in those flannel cutoffs; I wish I could get me a pair of shorts as righteous as that."

I made everyone laugh. The rope turned, never touching my ankles.

Before we got to her front steps I told Theresa we should put Kitty in the play.

"Are you nuts?" she said. "I thought we were just going to leave a flyer, then bolt."

But why hadn't I thought of this before? Lumberjack Kitty Thurman and that horrible accident in the woods of the Pacific Northwest. It wasn't an urban legend. We'd all seen it. We all knew it had really happened.

I knocked on Kitty's door.

"You didn't say anything about having her in the play. You're like totally springing this on me," Theresa said. "I should just leave you right here by yourself."

We heard weird scuffling, like someone skipping in clogs, then something falling, then someone clogging away. All at once she was there, in the same cutoff jean shorts we saw her in almost every day, the same T-shirt with a peeling decal of a wolf howling at a seriously large moon.

We all said hi.

We were all silent.

I wondered if we all smelled the air like mushrooms and charcoal wafting from her house.

"I think I know you guys," she said.

"Yeah," I answered. "I live down the street." But the very inside of me tightened. *Don't act like a nervous spaz. Make a joke about something.*

It was very different being right in front of her than it was watching her mass from a safe twenty feet away. For the first time I understood that if someone wants to kill you, there isn't a joke in the whole world funny enough to stop it.

I told Theresa to give her a flyer, then asked if she wanted to be in the play.

She answered fast. "No, not me." She ran her fingers through her stringy hair the color of concrete. I caught a fast glimpse of the patched-up hole on the side of her head where the bullet had taken off some of her body, leaving a pink gummy-worm scar. "There's no way I could be in a play," she said.

"We'd really like you to come and talk about your accident," I said. Then I swallowed hard and went for it. "Maybe bring your ear and show it to everyone. Or you could just give it to us and we'll show it for you." Not that there wasn't a kid on the street who hadn't seen Kitty Thurman's ear. When she first moved here she'd made it a point to carry the thing around in a baby-food jar and offer a peek to anyone who wondered. Part of me felt such dislike for that kind of suicide.

"No, I really don't think I can," she said. "I'm not allowed to take it off the property anymore."

I looked around. I'd never heard a kid use *property* to talk about their house.

"The play is going to be so good, Kitty," I said. "You're not even going to believe how many people will be there."

Theresa held up my lie. "Yeah, practically the whole neighborhood."

It went on like this for a long time, long enough to make me stop caring if she wanted to stand in my garage and show everyone she was more than just wood and growling. It was the same as Peter and Scott Smalls in my driveway—the girl wouldn't try.

I wanted to ask Kitty so much on her porch that day. I wanted to see what the inside of her house looked like. Did she have a room with secret books of what to expect when you're menstruating and swirls of plaster on the wall like unearthly faces hating her? What happened to her mother? Did she ever want to do anything about the kids who mocked her for reasons as obvious as they were invisible, or was it okay to keep shutting up and dream about other people pointing out your lights in the sky?

"Kitty," I said. "I have money. . . ."

When we walked home I told Theresa no, she couldn't hold the baby-food jar with the ear. "I'm the one who gave her two dollars," I reminded, and as the jar heated up in my grip I counted four times we had asked if she would please come and watch the play, to just be there when we did our newly made-up skit on hunting safety. But no, she couldn't, no she wouldn't. She said she had to help her father with his bandages.

"So where do you think her mom is?" I asked Theresa.

She shrugged. "Who cares. What I really want to know is what kind of dad points a shotgun so close to his kid's head?"

———

The shower curtain went up at seven, just like the flyers said. In front of two kids I knew from the neighborhood and two adults I had never seen save for Haj the Ice Cream Man, we began our show. Peter and I took turns emceeing the intros and outlines to each skit. One narrated the story into my Mr. Microphone while the other worked the boom box. For Theresa's skit of the mom who smoked and had to deal with a premature baby (a gasping thing crafted from blue Play-Doh and real doll parts) we chose Diana Ross's "Do you Know Where You're Going To" as the background music while my voice-over asked, "What kind of future will this child have in a world clouded by her mother's smoke?"

Theresa came through beautifully. With one of Kim's unlit cigarettes in her hand she leaned over the incubator crying, so much feeling in every line.

The enthusiastic clapping of an audience member filled a corner of the driveway, but due to realism of the subject matter, the crickety chain of a bike and its rider pedaling away was what we heard the loudest.

For "The Boy Who Went into Insulin Shock," Peter aced every word, hit all his marks. During the restaurant scene where I played the concerned sweetheart who brings him orange juice, rubs his back, and reminds him how important it is to eat foods like nuts and apples to keep blood sugar at safe levels, we heard someone whisper, "How inappropriate."

But we kept right on.

During Peter's dance, Theresa and I began preparing the props for the hunting-safety skit: a gun made from cardboard and aluminum foil, Bryan's old Davy Crocket hat with ketchup on it, and, floating in its little jar of circumstance and formaldehyde, Kitty's ear—a near-perfect specimen of what can happen when you have don't have a mother to protect you from a father who takes you into the woods.

Then the boy who knew every Neil Diamond song by heart and almost every dance step from *Can't Stop the Music* fell against the card table, knocking over all the props. While Elton John rang out—*If you think this fool could never win / Well look at me I'm a-coming back again*—I watched helplessly as everything on the table came sliding down, and Kitty's ear crashed onto the floor of my garage.

Peter put his hand to his mouth. "Oh my Lord," he said, then looked around for something or someone.

Haj the Ice Cream Man and our one remaining audience member stood to have a look. Someone said, "Whoops, did you guys drop a glass of water or what?"

Water.

Theresa and I scurried to the place where Kitty's ear lay dying its second death and glass shimmered like the tips of shiny swords.

"Oh my Lord," Peter said again. "What's happening to it?"

We all watched as my two-dollar foolproof idea shriveled up like a burnt Shrinky Dink.

Haj the Ice Cream Man asked if the play was over. I scooped up what was left of the disintegrating ear and made a mad dash for the house.

Theresa caught me at the door. "Wait. What do you want me to tell everyone?"

"What everyone?" I said. "There's only two people left."

In the kitchen I ran cold water into my cupped hands, over this—whatever it was now. It was hard to tell it had been anything. "Oh God, I feel sick to my stomach," I said.

Peter said, "I think I know what's going on here. I'm not a scientist or anything, but I think whatever kind of solution that thing was in wasn't supposed to be in the open air. Like, I did this experiment at school once. You take some rubbing alcohol—"

"Peter, I don't care about that!" My yelling brought a teary lump into my throat. "Just help me fix this thing or that girl's going to beat the living crap out of me."

We tried water. We tried window cleaner. When we realized we were just drying it out more we tried Vaseline, then baby oil. Nothing worked.

Theresa patted my back while I cried. "That one kid who was asleep wants to know if he can get his fifty cents back," she said.

———

They had to bring the doll into my closet because I wouldn't come out. All I wanted to do was breathe into my paper bag. I had watched a report on *20/20* about phobias, and it said if you feel faint, put a bag around your mouth and nose and breathe with your head down. But Peter and Theresa kept shoving Baby Alive in my face, explaining how we were going to cut an ear from my doll and pass it off as the real thing. I breathed harder, the brown paper heaving like mummy lungs while the sides of my life closed in a little. When Kitty found out what happened to her ear, she would hit me until I lost my life on a summer afternoon.

"We'll put it in this." Theresa held up an old sample-size mint jelly jar she found way back in the fridge.

Peter clicked open a retractable box cutter.

"Oh, there's no way," I said when we were done. "It looks completely fake." My chest was all prickles again as I imagined handing gigantic Kitty Thurman this plasticky-looking thing in a ridiculously small jar that smelled like dish soap and cough syrup. I put my head between my knees. I tasted stomach bile.

My good friend and my pretty cousin did what they could to reassure me. "She's totally not going to know the difference. But if anything happens, I think you're supposed to keep your forearms up to block your face."

When my doorbell rang it was lightning down my spine. I couldn't speak—of course I knew who it was. I held my paper bag with one hand and flapped the other hand while vigorously shaking my head to indicate that under no circumstance was anyone to open my front door. The next sound was my own pulse in my head while Theresa, who apparently didn't understand my spastic hand flapping and head shaking, ran down the hall to show Kitty that I was home without her ear.

Peter left me too.

All I had was Baby Alive, and Baby Alive had been cut, a part of her head just gone. Not unlike the girl at my front door who had come to hurt me. I looked at my once-loved—though not favorite and kind of scary as she got older—factory mimic of a real child, matted hair and a butthole crusted up with banana-flavored powder product because I never cared enough to change her diaper. She looked at me with shame and disgust. The open bloodless flap of all man-made material above her chubby little jaw was an alien mouth. *You've really done it this time. Now me and Kitty aren't the only ones with holes in our heads.*

They called me to come out there. They said she wasn't buying it.

"So what is this supposed to be?" Kitty held up our unclever trick. "I really need my ear back."

"Kitty, what are you talking about?" I managed to say. "This is so too your ear."

"Nope. It's definitely not." God, her voice was so calm.

"I think it is," I said. My knees shook. On that television show about phobias, I remembered the woman who said that if she stood on a balcony, she was scared she might fling herself over the edge, said her whole body felt like the Scarecrow flopping around the yellow brick road. At the time I thought, What a stupid comparison. Now, in front of Kitty and her slow words without anger, with that goddamn wolf on her shirt and the moon that in a million years could never be so big, I knew it was the truest thing I'd heard in a long time. I was turning into straw just like that poor woman, watching the balcony crumble in front of me.

How much longer till the girl breaks my nose?

"Kitty, that is your ear," Theresa tried again. "I don't know what you think we're trying to pull here."

"Okay, look, this is ridiculous," Peter said. "Accidents happen. I mean, what can we do?" He turned to me and said I should just apologize.

I had no control over my trembling, and it did not occur to me until later that Peter should have been the one to apologize.

Peter Veneko did not stand up straight and tell Kitty to fuck off or try to see where my sister was so she could come out to the porch and help us. He did not put his arm around my shoulders or write a play for practically just me so that people could see me doing something other than just being weird. He told the truth. He said to me, "It was your play, Traci, say you're sorry."

In a split second with a shot of heat in my arms, I wet my pants and my breath was gone. A salty fluid filled the insides of my cheeks. I swayed a little and went down. Kitty's arms reached toward me. The cold stickiness of her shirt decal pressed against my forehead, the knotty smells of her weird life in the fabric. I tried to make a noise but all I could do was watch how the moon shrank and shrank until it disappeared into the wolf's open mouth.

I would not bounce back quickly or entirely from this. From fainting. From that poor and awful girl catching me. Peter would go back to Novato and call me once to say he was coming down for the weekend but never show up. Kitty would go back to her house with her father. The next summer both of them would return to the understanding of their northern forests.

For me, it would take more than half my life to free myself of that memory—of the terrifying truth owning up to yourself lies at your feet.

Kitty's father came to our house that night. He apologized to my mother and said he was so embarrassed over how irresponsible his daughter was. My mom made me say sorry to a thick-faced man whose lack of expression—like his daughter's—showed us all how they cared nothing for California theatrics, how a dead mother, a missing wife, a shot-off ear, could turn you so inside out the crap happening around you was only a play.

I never spoke to my family about Kitty catching me. I held in that story for a long time, how she stopped me from hitting my head on the bricks, maybe even stood between me and my death. In fact, the next to know the details of Peter and Theresa's betrayal, they way I'd been forced to act outside of who I was, would be the people in my therapy group, the ones who would hear me talk about how scared I was of losing my breath again and passing out. In a circle of folding chairs and coffee in Styrofoam cups, Kitty would be immortalized. To my friends who would never really understand why I could no longer drive on the freeway for fear of fainting, or sit for too long in a movie theater where no one would be able to find my crumpled body on the floor until after the ending credits, Kitty would be the horrible girl who started all this anxiety-attack business. Her big hands and favorite shirt turning into a joke of what I couldn't control.

A laughing me making my problems as funny as a stand-up act. *Can we get some drinks down here!*

But when heads are thrown back and shoulders bounce and some-one asks you where you come up with this stuff, the truth makes you wish like hell you had *just come up with it.* So you could get over it. Instead, you replay that fainting spell over and over in your mind.

Some nights you'll have dreams about the girl you teased, the girl who was more like you than you realized, and you'll see her not catching you in her arms so that your brains spill out all over your happy white patio. You'll wake up in a sweat like water from a polluted sea, wondering how different your life would be now had that girl just gone off and smacked you cold in the face—anything to not feel yourself slow and floating, a shutter-lens good-bye—anything to stop making excuses for why you can't drive on the freeway, why you can't see a movie unless you sit in the aisle seat, why you can't chew food in front of other people, why cold medicine that makes you drowsy and forgetful will end up meaning so much. Anything, goddammit—whatever it takes to erase the day you collapsed into yourself.

6

two-pack conspiracy

*Elphaba to Fiyero: "Do you really want to know who is
pulling the strings to make you move?"*
—GREGORY MAGUIRE, *WICKED*

"Because I'm afraid it's trying to kill me."

That was the only answer I could come up with. The minute the
words slipped from my mouth I knew they were the wrong ones.

Dr. Schmidt rocked a little in his chair before he spoke. "So, is it
that you think the sun represents a person and the person is trying to
kill you? Or are you talking about sunlight, as in the sunlight will kill
you?"

I shrugged. "Uh, I'm not sure what I mean exactly." I only knew
that I had been having terrifying dreams about looking onto a horizon
that never seemed to end. My bed reeked of sweat and when we had
an assembly at school about Northern California's new water restric-
tions, I looked around the cafeteria at the wet bangs and red cheeks
and almost had a panic attack wondering which one of us would be
the first to die from dehydration. But I wasn't sitting in the office of my

new Someone to Talk To because my home state was running out of water. A week or so before my first real head-shrinker visit, I had come home from school almost on fire. My clothes smelled like an old heater and I couldn't catch my breath. When I sat in my closet and cupped my paper bag over my face it just made everything worse. What a terrible sensation to have to strangle yourself a little to keep from being strangled.

I called my mother at work and asked where she'd put my bathing suit.

"Oh, it's not warm enough to go swimming," she said.

The clinkety sound of typewriter bells in the background scratched me all over. "I don't *want* to go swimming," I answered. "I *have* to go. If you don't tell me where my bathing suit is I'll just jump in with my clothes on."

"Look, don't start this shit," she whispered. "I said no. It's not warm enough, the pool hasn't been cleaned. I don't want you to get sick, you got it?"

"No, I don't got it."

"Get Kim on the phone."

She hung up. I called back. She hung up. I called back. She said she would lose her job if I didn't stop.

My sister was in the kitchen baking cookies and sounded busy enough for me to sneak into the pool no matter if I'd been threatened with my dad coming over to show me what happened when I got carried away with my smart mouth. But halfway to the pool gate, the phone rang. In a split second Kim was running outside in her oven mitts.

"Get the hell in the house, now!" Her arm flung around my neck as she tried to scoot me toward the screen door. I screamed. I kicked her shin. "My skin is burning up! You want me to catch on fire! You have no idea what's happening in this country!"

"What is the matter with you? Have you lost your mind?" We shuffled inside toward the kitchen table. I knocked over a chair and grabbed the plate where two rows of Nestlé Toll Houses sat melting in their heat. I threw them against the refrigerator.

"Oh my God, I don't believe this." She picked up the phone and dialed our mother's work. I ran into my bedroom and slammed the door hard enough to knock down a little porcelain ballerina from my shelf. From my room I could hear my sister: "All I wanted was some nice cookies," she said.

What did she know about the dangers of drought, anyway? My sister didn't care. No one in my family did. No one saw the dreams I had about the never-ending sunshine, about people who just wanted to throw a Frisbee around at Golden Gate Park but ended up seared and black-nosed like scary marionette puppets in an evil girl's daydream.

For Earth Appreciation Week our class studied about ways we could help protect our environment. I had to write a list of how I thought my family might help conserve water. What I turned in was a list of lies. No one in my house was going to take five-minute showers, or wash their clothes on the quick cycle, or wait until the dishwasher was totally full before turning it on. That just wasn't us. If the water in our unheated pool caused the slightest discomfort we'd hook up the hose to the spigot in the tub and play Atari or watch *General Hospital*, all blue ghosts and pretty sighs while we waited for the water to change into something we deserved.

I did all those things too. And without any guilt until our class watched a movie about how when the Earth will become too hot, there will be no oranges and people will find out their mysterious rashes are called scurvy and they'll be crying and wishing they didn't let their kids play in the sprinklers because now blood vessels are popping up purple and oblivious all over their bodies and their kids are coughing like dirty screen doors slamming shut.

After watching that movie it was clear to me we'd all been living wrong, but when I tried to help, tried to make my family see this by putting egg timers in the shower stall with red fingernail polish indicating the five-minute mark, when I waited by the bathroom door and made lists of who let the water run during teeth brushing, all I got was my brother flinging his toothbrush saliva at my face and my mom telling me to shut it with the preaching.

"Get your ass in that kitchen." Kim stood in my doorway. "Clean up every crumb."

"The sunlight," I said.

She squeezed the back of my arms and gave me a shake. "Shut up. I don't want to hear a damn thing out of your mouth. Sunlight my ass. Just get in that kitchen and fix what you did."

"You don't care about anything but your stupid boyfriend and your stupid pot. I hate you."

She let go of my arms. Her mouth made a tight little O.

"Yeah, that's right. I hate you," I said again. The heat of not crying flushed through my face. Kim left my room and headed toward the bathroom—to blow her nose or wipe her tears about how mean I was or maybe let the faucet run while she held her lighter upside down into her pipe. When she returned she threw a glass of water in my face. "Not as much as I hate you." She tossed the glass at the wall above my head. It didn't break. "And pick that up too," she said.

Now here I sat in front of a man who knew nothing about how much I was on to myself. Only abominable children told their older sisters they hated them and pestered their moms at work to the point of their moms not even speaking to them for a whole twelve hours or even saying good night, sweet dreams, and girls who threw baking pans might even lock themselves in the bathroom and stare at a pair of scissors for a really long time and wonder what stainless steel would feel like in the fatty parts of their calves.

I wouldn't tell Dr. Nicholas Schmidt a damn thing about the night of the cookies and my wet face and me in my bed with my hands pulsating a hatred for everything but especially myself.

"I just don't like the sun that much anymore," I said. "It's like the sound a microphone makes when it's too close to the speakers."

"That's a really interesting way of putting it," he said. "I like how you describe things."

Most of the time I just shrugged and didn't say much. A stranger asking me if I knew why I acted so strange was just—well, strange. Plus, he was there as a paid have-to-be friend, and the last time I sat in front of a person my mother paid to talk to me was because I had locked a little girl in a hot car. Now it was me, and everything was hot, every door locked.

"I guess it really hurts my eyes," I told the doctor. "I can't see in the sunlight. It feels like needles."

He leaned over his desk and I hated it because he was cute, with a cool German accent. I could totally picture us holding hands in the snow.

"But no one can see in the sunlight," he said.

"Yeah, but me more than others." Because wasn't everything me more than others? Like last year when Theresa got her first pair of eyeglasses and everyone said she looked so smart and so pretty. I faked an eye exam to the extreme of bifocals and wore those ridiculous things like crystal balls pressed into my face.

In the car, after my first visit with Dr. Schmidt (with Kim and my mom and the windows rolled up and the AC full blast and their cigarette smoke), my mom asked if I made sure to tell him about the screaming and the cookies.

"Yeah," I lied. Actually, he'd hinted around as if someone sure had told him: *And do you ever get the urge to throw things or shout for no reason?*

Whatever.

Maybe I barely knew my times tables and couldn't keep track of more than two numbers in my head, but I wasn't retarded. I knew when someone had been talking.

"And the psoriasis," my mom said. "Did you tell him about the psoriasis?"

My dislike of sunlight had started the onset of a scaly scalp and knees like an old beaded coin purse. Gross and interesting at the same time, but I certainly wasn't going to let a complete stranger in on that nastiness. "Yeah, I told him," I lied again. "He said to just keep using my cream."

I tried to make little jokes around Dr. Schmidt. I suggested that since I had no desire to go outside maybe the best therapy would be to avoid dangerous situations such as going to school. Ha-ha. But all that did was start a bunch of questions on the subject of teachers and did I feel like they were there to help or hurt me, blah, blah, blah. . . . I spent so much time during the school day worrying about the notes going home, the fake sick days and how many more I could fake, the weird uneven symbol for long division—the last thing I wanted to do on a Tuesday night when every girl my age was at home watching Nell Carter was talk and worry about more school stuff. But I didn't really feel like talking about anything else either, like how the voices in my head were getting worse.

I had read Kim a poem I wrote in my ledger about people on fire and showed her a little drawing of a stick man with flaming shoulders. She said it would be a good idea if I brought my ledgers with me to my next appointment, then made a huge show of knocking on Dr. Schmidt's office door to bring in my journals after I purposely left them in the waiting room.

"What are you doing?" I said with big eyes.

She put the books on Dr. Schmidt's desk. "Didn't you need to show him these? Hi, Dr. Schmidt, good to see you again."

That night I felt an aggression that bordered on paranoia. "You did it on purpose!" I yelled. "You just want to embarrass me. Both of you do!" Mom and Kim sat at the table making out a grocery list. At first they didn't say anything when I tore out a bunch of papers from my ledgers and flung them all over the living room, but when the actual books started hitting the side of the walls my mom grabbed my shirt collar.

"I've had it with your attitude these past few weeks, missy."

"Well, I've had it with your attitude," I said. I tried to pry her fingers from my clothes but was soon warned that if I scratched anyone or threw anything else or slammed my door or cursed or whatever I had in mind to make everyone miserable, my television was coming out of my room and my father would be called.

"Call him," I said. "I know he doesn't know I'm seeing Dr. Schmidt. Call him."

She slapped me, hard.

Just as it had been with Misty in the car, I had promised my mom I wouldn't tell my father I was visiting a therapist. "It'll just worry him," she'd said. Same as when she came into my room the night I threw the cookies and said she thought maybe I needed someone to talk to. "But I'll be paying for the sessions, so we don't need to drag your dad into this."

After the slap, I didn't cry right away. She pulled back almost immediately, kind of surprised. My first face slap. A sunburn without the sun.

"Why did you let Kim take all my writing and barge into Dr. Schmidt's office like that? Do you even care how that made me feel?"

"We thought it would help you open up a little," Mom answered. "If you could maybe just read him some of the things—"

Kim appeared, wringing her hands, bursting with sisterly involvement. "Traci, some of the stuff you write in there, I mean, it's got us a little concerned."

"What stuff? The guy on fire?" It was the only thing I had shown her recently.

They looked at each other. How obvious. The story about the teenage couple who drowns their unwanted baby (it's what my grammie had said the song "Ode to Billie Joe" was about when I asked her what the lyrics meant). The little hearts I drew around Dr. Schmidt's name. The one entire page completely devoted to the word *sex*. Oh, I could totally picture the cozy scene: the two of them with their plastic tumblers full of Pepsi, smoke slithering over the table all grown-up and death swampy. Worried. Oh so worried. I had already overheard Kim's little joke about my fear of sunlight not even being real. "Come on, Mom, it's just something else for her to get attention. We should push her outside and lock all the doors," she said. "I bet that would put a really quick end to her tantrums."

I actually thought it was kind of funny then.

Not anymore.

I pointed to my sister standing there, her little burdens shining next to my mother. "Never. Ne-ver, e-ver go into my room again," I said. "And I will never share anything with you for the rest of my entire life."

"Oh well, okay, that's just fine," Kim said. "So, you know what? You can clean your own damn room from now on, you ungrateful brat." She started with the tears. "I'm the one who goes in there every day and picks up all your crap, all your food wrappings and the stacks of magazines you're taking from the library. You think it all just magically cleans itself?"

My mom nodded. "I know, right? You think anything's going to run smoothly for you if you don't shape up your act around here?"

I rubbed the spot on my cheek where my mom's hand had been. It still felt like something was touching it. Someone else's skin that had nothing to do with my own.

"I'm not acting," was all I could think of to say.

That night Grammie called to let us know she was bringing home some leftover tacos from her friend's nursing home where she'd been working. Actually, she was in the process of buying the care facility— the first time someone in our family would be a proprietor of something that didn't involve forged invoices or a pushcart. "Tacos sound good," I said. "I just got in from being locked outside so I'm really hungry."

"Locked outside? Are you there alone?" Grammie asked. "Where's your mom and everyone?"

"Everyone's here. It's just that Kim's trying to help me get over a little problem and locked me out of the house all day," I said. "When will you be home? Jeez, I'm still shivering."

When I hung up the phone Bryan was in my face like a super-fast zoom-in. "You're a liar," he said. "No one locked you out. Why would you tell Grammie that?"

"Mind your own business. You don't know what mom and Kim have been doing to me."

He grabbed my elbow. "I was here the whole time, you liar. I was in my room and totally heard you spazzing out all over the place. Now the minute Grammie asks, you're going to tell the truth. No one's done a damn thing to you. You've got to stop this bullshit."

"What bullshit?"

His hand around my arm was like a blood pressure cuff, in his dark eyes the anger of a man. "Making everyone totally nuts," he said. "Turning everyone into you."

At my next meeting with Dr. Schmidt I confessed about lying to my grandmother. He'd brought me my first ever piece of marzipan. I don't really know why I blabbed all over the place. I just wanted to tell him, I guess. Maybe I was happy about so much sugar. "I'm flaky," I said. "Look." I shook out the shoulders of my black T-shirt to let the silver-fish skin cells of psoriasis snow up the air. "I can make weather from my brain."

"Uh-huh." Clearly, he wasn't impressed. "So tell me why you think you were so motivated to make up such a lie about your sister locking you out of the house?"

Motivated. Head-shrink talk was funny to me. It sort of felt like one of those school assemblies where they showed slide projector pictures of winning Olympic athletes and played soft rock anthems to get you all excited about being a kid, or life, or however a kid's life is supposed to be exciting. "I just wanted Kim to get into trouble because I'm sick of her. She goes through my private stuff," I said. "Plus, she's going to marry Gil in a few months, so how come her and my mom can't just plan the wedding and leave me alone?"

"Are you upset about your sister marrying Gil?" he asked.

"No. He's a nice guy," I said, "but let me show you something funny." I grabbed a pen and quickly sketched out my new doodle sensation since becoming slightly obsessed with books on Marie Antoinette. "Look." I held up the paper. "It's a guillotine. Get it. *Gil*-o-teen?" Not even realizing my mispronunciation, I chopped the air with clapped hands and made a *shhppt* sound like something being sliced.

Dr. Schmidt's silence made the air like phlegm drying on a hot sidewalk.

"Don't you think that's funny?" I asked.

I was old enough to know how I should've been acting. Whenever someone said to me, *You know better*, of course I kind of had an idea they were right. I mean, what kind of person feels awesome about throwing around baked goods and telling her sister she hates her? What kind of zombie mutant are you if you keep repeating the word *hate* in your mind and keep a tally on a sheet of paper until the word adds up to three hundred, which is clean enough to stop saying the word altogether and switch to its antipode, which of course is *love*, so you write that word but doubling the number three hundred to show that your love—yes, Jesus, God, and Mary—is stronger than your hate, except that this sum leads to six hundred, which has a six in it, which you kind of understand is somehow related to the devil, which brings you back to probably why you are hurling cookies at the wall and acting like Bette Davis in *What Ever Happened to Baby Jane*.

My mom said this constantly: "Don't you know how hard it would be for all of us if Kim weren't here to look after things?"

Most of the time. Sure. There'd be no trips to Taco Bell after school, no one giving me a head-start push down the stairs in my sleeping bag, no one to tell my mother she was doing the best job she could do.

"But it seems like it bothers you that your sister does so much," Dr. Schmidt said. "Or maybe you wish she'd spend more time with you and less time with Gil?"

I shrugged and thought about that for a minute. What I wanted to say to Dr. Schmidt, what I knew as deep as my own instability, wasn't that Kim and her best boyfriend bothered me—it was Kim and her best girlfriend, my mother. In their combined presence I was as filthy as a demon, as invisible as a poltergeist. Where they had Rod Stewart concerts, a serious love of tobacco, and Mervyns credit cards that carried exactly the same balance—"Six seventy-nine for both of us, Mom, look at that. We're like psychic shopping twins"—I had skin diseases and a vile interest in scabs.

The older I got, the weirder I got, the closer they became. When my mother changed careers and took a position as lead sales distributor for a prominent winery, she needed Kim more than ever to be at home. After school the kids asked if the girl in the old-lady sunglasses and bitchin' Camaro was my mother. "Nice car," they said. "Was she like ten when she had you?"

It could be so good when it was just me and my big sister, us on the sofa painting our toenails in front of *People Are Talking* or her crank calling a boy I liked who didn't like me back, saying she was the school librarian and Mike or whoever had better stop checking out so many Judy Blume books or people are going to start figuring out he's a big homo. I loved looking at my sister's photograph books and finding pictures of just us when I was a baby and she was almost a preteen.

"I thought Mom brought you home from the hospital just for me," she would say. But then there's a photograph of the three of us: me, Mom, and Kim, standing at the entrance to Frontier Village. My mom's hand on Kim's shoulder, while only a half of me blurs off into the corner. My extended arm reaching through the static like a creature in a toxic fog. Just a few more seconds and I would've been in the entire frame; you could've seen all of me.

On a Friday afternoon Kim picked me up early from school to take me to my neurologist appointment. I'd had an MRI earlier that week and was asked another slew of stupid questions on account of I told the doctor I could hear things others didn't. Everything from *do you have regular nosebleeds* to *have you ever experienced furniture/buildings/ people changing shape in front of you*, all answered by the neurologist having to look at my mom and Kim first before accepting my replies: "No way. Uh, I think I would totally know if I fell asleep in public places or had the urge to bark."

And now the results were in. Dr. Mojir told me to sit in the waiting room. He said he needed to talk to a grown-up. And *he* wanted to do the talking. I understood enough of the serious medical world to know that if a test shows you're not contagious/in need of a different drug/ getting ready for the mortician to stitch your eyelids shut, then it's the nurses who call and say you're in the clear. When the doctor wants to talk, you're in a gown without a butt cover and asking for a priest to help you get a few things off your chest.

"I'd like to give your mom a call tonight," Dr. Mojir said to Kim. "What's the best time for us to talk?"

Kim touched the ruffled collar of her blouse with worried fingers. "Well, whatever needs to be said, you can say to me."

But the doctor said no, he needed to talk to a *parent*. I watched my sister's face. Her dark brown eyes turned to little hard slits. She pressed her lips and took in a big breath to make her spine straight, like a bird showing another bird how it is not scared. "That's fine," she said.

God, that little piece of defeat was so pleasing to me. It was almost enough to make me forget I obviously had something very serious. Maybe even fatal.

That night on the phone with the neurologist my mom began to cry. She pulled the cord to talk in the hall and sucked in wet air with her cigarette smoke. "Yeah, I understand what you're saying," she whispered.

I stood by my bedroom door and listened and plucked at the scabs on my head until I saw blood under my fingernails. My heart beat fast. I knew we were coming up to the part where me being able to hear a booming radio in a parking lot had nothing to do with superpowers and everything to do with me moving closer to where ghosts live.

My mom said, "Come on and sit down, honey." She and Kim lit up cigarettes at the kitchen table. I waited. Someone had to just come out with it. So my mother did. "Dr. Mojir thinks you may be schizophrenic."

Kim gasped.

"What?" I asked. "Sitz . . . oh . . . pent . . . What?"

My mom dabbed under her eyes with a napkin. "Schizophrenic. It's a mental condition. Schizophrenia."

Kim said, "A bad one."

I made a quick check in my knowledge bank of mental conditions: not a whole lot. Infectious diseases were more my thing—the bleeding eye sockets of the Ebola virus being way cooler than grandma padding around in a housecoat wondering how she came to be in a place with all that bingo. Okay, so, heads spinning and green vomit: demonic possession; stealing I knew as kleptomania because Theresa called me Klepto and said she wasn't going to shop with me at Kmart anymore if I didn't quit it with the five-finger discounts. What else? Alcoholism? An ABC after-school special and my uncle Tony falling from a two-story window on New Year's Eve were pretty much my frame of reference for heavy boozing. Murdering people—was that sociology or pathology?

"So am I going to die?" I asked.

"We need to talk to your father about what's going on," my mom said. "Dr. Mojir's going to talk to Dr. Schmidt. We all want to be clear about what the voices are telling you and if we need to—"

"Wait. Voices? What voices?" I stood up. "I never told anyone about hearing *voices*." Not once did I ever let Dr. Schmidt in on my touch-this, touch-that check marks or my responsibility to listen to each stove-top burner after turning it off because gas makes sounds and it also helps if you press down a little on each burner but only on the left side. None of that had been discussed.

I especially never said a damn thing to Dr. Mojir, who called me Stacy all the time and didn't even look me in the eye when he spoke.

"You mean the bass and the music sounds I hear? From when I had the toxo? Those aren't voices," I said. And still nobody cleared up if I was going to die.

"No, honey," Kim answered.

I didn't want her bogusness now, calling me honey because my mom was there. Right now I wanted someone to tell me what the hell was going on.

"No, I'm not going to die, or no, those aren't the sounds you guys are talking about?"

Through a cloud of cigarette smoke they sized up how their words dug into me—a fine angle, an easy reel. *Look how pretty that stupid fish is in our sunlight.*

I spent the better part of the evening searching through various fiction and nonfiction books about a new mystery called schizophrenia. I hated that I'd never heard of it before. It was too late to go to the library and I wasn't finding much in our outdated family health books. By the time Johnny Carson came on, I was so wound up all I could do was pace back and forth from my room to the bathroom. I pulled squares of Charmin from their perforated edges and counted how many pieces of toilet paper it took to fill up my palm so that the sides of the paper weren't overflowing out of my hand. When I went back for a new piece

I said in my mind, If there's an even amount of paper fibers hanging from each piece I just tore, that means schizophrenia isn't really all that bad and maybe Mom and Kim are even lying. If it's uneven, I should just kill myself.

"Come on now," my mom said around midnight. "Look, you just try and relax in your bed and I'll read you something interesting." I chose an article from her *Redbook* magazine about a woman who had to give her adopted baby back to the birth mother because everyone involved was the wrong color for everyone else involved.

"Can you imagine?" my mom said into the printed words. She lit up a cigarette. "How awful for that poor kid." Something in the way she said *can you imagine* sounded too high-pitched for my bed to feel nice, like an actor on a stage who isn't sure that the audience can hear her or even knows who she is.

"I never told Dr. Mojir or anyone that I heard voices, Mommy."

She leaned her elbows into my covers and kissed my forehead. "We're going to figure this all out," she said. "We're going to get to the bottom of what's going on, and you're going to be just fine."

"I'm already just fine."

"Hey, you remember that movie we watched with Sally Field? *Sybil*, the one where the girl was very ill and you said what a great actress Sally Field was?"

Of course I remembered. It scared and fascinated me. Sybil was a hundred different people in her head and could even do the voices of whoever was doing the talking at the time. For months after watching that movie I worried that if I pretended to be Mary Poppins—like I did all the time—I might really start to believe in flying umbrellas and sidewalk art afternoons.

"Well, that girl was schizophrenic, and you certainly don't act like her, do you?"

I shrugged. "Sybil didn't count a lot, did she?"

"Not that I remember. Do you count a lot?"

"Not really." I didn't want this now. This mother/daughter love and understanding at bedside. I wanted clever remarks and everything okay in thirty minutes or less. Like on *The Facts of Life*, how Mrs. Garrett found an answer for everything from date rape to anorexia and she'd make it so it was never just *one* girl's fault.

When my dad took me to Dairy Queen he looked at me with his eyes all squinty, tilting in his chair, trying to see me from different angles as if I was blocking his view of the middle. Maybe he was waiting for me to morph into a different personality or jump up and start a conversation with the voices like those guys in Santa Cruz who walked around the beach in seagull-shit-covered army jackets asking people if they knew Jesus, then answering for them.

"What?" I said. "Stop looking at me." I tried to make things funny. "Why don't you look at how fat that girl is over there? Man, she must have swallowed the dairy queen *and* the king."

"So you're okay then?" He blew a stream of smoke from his nostrils and said that what would make him very happy was to see me do well in school and to mind my mother and to finish my sundae because it was just so horrible to spend money on food if you weren't going to eat it.

In the days before Dr. Schmidt was to speak to Dr. Mojir and discuss the possibilities of *yes she needs to be locked away* or *maybe if you all just laid off her she'd act differently*, my mom cried in her room almost every night. She tried to be quiet, tried to keep her door closed and turn her television up and play it off like the ragweed outside was making her eyes all watery, but my mom only closed her bedroom door when she needed privacy with Frank on the phone or if she and Kim were in there with Kim's pot and problems. One night I opened her door without knocking. I smelled the smells of Jergens lotion and smoke and a menstrual cycle. She was facing the wall over her bed, sitting backward and sniffling with a Kleenex pressed to her mouth. I almost expected to see a vision of the Virgin Mary on the wall, the way her eyes were fixed like if a person was in front of her saying, *Listen, here's what you have to do—*

"Mom?" I said. "I'm not like that girl from the movie. I want you to stop crying."

She flung her legs around the side of the bed, stood and smoothed out her nightgown. "I know. What movie?"

"That one with Sally Field," I answered. "That's not me."

"Oh, I know that." She disappeared into the little bathroom in the corner. I heard the sizzle of her cigarette in water, then the toilet flushing. "I wasn't crying because of that," she said, "It's just one of those days when I really miss my dad."

It was hard to tell if she was lying. My mom did cry a lot over her father who died when she was a kid. A few days after my grandpa Antonio Bettencourt found out he had throat cancer he stuck a gun in his mouth and pulled the trigger. My grammie got the telegram while vacationing in Mexico with her second husband and my thirteen-year-old mother. In the car on the way back to California she broke the news to my mom that her father was in heaven. Maybe it didn't even come as a complete shock, because there had been two unsuccessful suicide attempts, which my grandmother tried to keep from my mom. "But you can't keep things like that from kids," my mom always said. "Kids know when something isn't right."

———

Dr. Schmidt suggested I practice just sitting outside in the sunlight and take my ledgers and write about how it made me feel. "Take your cat out there and watch him play. Take notes about the things he does. Maybe even write a poem about all the wonderful things sunlight does for the Earth."

I grumbled and said I could do the exact same thing inside.

"But didn't you tell me you have this huge swimming pool? So start swimming again. If you'd like, I'll talk to your mom about letting you swim more often. Even when it's chilly out. You know, in

Germany, if we had to wait for good weather before we went swimming, no one in the whole country would even learn how to doggy paddle." He leaned in close and maybe even winked at me. "Just let me talk to her."

"And I want you to talk to her about what I told Dr. Mojir," I added. "I want you to tell her that I never said a word about hearing any voices. I seriously don't like that guy. He never listens and I don't like—"

"I already spoke to Dr. Mojir, and that's why I'm going to have your mom come in now and we're going to clear this up."

My mom took a seat in the chair next to me and reached out for my hand. Of course Kim had to sit on the love seat in the corner. Dr. Schmidt said he would run a few more tests, talk to another colleague who deals specifically with juvenile personality disorders, but from what he gathered by speaking to Mojir he was almost 99 percent positive I showed no signs of schizophrenia.

My mom pulled a wad of tissue from her purse and cried into it.

Kim said, "I knew it." She crossed her legs and folded her hands on her knees. "Didn't I tell you, little miss?"

Yes, she did. My sister was the one who suggested that my mom call Dr. Mojir and ask for the *exact* words I had said to him during the visit where he claimed I said I heard voices. But now nobody would have to; it seemed as though Dr. Schmidt already had that answer, and he was about to share it. But when he finished, our little victory scene changed completely.

It was Kim who spoke and got all upset first. "What in the hell is that supposed to mean?" she asked Dr. Schmidt when he was finished talking. Then she turned to me and said, "Me and Mom are against you? *That's* what you told Dr. Mojir? That me and Mom are constantly talking about you behind your back? How stupid. We're the only ones who are in your corner at all times. Through everything, all the little stunts you pull, all the shit you stir up—"

My mom stood from her chair and walked over to Kim. She put her arm around her. "No. We're not going to do this, okay? We're here for Traci, we're trying to figure this whole thing out."

"Here for Traci. Here for Traci," Kim mocked. "That's what we're always here for."

I looked at Dr. Schmidt, my eyebrows raised in an expression of *well, there you have it.*

"Okay, look," Dr. Schmidt interrupted. "The most important thing we're trying to establish right now is that after speaking to Dr. Mojir I understand Traci told him more about the way she feels ganged up on at home and not so much about hearing outside voices, which would be consistent with a diagnosis of paranoid behavior." He paused and wrote something on his pad. "So this is a good thing."

"Ganged up on?" my mom asked.

Kim said, "So how is catering to your every whim ganging up on you?"

"It is extremely common for kids of Traci's age to feel this way toward authority and family members," Dr. Schmidt said. "It's typical behavior of one who is trying to gain her own sense of self. We might need to talk about boundaries, let's say between what a sister should do and what a mother should do. I'm wondering if we should start scheduling some meetings for all three of you together."

"And how much would *that* cost?" my mom said.

Kim stood and fiddled with her purse like she was going to leave. "Oh, this is bull, total bullshit." She sat back down again. "This girl can't even be left alone for a second." She whipped her pointed finger hard in my direction. "She's unbelievable."

"Why are you even here?" I said to Kim. A hot wave of anger rose into my face, giving my sinuses their own pulse. "Why can't I have anything or say anything without you butting in? You're so jealous that someone is going to know something you don't."

"You shut it," my mom said to me. "You need to quit being so damn ungrateful and driving your sister crazy."

Now Kim held her hand out for my mother's wad of tissue and wiped her face with it. Dr. Schmidt handed her some clean ones. She shook her head and lifted her hand. "I've had it with her. I've just had it," she said. "I mean, I'm cleaning her room because she's a complete pig with crusted-up cereal bowls and these weird insect experiments all over the place. She won't dare clean that up, but she'll go around rubbing everyone else's stuff with bleach."

"I don't have any bugs in my room," I lied. There were snails on salt rocks and roly-polies in Tupperware containers. Not that I'd call any of those things experiments. What I really wanted were some reptiles. I loved being around the snakes and lizards we had in little aquariums at school. The grainy smell, the way they had no choice but to always be so close to the Earth—it all gave me the urge to run outside and lick the sidewalk in the rain.

But to hear someone say it out loud, to talk about my bugs and okay, maybe a few cereal bowls I'd forgotten about, made me see it all so ridiculously, made me think of myself like a mad scientist, my lab coat reeking of molded Cocoa Puffs while I pulled the eyes from helpless slugs under the purple shocks of electricity that carried my wicked laughter up toward the thunderstorm above my dungeon. And to hear it all come from my sister's mouth, all my secrets in front of Dr. Schmidt, made me sick to my stomach. I looked at him, his pretty blond hair hanging wispy in his eyes while he scribbled in his notebook as fast as I'd ever seen him.

"I know this is something we should all explore at a later date," he said. "Obviously we've struck some nerves here."

"Nerves," Kim said. "Ours are all shot. Living in a house where every damn appliance gets unplugged every damn day, and I'm up at four A.M. making sure the coffee gets turned on so my mom can make it to work without a major meltdown."

I buried my face in my hands and swallowed down tears, but I couldn't keep them all in. This was *my* doctor, this was *my* session, *my* sort of friend with his marzipan and the Rubik's Cube he let me take home. This was *my* life and everything I had spun from it. Damn her.

I got up quietly and said I was leaving. "I'll take a bus home."

"You're not taking any goddamn bus across town." My mom headed for the door but Kim stopped her. "No. Let her. She always thinks she knows everything . . ."

"We all need to sit down and take a little breather," Dr. Schmidt said. "Traci, why don't you go to the vending machine downstairs and get everyone something to drink." He opened his desk drawer and pulled out a handful of change.

"Oh no, Doctor." My mom took out her wallet. Just as polite as you please.

"She'll take off," Kim said. "She'll just run outside and make some big scene."

"Shut up," I said.

Dr. Schmidt looked straight at Kim. "Why don't you calm down for a second and let your sister get us some drinks?" Now his voice was harsh. Beautiful.

But in my family we didn't *just let* people do anything. My brother tested his boundaries of where he wasn't supposed to be, with the women he wasn't supposed to be with; my father looked for loopholes in the eyes of the girlfriends who didn't like the idea of stepmother; my mother poked and prodded at my grandmother, saying all the time that her Okie twang and mispronunciation of words were embarrassing and why couldn't she talk like someone she wasn't?

There was no "well enough alone" in my house.

I guess that's why Kim sprang out into the hallway and tried to pull on my shirt when I was halfway to the elevator. Maybe it's why I called my sister a bitch for the first time ever so that I started crying because that word stung and the look on her face wasn't at all like something I had thought I wanted. Why all at once I hated everything and was sorry for everything and wanted everything to disappear.

"All right," Kim said. I'd shaken her hand loose of me. "If I'm such a bitch I'll tell you what, the next time you get caught in the bathroom with a boy at school or a bunch of girls are waiting to kick your ass on the playground, you just have someone else get on the phone with the principal pretending to be Mom."

When I turned to take the stairs I slipped a little. I reached out for my sister as a blind girl would if she needed to borrow someone else's balance.

In the hallway I heard my mother. "What bathroom? What boy?"

7

born freak

*And the creature crawling from the abyss may be eased by the
radiance from above.*
—THE MOON IN MAJOR ARCANA, RIDER-WAITE TAROT DECK

For weeks after that pretty little scene in Dr. Schmidt's office, the
air between my mom and Kim was thick with alliance, while the air
between my mom and Kim with me in it went thick with stuff that felt
like throw-up. I stepped over my complaints of being excluded while
the two of them interviewed wedding caterers. I kept my dress dissat-
isfaction tucked away in a pastel green garment bag until my grandmother was damn good and ready to hem the damn thing goddammit.
While my mother and sister overruled Gil's thoughts on flowers and a
band and whispered at the kitchen table in his presence, I flashed him
knowing looks and actually felt sorry for my soon-to-be-brother-in-
law, who was coming into this family on purpose.

Most of the time I just stayed in my room or hung out at Theresa's.
Grammie had come away nicely on several racetrack days and was
more than happy to dish out five-spots in my palm to keep me out

of the way. "Here, you and Theresa go to McDonald's or something. We're up to our ears in this wedding nonsense and we don't want you a-twistin' up our sanity."

The wedding kept everyone busy enough to forget about me for a little while. I wasn't entirely certain I liked that very much until the big romantic day came and I totally aced the whole toss-the-rose-petal-here gig. I didn't mess up once or make any kind of a scene like everyone thought I would. I did have a brief and weird feeling in the limo like something bad was going to happen. Maybe I'd stand up in the church and yell, "God is a liar!" or something filthy about Jesus. I got all panicky over the thought until I watched how my mom and Kim cried pretty much all morning and dabbed each other's eyes and laughed in between the crying, which gave me a really good idea. If by chance I started counting the buttons on my sister's gown or got into a tizzy from the sunlight and warm weather, I could just start with the tears and no one would even care. From watching my mom and Kim star in "Putting on the Veil" for the photographer all the way up to, "Do you take this woman," blah, blah, forever and ever amen, it was plain to see that tears were totally normal for weddings. If I had to collapse into the bathroom and breathe into a paper bag while trying to sniff up a breath I could say, "Oh, what a beautiful day, I'm so emotional," or whatever lovely words come with lovely unions.

Thinking about that helped me to relax a little, to smile, to actually kind of enjoy myself. Also the glass of champagne I downed while playing pool with my brother in back of the reception hall helped kick the *really*-enjoying-myself part up to notches I'd never before experienced. "Holy moly," I said to Bryan as we twirled to Donna Summer. The swaying taffeta dresses beside me were zigzag daisies on a high plain. "I feel like Alice down the rabbit hole."

Kim and Gil were to leave early the next morning for love and romance in Hawaii. When your sister's about to take off for a new life where there will be much less you, the Tilt-a-Whirl happy of a first booze sure doesn't last long.

Good-bye! Good-bye! Have fun with your fun husband. We threw rice and cried again and then my father got red wine in him and bothered the DJ for the rest of the night to play more disco than should ever be allowed in a single evening.

I said my stomach felt pukey and was sent home with Grammie and Bryan.

When the front door opened I was instantly struck with grief. That old flower from a dead prom queen crumbled inside my chest. Just like the time I came home from the hospital and cried all week for reasons I couldn't explain. While my grandmother folded laundry and Bryan asked some girl on the phone if she wanted to come over and see how killer he looked in a suit, I walked into my sister's room full of sand castles.

Most everything in there had been packed on account of she was already staying at Gil's apartment (slowly turning into *the* apartment—now overheard at the reception hall as *our* apartment). For weeks I'd been watching my sister fill boxes and label things and hum the Carpenters song "We've Only Just Begun." I couldn't help but think of all the times we'd moved out of here, moved into there, all of us bubble-wrapping old problems into new and better ways to survive, all of us wondering what things would be like. Now she was the only one packing, bent over a cedar chest of embroidered sheets and delicate beginnings. Ambitious and promising as a new religion. She had taken the big stuff first, the good stuff: clothes, makeup, her collectible Avon perfume figurines, all her romance novels and albums. But the posters of John Travolta, her bulletin board with her high school graduation picture and caricature drawings of friends on Fisherman's Wharf, all the stuff that didn't matter anymore was still there. The first time I saw her walking down the stairs with her arms overflowing with new-life things I said, "You look like you're going to be gone a long time."

She laughed. "If it works out—forever."

I thought, How dumb. Forever. Nothing's forever. The women

in my family had never found marriage to be the kind of good that requires forever. But in the phantom aura of her almost-empty room, that infinite word was as exact as my own big nothingness. Sprinkles pranced quietly through the doorway and I swear to God, he looked liked he cared about our new missing pieces.

"Well, kiddo," I said to him, "I guess that's that."

He jumped on my sister's bed, just a mattress now without a cover. I kneeled and petted him while he nuzzled my face.

"If I got married would you miss me so much you wouldn't even be able to stand it?"

I buried my nose in his dusty fur and tried to imagine what my house would feel like without me in it. Dr. Schmidt had a big fat pen from some head-shrinkers' convention that said, WHEREVER YOU GO, THERE YOU ARE. So then, if my sister wasn't technically here, did that mean none of her was here? The body goes off to all kinds of new and exciting places, takes all its clothes to Our Apartment or stays at the old house with a midlife crisis and new girlfriends—then what? Is everything of that person just supposed to exist lightly in the places where the entirety used to be? There was a story in one of my reincarnation books that said after we die we're supposed to find the bellies of our new moms, jump into the baby inside her womb, and wait to be born.

But what if we're not dead—what if we're just gone? Does someone come along to take our place? Maybe they pick us, see what we're carrying inside, then leap right into the clumps of lidless eyes and question-mark spines.

Maybe it's all a bunch of shit.

I squeezed Sprinkles and watched a million charm bracelet sisters floating behind my eyes, dropping down from wherever shiny new souls drop down from.

Pick me! Pick me!

Oh, but I would learn just how many ways there are to replace those lonely spaces between poor, poor you, married sisters, and dads in old houses—you can make out with boys you hardly know, you can sneak cold medicine into your locker at school and drink it all day on those rare occasions you actually show up to school, you can even run as far away as you can get on fifty bucks—run from the places and people you hate even though you know damn well you're still stuck with thoughts that aren't right, with a You that isn't right. Sometimes the only thing you can do is just sit around and feel it all, and nothing is going to make those things *not* happen, not even if you've had too much champagne at your sister's wedding and you lie on her mattress facedown trying to smell her smells but the only thing that comes up is a cold flush of air like someone opening a door, someone trying not to be wherever they are.

—————————

That was my summer on the roof with Sprinkles. The season of the cat. Kind of. The more time I spent waiting for my sister to divorce Gil, the more I thought hanging out with humans wasn't something I was totally into anymore. I followed Sprinkles around the house and yard, crawled on my knees and took up his trail just about everywhere he went. When he napped I laid my head next to his warm little pocket of belly. By the end of the summer I got very good at making vibrating sounds with my tongue purring on the roof of my mouth.

"What the hell is that constant humming noise?" My mom looked up from her cigarette and her copy of *Your Erroneous Zones.*

"It's just us," I said, low enough to make sure no one heard. "Just us purring. Loving life."

On a PBS nature special I watched a pride of lions—"Our cousins," I said to Sprinkles—crunching through the jugulars of zebra necks, then dragging off the bodies to share with everyone in my extended family. Oh, the hunting—that was our favorite part: the harshest element of survival was anything but harsh to me. It wasn't bad or gross. I pointed to a wildebeest thigh dangling from the branch of an acacia tree and asked Sprinkles, "Don't you think I'd be good at that?"

When I wasn't sitting on the roof with my cat trying to copy his squeaking bird imitation, I spent entire Saturday afternoons combing through books in the library on how the big cats stalked, fed, loved, and lived. In the backseat of my mom's car I closed my eyes and pretended the heat rolling off the rear window wasn't there to singe my skin but to beckon me back to the viscous savannah where I roamed with my lion family, tearing through head and hide, lightning sounds striking the ground where we growled and feasted like the killers we were.

Trying to keep my footing on top of the house was a lot harder than Sprinkles made it look. There were a lot of uneven parts where the roof came to a triangle above the garage, where Kim's husband patched a hole that we never told our landlord about on account of when he called asking for the rent we couldn't come up with we were supposed to say our mom was on a business trip until such and such date while we waited for her pay raise to kick in or a goddamn child-support check from my father.

Earlier in the week Sprinkles spotted a nest near the gutter. One by one, he'd brought down the babies. First for show-and-tell: "Oh, Sprinkles, for me?" Then the ice-chip crunch of vertebrae snapping. I took Polaroids of the gnawed-off pink heads and egg-sac entrails decorating the yard like a stillborn Christmas.

On an afternoon Kim was over she yelled, "Oh, Jesus! He's got another one!"

She and Bryan and Grammie were pulling weeds in our front garden when Sprinkles pranced by with a struggling thing in his mouth. "That's the second bird today," she said. "Oh God, how disgusting."

"Third one today," I corrected. "Pretty good for a guy without claws. And I helped, you know; we've been waiting all morning for the mom to leave."

Grammie said I wasn't to be playing on no roof.

"I wasn't playing," I answered. "I was hunting with my brother." But I left out the part about almost falling and how the Separate Animal God, the one who had no patience with humans due to their inability to listen and stay, had watched over me and smiled on my efforts.

Hunting was so much harder than I counted on, but Sprinkles didn't keep an eye on my limitations the way teachers and mothers and married sisters and even Dr. Schmidt sometimes did.

I knew that no one, not even my grandmother with her shoeless childhood who once pulled out a chunk of honeycomb from a beehive only because some boy said she was too scared to do it, would understand my dangerous and feral ways.

I certainly wasn't surprised when Kim didn't respond in her usual spastic hand-flailing manner after I looked directly at her and said how lucky I was to still be alive. "It's hard to keep your balance on ivy trellises, huh?" I said.

But Kim didn't answer because Kim was now Mrs. Johnston, with roast beef recipes and colorsafe bleach. Though her and Gil's apartment was across town she came home a few days a week to help with dinner and clean things up and make sure I didn't start stuff until Grammie got back from taking all her classes to get her nursing home license. Every evening before she left seemed like a battle between my mom and grandmother to see who could give the best advice on the feeding and care of husbands.

"Now you remember to put those onions in during the last half hour of roasting, otherwise they'll turn the whole thing bitter," my mom said.

"Mix the cornstarch in a cup of cold water before you put it in with the rest of the gravy," Grammie said.

Mostly it was eyes rolling and heads shaking behind my grandmother's back because no one but Bryan and me loved Grammie's Southern cooking. My mom's food was good in a way that your mom's food is supposed to be good because your mom is your mom, but Kim's cooking was pretty much flavorless. She cooked liked she acted around my mother.

I preferred the first imperfect pancake and ravaged down anything with hunks of bacon fat and gravy. Pink metallic meats and the coagulated heels of pigs' feet suited me just fine.

"You eat like a disgusting animal," Bryan said. So when I finally made up my mind to live as a cat, I figured I already had enough jungle know-how to excel at a real wild life. When I couldn't rough it enough to watch Sprinkles and his dinner of death, I sat in my room on my haunches and ate strips of beef jerky sideways, tearing up the pieces, sometimes two, three at a time, imagining blood dripping from my canines.

But on this morning I couldn't eat with my cat. Or even with myself. I was just too nervous.

On a visit with my psychiatrist I'd been given another stupid set of questions, this time with pictures to see how I responded to different scenarios. Obvious, easy stuff. A girl bent over crying in front of a tombstone. "And what do you think she's feeling?" Dr. Schmidt asked.

"She's happy," I said, trying not to giggle. "It was the teacher who gave her an F out of jealousy. Poor teacher, it happened on a slick and rainy freeway."

I was told to get serious, that every minute I wasted time trying to be a comedian was one step back from understanding my real feelings.

Some questions were really weird and actually kind of spooky, even for me: "Do you ever see people's faces changing in front of you?"

"Like changing expressions?" I asked.

"No," Dr. Schmidt answered. "Perhaps like melting or dripping like wax or morphing into mannequins." He said it so, you know, whatever-like, as if there are people walking around seeing morphing mannequins every day. No big deal.

Other questions were just as bizarre, something right out of *The Superfriends* or a Sid and Marty Kroft show.

"Do you ever feel you are being watched/followed/spied on by government officials or authorities?"

"Huh? Those big mirrors on the wall in the front and back of Thrifty's were pretty much unavoidable whenever I stopped in there after school to swipe some Pop Rocks or a pack of bobby pins, but I don't think the old lady behind the counter could seriously be considered governmental.

So, no.

"Do you ever feel as if the happiness and prosperity of others depends solely on your actions?" This Dr. Schmidt explained to me in a kind of little-kid narrative, even though I totally got it. What the question should've asked is, *Do you ever think, while you're chewing bubble gum, how cool it would be to blow a gigantic bubble and let it smoosh all over your face but you can't because something inside of you warns that the minute you hear the popping sound from your gum will also be the exact minute a chemical mushroom explosion blows the roof off of the printing press where your father works?*

"No," I answered. "I never think that."

The next question I had to be extra careful with: "Do you hear voices of people who aren't there?"

"What do you mean exactly by voices?" No way was I going to say anything to Dr. Schmidt about the voice I really *did* hear: my own. Insistent, panicky, telling me I was going to faint, I was going to kill someone if I didn't listen up. I watched Dr. Schmidt watching me, waiting for my response.

Don't mess it up just yet. "Of course I don't hear voices," I said. "And I'm not delusional, Dr. Schmidt. That would totally freak me out if I heard voices."

He put his pen to his mouth in thought. When no one was speaking in Dr. Schmidt's office you could hear the fountain in the main lobby atrium and the music from the Mexican car dealership across the street. Ranchito bass drums and tubas like a cinnamon circus shared the same air as water falling onto Spanish tile. If you closed your eyes you could smell a vacation.

"Well, what about last week?" Dr. Schmidt finally said. "The incident with the knives? Was it voices telling you to get out of bed that night?"

"Oh God." I giggled into my palm. "I really feel so stupid for sharing that." It was hard to tell if I'd confessed about my fear of knife swallowing only to fill up the spaces of having nothing interesting to say, or was it that when I felt the slightest glimpse of hope or happiness I babbled on like an idiot? I had shot my mouth off about the night I got it into my brain that there was a firm possibility I would wake up and randomly stick things into my mouth if they were too close to my door frame or the hallway outside of my room. I tried to explain it the easiest way I knew; I tried to tell him that the idea of swords and knives somehow finding their way into my mouth had seriously just appeared in my mind, but I couldn't even find the correct words to tell my mother that night when she caught me putting a piece of masking tape across the carpet by my bedroom doorway.

"So let me see if I understand what you're telling me," she said. "You think you might get up in the night and start eating something?"

"Not exactly," I answered. "I mean, I think I'll put something in my mouth."

"Like a cookie or something?"

"No. Not exactly a cookie."

"Well, what then?"

Of course it was almost midnight. Of course my mom had an early meeting at work the next day.

"I'm not sure," I said. "But what if someone accidentally leaves a sword by my bedroom door and I stick it in my mouth and I choke or cough up blood or kill myself?"

When I told this to Dr. Schmidt he smiled and pressed two fingers against his lips, as if he wanted to laugh. "That sounds like it would make a good science-fiction story," he said. I kind of liked that.

"But you haven't worried about putting things in your mouth since that one time, correct?"

"That's right." Just like everything that happened under my skull, I had no understanding of my sudden panic regarding sharp-object eating. However, I did quickly learn that nothing cured a bout of nervousness over such a nugget of disillusion faster than Bryan sitting on me and slapping my head because I had thrown away his baseball cleats when I discovered they were too close to the No Setting Things

Over Here Because I Might Put It In My Mouth When I'm Sleeping zone.

After my appointment, Dr. Schmidt met Kim in the waiting room and handed her an envelope of his evaluation declaring me schizo-free (not any kind of a real diagnosis, but I think by law he had to sign some sort of a statement saying I wasn't going to kidnap the president or open fire on a bunch of preschoolers or whatever).

When Kim tried to take the envelope from him he pulled it back. "Oh, wait a moment, you *are* eighteen, right?" He went on to say that he wasn't supposed to be releasing these papers to anyone who wasn't a parent or legal guardian. "But you'll give them to your mother, correct?"

This made my twenty-year-old sister upset like a ten-year-old. "Of course I will," she said, kind of pouty. It had always made Kim mad not to be considered a fully fledged adult—to not be thought of the same as my mother in practically all ways. Once when I was four we were all waiting to be seated at Golden Gate Pancakes when the hostess looked at me, Kim, and Bryan and asked if we needed three children's menus. I remember how my sister cried about it and said it was Dad's fault because he didn't let her wear as much eye makeup as she wanted to and how she and my mom whispered at the table so much that my dad had to go outside and have a cigarette while Bryan and I played Olympic Balance Beam on the edges of the flower planters.

"I already looked at my papers," I said to Kim. "And I'm not to be considered for further evaluation for psychotic paranoid personality disorder." Then I did a little spinny ballet move and felt stupid immediately after. It wasn't so much that I was happy about the prognosis, but that I had shared a kind of secret with the doctor. Me. Alone. Even if it was only for a few beautiful minutes before my mom and Kim got their hands on the words that confirmed I wasn't as hopeless as everyone said.

When we stepped out into the bright light of the late afternoon

Kim put on her old-lady sunglasses and lit up a cigarette. Before we crossed the street to get to the parking garage she tried to grab my hand. I guess she'd been doing this for the better part of her life, tending to my safety through duty and instinct—two things you don't mix up with the word *want*. But now her hand jerked away before it actually touched my arm. If a car was going to hit me, I'd see it. I was old enough to get myself out of the way.

———————

It was my understanding that we were going to celebrate my not being that crazy by going to the Burger Pit for one of their jumbo grilled hot dogs, but in the car a problem came up. Mom and Kim had an argument because I needed to be watched on Friday night so my mom could go to Carmel with Frank Ranaldo. Bryan had to work and Grammie had to work and my dad had to work out which silk shirt for which girlfriend.

"But Gil and I had plans to rearrange the living room furniture," Kim said. "We got this new oak entertainment shelf. We've got to figure out where it's going to go."

"Gosh, that must be nice to run around and spend money on brand-new furniture," my mom said. "I wouldn't know. I haven't bought a new piece of anything in a long while."

I pretended I wasn't listening. I took out my Vicks inhaler wand, stuck it in my nostrils, and drew pictures in my ledger about my new obsession with scientists in the Congo. Almost every day for the past month I'd watched *Born Free*, the 1968 film that documents the life of biologist Joy Adamson and Elsa, the lioness she raised from birth. At least twice a week I begged my mom to rent the movie, and every week, when it was due back, we'd call the video place to ask if we could keep it another four days. We'd send a check in the mail so no one would have to make the entire two-mile drive to the Alpha Beta shopping center and put out their cigarette long enough to walk into the video store. When the store owner realized there just wasn't a huge audience demand for the true adventures of scientists, he agreed to sell it to us for sixty dollars.

"Bargain, my ass," Grammie said. She put the money in my hand and told me to go inside and pay the cashier. "Your mom's nuts for letting you get away with this horseshit. Sixty dollars for a movie of a goddamn lion. Hell, we can go to the zoo and see some real animals for less than that."

But I barely heard her ramblings over the bliss and satisfaction of knowing Joy and Elsa now belonged to me.

That's pretty much all I did as summer rolled into another school year: watch my movie, read books about lions, write stories about lions, tell people I really was a lion, see what it felt like to attack and hunt like a lion.

"I don't think it's natural to be so absorbed in just *one* thing," my mom said. She was watering the jasmine bushes under our front window, trying to keep her cigarette from getting wet while I scratched my back against the willow tree in our front yard. "I guess it's nice that you've finally realized being outdoors is healthy, but why don't you see if Theresa wants to come over or put on your roller skates or something?"

But Theresa wasn't willing to understand the beauty of wild feline culture. I had in fact talked to her at school that day and asked if she wanted to come by later.

"I'd say yes but you have to swear to God you won't make me watch that movie again," she said. While she and Emily Gomez passed around their Wet N Wild fingernail polish, I balled up wet toilet paper and threw it against the ceiling of the girl's bathroom.

"Just forget it," I said. Besides, what hell did she know about the business of jungle life? The last time we watched *Born Free* together she'd made some snippy remark when I said I wanted to live in Africa. "So you want to be black now?" she'd said, then laughed a hissy laugh through her teeth.

Not that I could find much more support in my mother. She

grabbed my arm and yelled at me in front of the ice cream man for sitting in the driveway in my nightgown with Sprinkles while he ate a steak I'd heated up for him in the microwave. We're talking about a woman who thought a glass of ice water on the coffee table without a coaster was wild. When she was a teenager my mother tore down the Exit sign from the third floor of a San Francisco hotel where Elvis was staying. She wanted something to show she'd been inside the place where the King had slept. But now, wild and reckless meant giving yourself a Toni home perm without enough of those little tissue paper things to protect you from split ends.

Joy Adamson wouldn't have given a damn about me and Sprinkles outside in the rain or split ends. From all the books I read about her free and primitive lifestyle, and from my limited knowledge about the possibilities of life after death, I was pretty sure being cast as my mother's daughter could have very well been an oversight on the part of God or whoever's in charge of stuff like that. The fact that I spent most of my afternoons in remedial math tutoring and not in an acacia tree gnawing meat from a wildebeest's thigh with my real mother was probably just some cosmic mix-up.

I even told Drew Larson my secret about the thing I wanted to build to keep next to my bed. Drew was the best artist in our sixth-grade class and very into architecture. I thought for sure he'd appreciate my idea. Maybe even give me some pointers. If he wanted to come over and show me about hammers and nails and watch *Born Free* and maybe kiss, that'd be fine too.

"A litter box?" he asked with his face all screwed up. "You want to build a litter box? Like, to take dumps in?"

"Yeah, like that," I answered. "But not just a regular old litter box. Giant-size. And I'm not going to go to the bathroom in it, silly."

"What are you going to do in it?"

I hadn't really thought about it. "Maybe sleep. Or eat. Or whatever."

"Eat what?"

"Well, food, what else? But straight from a bowl, because using

forks and spoons sucks. It's not how they do it in the animal kingdom."
Actually, I'd been doing the no-cutlery thing for some time now. I'd sit
in the garage by Sprinkles's cat dish while he munched his Nine Lives,
close-eyed and bored; then I'd lap up a nice serving of tuna from a
clean dish. Afterward I'd lick his fur and let him do the same to my
hair, though sometimes he'd get a lot more into this if I put a little tuna
juice in my bangs.

When Drew said, "That's got to be the gayest thing I've ever heard,"
I felt myself shrinking back. I shouldn't have said anything to anyone.
I don't know, I thought maybe he'd think I was cool, or kind of into
building things like him. Instead he held his sides and commenced to
have a long, loud laughing fit. "What a freak. A total freakazoid, man.
Are you totally serious? I mean, is this a joke or a dare or something?"
He wiped his eyes and blinked at my paper. Another boy came up and
asked what was going on. "Look." Drew handed him my sketch. "She
wants to shit in a litter box."

I spent the rest of recess in the bathroom, telling a second grader
who I didn't even know that her hair was ugly. I wished I could dig into
something with real claws.

On our walk home I told Theresa that Drew called me a bitch and
laughed at me because I showed him this picture I'd made.

"Well, who knows what the heck his problem is," she said. She
pulled two Rolos from her pocket and unwrapped one for me. "I've
never liked him. I saw him smoking behind Saint Julie's once."

"Really?" I was kind of shocked. Drew wore shirts with buttons on
them and his hair was always cut so short. Once he sat behind me at an
assembly on Memorial Day and went on and on to the kid next to him
about a letter President Carter had written only to him, saying how
great it was to see a young person so involved in their community and
a bunch of junk like that.

"He prank calls me too," Theresa said. "I can totally tell it's him and
his bogus friends. Nothing bad or whatever, pretty much he giggles
and moans and says he's coming over to pet my pussy."

It took a few seconds, but as we walked atop the rim of a canyon where new pink and tan condos sprouted up like hard pieces of birthday cake, I realized my cousin had seriously thought that disgusting boy wanted to come to her house and maybe spend a little time with her cat.

The next day we both waited after school for Drew Larson.

"What blueprints?" He walked backwards, smiling while we stepped slowly in front of him. "What are you guys talking about— blueprints? You never showed me anything but a stupid drawing of a crapper pan, Traci."

We came to the back fence where a person-size hole allowed for easy entrance to the street and homes behind the school.

Theresa said, "You know what I think, Drew Larson?"

He turned and dropped his book bag, his green eyes squinting against the sun. How weak of me to think that a boy could still be so cute even if he doesn't give a damn what he tears apart. "I don't really care what you guys think," he said. "So, do both of you like me or what? Why are you following me? Because you want to take your clothes off with me?"

I laughed loud, like he had done to me in front of that other guy.

Theresa wasn't laughing. "Not quite," she said. "What I really think is that you should apologize to my cousin for acting like an asshole." She hardly ever cussed. "And you're also going to stop calling my house."

"What?" Drew smirked and looked around. "I'm totally sure. And then you woke up, right? Like I'd even care about calling you." He picked up his book bag and flung it over his shoulder. "You guys are mental. I need to get home." He started to duck into the fence hole but Theresa pulled him back by his shirt. Drew yelled something and tried to turn but couldn't. Theresa was just—on him, all over him, his back and his neck; she spun him around so fast she looked like a cop on the news. I had no idea what to do when she sort of propped him up in front of me, her hands holding his arms tight against his back. "Beat the shit out of him!" she yelled.

I stood there and did nothing.

"Hurry, Traci, kick his ass now!"

Drew Larson screamed. It was a scary baby sound like the time Sprinkles sank his teeth into a rabbit's head. He tried to kick Theresa in the place where she stood behind him. Grass blades and white gnats flew up from the heels of his shoes. I felt my fingernails press into my palm, and all at once I swung at Drew's stomach. He lurched a little, but I could tell from the times I'd played Rocky with Bryan that I hadn't done much.

These are the words I used to explain my actions to Dr. Schmidt: *like a blurry dream.* Except that wasn't entirely true. Yeah, when I lunged atop the boy and went completely nuts scratching his face and puncturing his skin with my nails, it was sudden, but *not* blurry. Oh man, it was so much the opposite. I saw the blood pour down from the open wounds I slashed across his face and neck. Not a single thing in me felt wrong.

But you can't say stuff like that to your psychiatrist.

I was asked if I knew what the words *coping mechanism* meant. "With Kim's new marriage and your grandmother spending a lot of time getting her business together," Dr. Schmidt said, "I think we can say that you've been acting out." His dark blue eyes narrowed in a sad way. "I don't like to hear that you're doing these things to other kids, because I don't think you really want to act like that."

I shrugged and rubbed my hand in the spot where my mother had stuck my fingers in her mouth and bit down. "I guess I don't," I said. But there had been such a huge thing made of what happened that day near the fence. First, Drew Larson's mom called the school and said she would press charges; then the school called my mom; then my mom cried all night; then Kim went to the school and said my mom had to leave town for a business meeting (total lie); then we picked up my mom from work due to her saying she was too panicky to drive and her chest felt tight from me acting up so much.

Up in the smoky front seat Kim rubbed my mom's shoulder and

gave her the news that I was receiving three days of in-house suspension. In the course of the next eight or so hours my mom would only look at me once. She would turn to me in the narrow hallway as we both tried to pass the same place and say, "This makes you happy, doesn't it?"

It would be a long time before I understood those words meant I was blocking her way.

Dr. Schmidt asked me if I knew how serious suspension was.

"Yeah. I know."

"Well, I'd like you to try and tell me how you felt when you were scratching up that boy."

"This is dumb," I said. "He wasn't really hurt. He shouldn't be teasing people like that. I don't know how it made me feel. Calm, I guess. I don't know."

"But you know that was wrong, don't you? To hurt another person is wrong."

"I know. That's what I was trying to show him."

Same thing, I guess, as what my mom was trying to show me the night I got suspended and she sat on my bed trying to talk to me but I wouldn't pull the covers from my face. Even when she yanked as hard as she could, I pulled with opposite force until I heard a little crinkle of seam separating on my Strawberry Shortcake comforter. I wouldn't get out from under my blanket.

"We're just going to talk, okay?" my mom said. "I'm telling you right now to get out of those damn covers and act your age." She pulled on my fingers and tried to pry them away one by one. "You can't just hide every time you do something wrong!"

Finally she freed enough of my hand to stick into her mouth and bite. "Yeah, you see that. You see how you're making me act?" She stood up.

I'm not sure how I knew she was trembling, but I did.

"Now you can just fester in there all day and think about how that felt."

So I festered. And I thought. I also must have fallen asleep, because when I finally lifted the covers from my head it was dark outside. The odor from my body was like saliva just before a bad cold, the red spot on my hand so small I thought about killing my disgusting self.

This is all the damage I can do, the little mark said. *This is as far as I hurt.*

8

can you dig it?

There is never just one zombie.
—KELLY LINK, "SOME ZOMBIE CONTINGENCY PLANS"

No one thought my being suspended from the sixth grade for *violence while on or near school property* was cool. That didn't surprise me. People were given orders not to help me indulge.

"I don't want you talking about it with her." To my brother in his room when she thought I wasn't listening.

"The less attention we give to this, the less she'll thrive on it." On the phone to Kim while I was supposed to be sitting quietly in front of *The Great Space Coaster* organizing my Legos.

"I'm so sick and tired of this girl, I wish I would've had an abortion when I was pregnant with her." Probably to Dr. Schmidt—though I had no way of confirming this, really, except that he said it was the most shaken up he had ever seen her.

"Maybe because we're moving and packing and everyone's running around trying to get things done." That was all I could offer. Of course I knew the *most shaken up* part was because of me.

When you're little and told all the time that the world doesn't revolve around you but all you have to do is take a look at all the upset faces and eyebrows turned down and naps being taken for nerves that can't get settled—it doesn't take a genius to figure out that, though the world may not be revolving around you, it sure is a pretty damn fucked-up place because you're in it.

That's a hard thing to put into words and explain to your shrink.

We had uprooted again, moved into another house on the southernmost side of San Jose, where the rent was a little cheaper and the stucco walls were older.

Dr. Schmidt mentioned that another move could have been making me act out.

"I'm still going to the same school," I said. "I still have all my old friends." Meaning Theresa.

"And have you been writing down your sentences?" he asked.

"Yes," I said. "I don't really know what I'm supposed to be doing, but I guess I'm doing it."

This is what he was talking about: three questions I was supposed to list in my journal, think about, then answer myself.

1. How are my words making people around me feel?
2. How are my actions making people around me feel?
3. How am I even supposed to be caring about making friends
   if we have to keep moving?

That last one was my own. I knew Dr. Schmidt probably wouldn't think it was funny, but it was still valid. I wrote it in my ledger underneath those gay questions I was supposed to be asking myself every day. Half the time I didn't have any real answers to many of them. Like number two, for instance. In the moving van on our way to the new house I got to sit up front while Bryan drove. At a stoplight some girls giggled when he waved to them. One had all her fat hanging out the sides of her jeans so that her half shirt was like the top of a volcano while disgusting lava oozed down the sides of her.

"How sleazy," I said. "Like I'm sure some guy would totally be interested in her with all that whale meat."

Later, when we saw her again in the Alpha Beta parking lot, it was clear by the way her mouth hung open that something was wrong with her. I kind of felt bad, but I wondered if that thought was something even worth journaling: *2. How are my actions making people around me feel?* In my ledger I drew a picture of a round humanoid thing discharging fat balls like rubber bands clumped together through superhero death-ray eyes.

People who are not normal have feelings too, I wrote. *Someday they should all get the power to shoot down whatever gets in their way.*

On our new street was a six-year-old boy with four webbed fingers and a teenage girl on the next block who'd been born with one eye looking in the back of her head like a trick. Around the corner were the Harper twins, both deaf, but one had backward kneecaps. Dee Dee with the leg braces lived next door.

This was our new neighborhood, the Los Paseos area of South San Jose. Long before we ever moved into our extremely small three-bedroom rental on the tumbledown humble-up street, methyl chloroform had seeped from a local factory into the well that ran straight into the area's water reserve. My neighbors blamed it for the high rate of an affliction of miscarriages and birth defects in the area. The papers said the leak happened only the one time, but everyone said that was a lie, a conspiracy of some sort, that for years the whole neighborhood had a radioactive ringing in its ears. Whenever someone came down with a mysterious anything or a little kid couldn't maintain his attention span long enough to sit through a game of Pac-Man, we said, "You're a Water Baby."

I thought maybe I was one.

We were just a few weeks into our new place when a neighbor woman—all afternoon Chardonnay smiles for my brother who was now something like The Terminator from weight lifting—chatted with my mom in the driveway. She said our area of the city had the highest number of recorded birth defects of any place in the Bay Area, then went on and on about the horrors of chemical-plant carelessness. She even told us about her own little gelatin bundle who'd slipped away into the toilet.

It had to be explained to me on more than one occasion that the chances of my being a Water Baby were slimmer than zero. Aside from the fact that the dates of the spill (or spills) didn't align at all with my birth date, we had lived nowhere near the area when my mother was pregnant with me.

Still, I worried. I had a tendency to rock back and forth. Plus my head was only slighter smaller than a football helmet, so of course I wondered. My brother wondered too: "Why is your head so big?" He said this almost every day. Once, a teacher told me to smile more, tried to reassure me that big teeth and a big head were signs of intelligence. By now, most of my mouth was full of jagged yellow squares and spaces like rusty jailhouse bars spread by a prisoner who'd found their weak parts. I was continuously teased about them.

Mr. Ed.

The Black Stallion.

Jerry's Kids.

Now that I was *almost* in junior high school, I could *almost* get away with wearing makeup on a regular basis. But there just wasn't anything I could do about my crooked chromosome features. I tried to do up my eyes all black mass or Pat Benatar, like the cholas and punkers who waited on the corner of my street for the high school bus.

"Normally, I'd like this," my mom said as she ran a washrag under hot tap water. "But on you? No way in hell."

Theresa brought over her *Seventeen* magazines and steam curlers. She showed me how to push the rubber holders just far enough into my scalp so the chunks of hair that came out when I rolled down the curlers were just a little less upsetting than the time I rubbed Nair all over my eyebrows. Also, I'd upped my showers to four nights a week and experimented with a combination of Jean Naté and Love's Baby Soft until the only detectable scent under all that perfume was the metal clasp of alcohol and something like a chalkboard. But as semiclean and conditioned as I was keeping myself these days nothing helped my psoriasis. I had horrible breakouts on my scalp and legs. I went around scratching my head with both hands like a chimpanzee in a show.

"Do you even realize you're doing that?" Bryan asked.

No, I didn't. I just knew my head itched something fierce.

He cocked his eyebrow and told me to stop. "It seriously looks like there's something the matter with you."

Maybe an increase in my skin abnormalities and higher primate actions were part of the water poisoning, like how people in eighteenth-century France who ate moldy bread started to howl and scratch at the ground, and that's how the whole idea of werewolves started. In my ledger I wrote, *Monkey see monkey do, stop scratching your head and be a normal you.*

From my afternoon chats with the Kaiser help nurse, I learned that birth defects only happened before birth. "No, honey, you don't all of a sudden come down with spina bifida. Is your mother there?"

But still. What if having the toxoplasmosis did something to my system, weakened it or something? That I seemed more susceptible to illness than the average person wasn't always in my head, no matter if Dr. Schmidt pulled out his dictionary and told me to read the definition of *psychosomatic.*

"But that neighbor woman who told us about the chemical leak said the government was covering it up." I said this to Grammie on one especially crybaby night when my hands seemed to tingle for no apparent reason and I wouldn't stay put in my bed. "I was standing on the lawn and heard her say that. 'A government cover-up,' those were the exact words she used."

"I don't know nothing about no government cover-up," Grammie said. She was elbow deep in the paperwork for her nursing home license, not really excited about having to come over and manage my dinner and also to make sure Bryan didn't have sex in the house with his new girlfriend while he was supposed to be watching me.

I shoved my forearms into her face. "And look at these bruises all over me. Who knows what they're from? Some kind of bad mutation in my blood, probably."

She pulled off her glasses and dropped a stack of envelopes into her purse. "Hell, you don't gotta be no doctor to know falling off a balance beam and doing those dangerous flips off the jungle gym, well, you're bound to be purple and green," she said. "I think the only bad mutations taking place on you, girlie, is in that brain of yours."

Exactly.

So was it any surprise that I would soon find myself in a classroom for special-needs children? With my big intelligent head and mouth of Jerry's Kids' teeth of course I'd be the obvious candidate for a teacher's assistant in Mr. Delgado's fifth-grade special-ed class. What was less obvious, though, was the fact that calling the pupils "special," or saying "special ed" or "special needs" or special anything was against Mr. D's policy for all his assistants. We could call the children in his class "the kids" or "the students" or "the Dig Its."

On a cold Friday afternoon, with the sun in a gray gossamer wrap and a spicy fog from the garlic fields, I skipped across the blacktop to the portables, I was that happy to start my new teacher's assistant job. Almost right away, Mr. D gave me my own red felt pen and handed me a file folder of dittos that reminded me of kindergarten. But before I even had the chance to make the check marks I'd been fantasizing about or suggest that someone *see me after class,* he called me into the adjoining portable where he had his office.

The problem was this: the Oak Grove School District wanted to retract the article I had written for the district paper about the Special Olympics because I used the word *special* too much.

"Take a seat, Traci." Mr. Delgado was hairy like my dad and wore pants like my dad would wear if he dug up dinosaur bones. I'm not sure how I knew this, but naming the Santa Teresa Elementary special-ed program the Dig It program was entirely his idea.

He said my paper wasn't going to be published because I had made fun of mentally handicapped children. "You've used the phrase *special education* repeatedly," he said.

"But it's a special-education class," I answered, totally confused. "I didn't mean it to sound any way. I don't call them retards like a lot of kids I know." I felt defensive. I had worked for two damn weeks on that article.

Mr. Delgado got up and closed the door. "No, no. We don't want you saying words like that." He sat in a chair with a crotcheted pillow on the backrest. "Let me explain about the things in your article that sound a little—" Of course the word *inappropriate* was coming next. Wasn't that the drill? Wasn't that a huge chunk of my life on the opposite side of a grown-up's desk: me being quizzed on the differences between inappropriate and how normal people act?

"What I mean is," he continued, "I can see how hard you tried to say all the right things, but the problem here is maybe you tried a little too hard."

I felt my new red marker in my hand. A bona fide teacher-style felt pen. I just wanted to get back into the classroom so I could write, *what's this* and *please follow instructions*, because those are very teacherish things and they don't let just anyone write things like that on students' papers.

I tried to calm myself and not flip out at whatever reasons Mr. D was going to give for not loving my work.

"It sounds like you're making fun of the children," he finally said. "By trying so hard *not* to make fun of them, you've done just the opposite. Does that make sense?"

It did a little. So what he meant was that I sounded sarcastic, right? Okay, I could kind of see that. Over the past year I had become acutely addicted to the wry comedic styles of Bob Newhart from his show *Newhart* and Roseanne Barr from the stand-up skits I watched on *Caroline's Comedy Club.* The parodies on *Saturday Night Live,* like Mary Gross as the Sarcastic Nun and Julia Louis-Dreyfus as the television evangelist named April May June, were so meaty and brilliant, I taped every episode and spent hours pausing and rewinding, trying hard to imitate the voices, expressions, and timing of these talented people. Though I didn't quite grab the concept of "indirectly funny," the whole process of no punch line equaling the best punch line was a kind of Mensa clever I felt I needed to get in on. Even if this sleight-of-hand ha-ha wasn't something I was fully ready for (on Julia Louis-Dreyfus it was smart and sexy. On me it was "uncross your arms and wipe that look off your face.") I was pretty sure that's what Mr. D was referring to.

"I think—yeah, I can totally get that," I said. Then I forced myself to shut my mouth because in the corner of his office, next to a creepy collection of ceramic owls and clay things made by his special (not special) students, was one of the main reasons I had said yes to tutoring Mr. D's class. The laminator.

Besides the fact that I just liked the way everything looked and felt with plastic over it, the health benefits of lamination were obvious. On the immediate home front I thought about the kids in my neighborhood and worried that my bathwater would turn my hands into tentacles, but there was a more pressing problem on a wider region: all the gays were coming down with AIDS, a blood disease that turned off your immune system and reduced you down to holocaust eyes. No one was entirely sure if it was limited to just the homosexuals or not. Living in the San Francisco Bay Area meant that the gays were everywhere, that AIDS was too. I was afraid if I left my window open the disease would blow right into my room, right into my mouth and nostrils, right into my blood.

I told Mr. Delgado I completely understood what he was saying about my paper, even though I only understood a little bit. I said I didn't mean my words to sound how they sounded, though I wasn't entirely sure how they sounded. "But what if I change the parts that aren't right?" I said. "If you just tell me where I'm making fun of the disadvantaged children, I could—"

"Well, look, there's an example right there," he said. "The way you said *disadvantaged children*. I don't know, you seem a little—do you know what the word *insincere* means?"

I looked at the laminator machine behind him and thought about how he said as long as I was working in his class I could use it whenever I wanted. My plan was to cover my posters first, then bring things from my room that would be of more use to fight the death cells of AIDS on my window screen. Pillowcases, sheets, curtains, can you laminate venetian blinds?

Stay calm, don't smart off, just think, if everything goes well you can bring in shirts and nightgowns, which will also work out for flu season. "Okay, Mr. D, I think I get it."

"I don't want to discourage you from writing, because you've got some real good stuff in there," he said. "I love your enthusiasm for the kids. I can see you really tried to write from your heart, but maybe if it were a little more reporterlike, more facts, you know? It would be great if you mentioned the details of how Myrna Chavez aced the twenty-meter freestyle, rather than saying how horrible it must have been for her parents to find out their only daughter would be faced with terrible challenges for the rest of her life."

The sentence actually read, *How tragic to find your only child would have such horrible challenges for the rest of her life.* And it took me something like a half hour just to get that one sentence so perfect. "I guess I can reword that and do it how you want." I tried hard to hold onto the vision of myself hanging up my freshly plasticized curtains, satisfied with my measure of prevention as solid as any doctor or scientist could have come up with. Maybe I would even write a letter to the CDC explaining these innovative procedures. Plus, I figured that laminate was fireproof in some way, and I almost felt excited at the idea of getting real sleep without worrying about my room burning down.

I came out of Mr. D's office promising a new article with facts and stats and all kinds of safe words to help parents and students alike understand that the Dig It kids weren't like any other children . . . or they were . . . or they should be . . . or maybe they should be thought of in that way. . . .

I don't know. I really couldn't wait to use my new red felt pen.

Envy in a bad kid has no boundaries. The lines of what other people have and what other people are burdened with are so blurred that even a fourteen-year-old who's still in the sixth grade and can only see out of one eye is a potential threat. To me, most of the Dig It kids were just the same as every other thing I thought I needed. Somebody at all times hovered over them, asked them how they felt, slapped them high fives for tying their shoelaces or not eating hair. With the way my scrambled-up mind had such a hard time with a lot of the basic things like when to take a shower and when not to cry over $13 \div 5$, sometimes it seemed logical to wonder if those kids were the same as me somehow.

But where was *my* hippie teacher with the weird ceramic owls to tell people that by making fun of my teeth they were really making themselves look bad? Where were all *my* high fives for the times I choked back the swell of screams in my throat because I couldn't stop thinking about the number three but still forced myself to finish an entire page of math without raising my hand for the nurse's office?

When my mom said, "Oh I'm so proud of you, tutoring those kids and helping them," her words made me feel as synthetic as the plastic I wanted to cover myself in. Sure, every once in a while I almost caught sight of myself being as good as good can be, as if a true and natural part of me was born to correct their grammar and secure the locks in the wheelchairs that hit my shins whenever I leaned over someone to check their work—all the while ignoring the smell of spit like old bathwater or the dairy/wheat/meat allergy flatulence that filled the classroom after lunch.

But those glimpses didn't stick.

My entire article had to be rewritten. I had to look past neck acne, foam in mouth corners, and those pure and constant smiles to see the words I was supposed to use, the paragraphs I was supposed to *feel*.

Guess what? I wouldn't be able to do it. The repulsive reality was that, more than being a good helper, more than trying to understand how lucky I was not to have to wear a helmet, I wanted plastic over my stuff so I wouldn't get sick. I wanted to hear Mr. Delgado read my article with tears in his eyes.

At the end of a long afternoon of grading papers and glandular voices behind me saying, "Thanks for your help, Traci," I walked home the same way I always walked home, thinking the same things I always thought.

———————

Theresa said it was stupid to spend all of Saturday afternoon in the library.

"Then why'd you come?" I turned the pages of a book almost the same size as my outstretched arms. *The American Reference of Pediatric Congenital Birth Defects* kept me inside on a sunshiny day of cute-boy-at-the-mall promises. I'd bribed Theresa with some money to help her buy the new Police record if she came along to be my research assistant. I told her maybe the Oak Grove School District newsletter would print her name in the credits as assistant to Miss Foust (though I knew for sure that would never happen).

She pulled her comb through her thick feathered hair and answered honestly, "I only came because you're giving me money." She squinted at my book, "God, does it really have to be so accurate? Why don't you just make something up? You can do that, you're good at making things sound worse than they are."

"Whatever," I answered. "I have an editor now, okay? It's got to be perfect."

Theresa clicked her tongue. "I'm sure."

"How many newspaper articles did you find?" I asked.

"Find on what?"

"Didn't you tell a librarian you need to use the microfiching thing for the newspapers? I need to get some stats on when that whole chemical leak happened."

"Stats?" She giggled through the side of her mouth. "Are you like Cagney and Lacey now?"

I shut my notebook and clicked down my pen. It was time for separate tables. "Forget it," I said, "I'm just going to sit somewhere else."

But there wasn't any place big enough to sit with all those excellent words about cleft palates.

Theresa said I was being a jerk. Then she said I was being tricked. "I mean, seriously, haven't you thought about why you're helping out the Dig Its? Besides English, your grades are like all F's practically."

"No they're not."

"*Practically.* I just said *practically*, okay? Don't get all in a tizzy. I thought you were failing almost every class?"

"Why are you being so mean?" I flicked my thumb and forefinger hard against the magazine she was reading and she went, "Oh my God." Theresa knew how I struggled in math. Maybe she didn't understand about how numbers could sort of come to life and ask to specifically not stand next to another number, like when nine didn't want to touch the poky parts of four because sometimes nine looked liked a pregnant woman and if four hurt the baby then someone who was *really* pregnant, like how my gymnastics instructor now was, would lose her baby or the baby would be born like one of the Dig Its.

But she was completely wrong about the failing part. D's aren't failing.

"For someone who has her face in a book all the time you can be so stupid," Theresa said. "Don't you see? You're in the Dig It class because you're a Dig It."

"That's retarded," I said. "I'm not a Dig It."

She scooted my book toward her and pointed to a picture of a girl sitting on a doctor's table in a paper gown. The girl held out both hands, some kind of balance test or something. The doctor in front of her seemed pleased with her arms, or her balance. "Does that girl look like a retard to you?"

She didn't. I read the caption under the picture: *Insufficient growth is a common result of cystic fibrosis.* I saw the girl's face clearly in the photo. She looked liked anyone from my own class—not Mr. Delgado's. She wasn't all super smiles or wearing an expression like how someone would look if it was their birthday every day. She just looked—normal.

"Well, she's not retarded," I said. "Of course she's got some kind of something or she wouldn't be in this book."

"That's totally what I mean." Theresa smiled and shook her head. "Don't you get it? She doesn't *look* sick. How much you want to bet she doesn't even know she's sick?"

I peered into the page, tilted my head a bunch of different ways. "I'm sure."

"You think all those kids in the Dig It class totally and completely *know* why they're there?"

"I don't really care what the Dig Its—what the Dip Shits know."

Theresa put her hand to her mouth. "You're going to go to hell when you die." She let that hang there for a moment before telling me I had deep problems. "I bet you are a Dig It, Traci. I totally bet they just stuck you in that class and gave you your little teacher pen and said they needed your help."

I looked at my cousin. We were both quiet long enough to let a devil hand with sharp fingers scratch the length of my spine.

Theresa leaned back in her chair, so pleased with her epiphany. "I mean, when you think about it, you do a lot of Dig Itty things," she said.

That night I sat up in bed, thinking. Out loud I said, "I'm a Dig It and don't know it. I'm exactly like those kids," just to see if the gravity of the words in the air gave my cousin's stupid accusations some truth. I took out my Trapper Keeper and found my article. It was almost finished. Despite Theresa and her attempts to distract me, I'd pretty much chocked the whole thing full of the reporterish stuff Mr. D asked for. Even if my paper had to be completely changed, it was weird and slightly wonderful to have direction about something I'd written. A real teacher asked me to specifically write something, change something, make something better.

I balanced my binder on my knees and held my paper at all different lengths from my face, trying to see my words for all the things they weren't.

Alone in my tiny bedroom, with all my Michael Jackson and Ramones and big jungle cat posters, I let the steadiness of words hold me. In the safety of sentences and white spaces as clean as a second chance there wasn't anything I couldn't handle. No one telling me how big my head was, how ugly my teeth were, how out of control my mind spun.

I opened my curtains to the window that looked right out onto the street—something I had always wanted but never had before: a wide-lens view of what was going on outside myself. Even if this new house was so much smaller than what I was used to and adjusting to a new neighborhood wasn't something I was particularly good at, there was always my window at night. My secondhand desk sat underneath the cracked and splintery sill, and while everyone slept I stayed awake with the hum of my typewriter keys and the blue pulp of light from MTV on my little television keeping my room churning in the hope that someday I would be someone better than who I was.

Most nights, I would pick at my psoriasis and try to get inspired by what my window showed me. I wrote little poems about the way the broken streetlight blinked and shivered in its dirty glass cover. If the reflection was just right, you could see how the shadows mixed into the sparkly asphalt like eggshells from throwaway chickens too ugly to make the cut. In the gray distance I heard barking dogs and the shouts of alley cat kids who ran around the neighborhood deliciously unsupervised.

But even when it was hot, I kept my window closed. It was totally insane about the AIDS virus in the air, I knew that—I *kind of* knew that. Though there wasn't much to read on the subject, I'd seen just about every special aired on cable about the terrible disease that got into your blood and ate up your immune system.

Maybe you could die just from kissing a friend.

I knew malaria was carried by mosquitoes. I knew when they bit you, you got sick. So even though the media, my mom, and all the helpful people on the phone at Kaiser reassured me I couldn't get AIDS from mosquitoes, I wondered if it was all a lie, a government conspiracy like that woman talked about when she told my mother how the bad water had ruined her life.

I'd also begun thinking that maybe the Dig It kids could give me what they had. Though everything I read about cognitive birth defects proved something entirely different, I started to worry about getting too close to them. Maybe their breath would bend my chromosomes or make some disappear or give me five where there should only be four. What if one of them coughed on me and I ended up like the kids on my street who could only walk if metal held up their muscles? What if everyone within a ten-mile radius was infected with something from the water and it was just a matter of time before we all started dripping out our eyeballs or acquiring a taste for raw flesh?

I hadn't made any friends in my new neighborhood yet. One Saturday my dad drove me around to garage sales trying to find something that could work as an exercise bar he could bolt into our garage wall for when I practiced my dancing. I had not given up entirely with my

New York/LA stage dreams. In a floaty leopard-print bathing suit that required curves I didn't have to fill up all the floaty parts, I danced on my front lawn while Theresa squirted me with the garden hose. To the galloping synthesizer sounds of Michael Sembello's "Maniac" I flung my wet hair and banged my fists on a patio chair until I felt my mother's fingernails in my arm, "That's enough of that," she said. Theresa giggled under her breath while I was led away to the front porch. "Are you trying to attract every child molester in this neighborhood? Why don't you go find someone who likes to play Monopoly or something nice and quiet like that?"

When my dad asked me if I'd given any effort to making friends I did not tell him how hard it was to hook up with kids who understood the importance of attracting an audience. I said, "Not really," then stayed quiet. The chair/hose/leopard-print bathing suit thing had been my only effort. But not one—not a single curbside spectator said, "Awesome, she's almost like a professional dancer." The kids in the Los Paseos area were a little rougher than the kids I was used to. Candidates for zombiness in their own right, a lot of them dressed all in black like bad cowboys in bad cowboys films and cussed and did this thing called tagging where you pulled a fat Sharpie from under your sleeve and wrote your street name on a piece of property that wasn't yours. Names like Raven and Oozie, Kasper and Goat bejeweled the sidewalks and sides of green cable boxes, all written in swirls and gender symbols like Prince.

One afternoon I fell almost instantly in love with a boy I met in the park. He wore black pegged jeans and big white sneakers with fat red laces like the guys in Run DMC. I startled him while he was tagging the door to the men's restroom.

"What the fuck?" he said, turning quickly. You could see his biceps just under the rolled-up sleeves of his black Local Motion T-shirt. Around his neck hung a five-pointed star on the same gold chain as a very detailed crucifix. "Sorry," he said when he saw the look on my face. "I thought you were someone else."

And before I had time to open my mouth, Someone Else appeared in a pink leather miniskirt and the leftover fog from a Whitesnake video. "The playground isn't over here," she said to me, in the same tone Bryan used when he wanted to make huge spaces between Big Cool Brother and Possibly Handicapped Little Sister.

So I was back at square one in a new neighborhood. I watched my television and wrote my stories and spent most of my time in my room worrying about illness and poisoned water. What if AIDS hung out in the bathroom stalls at Roundtable Pizza? What if I decided to take a shower every day but my hair fell out under the chemicals that came from our pipes? What if Theresa was onto something about me being a Dig It kid?

Always square one.

Always what if.

I closed my binder with my revised article and stuck it in my backpack. I also threw in the first of my belongings to be laminated; a pinup of Rob Lowe, a Mickey Mouse T-shirt, and a pillowcase. When I climbed into my bed I could hear the kids across the street breakdancing in their driveway. A boom box was turned up all the way, so the sound track to *Beat Street* was the only thing I heard as I pulled my covers up to my neck and waited for my mind to turn off.

Casey Blevins had cerebral palsy and something else I wasn't quite sure of, but I guessed it came from the water. Her head hung to the left and her shoulders turned the whole upper part of her body into a lowercase *r*. She called me Pie and sucked on both pinkies like she was at a concert whistling. The good thing about Casey was she could only do math if other people weren't looking at her, so my regular thing was to stay with her in Mr. Delgado's office while she sat at a study table looking at the addition flash cards I'd made for her.

The laminator machine sat waiting for me on a corner table. Here was my chance to be alone with hot plastic.

Casey said, "Good frogs, Pie!" and held up a card with the dancing amphibians I drew over the problem 2 + 2 = ? They were all like that: five astronauts take away two astronauts equals how many astronauts? And so on with bees and friendly vampires and frogs (which I guess she liked the best, because each time she saw one she'd smile extra hard and pump her hookish hand in the air like a stuck bird).

"Yeah, I like the frogs too," I said. I turned on the laminator machine. "You just keep up the good work and let me know if you get stuck." The fan in back of the machine started up. A clean factory smell began to fill the room.

Mr. Delgado said that me making Casey's flash cards on my own without being asked showed focus and maturity. I thought about that while I slid Rob Lowe as Sodapop Curtis onto the rollers of the little open mouth. I wondered if he'd say the same thing about my corrected article I handed in this morning.

In a perfect warmth of synthetic armor, Rob came back to me. I shook him lightly until he cooled. I smiled into his germ-free face. Mr. Delgado opened the door and made my spine jump a little. "Traci, why don't you come on into the classroom for a second."

He saw my poster, sniffed, and said I should keep the door open when I used the machine.

"It's all right if I do a few of my posters?" I asked. "You said it would be okay, right?" Something felt weird.

"Yep. I did." He put his arm around my shoulder as we walked to a corner of the classroom. I knew what was coming.

"I'm just so impressed by all your work and your attention to detail," he said. "And I'm really sorry, but it's just not—well, it doesn't seem like this time we can use it for the newsletter."

Hot salty fluid filled the insides of my cheeks. It was all I could do to stop myself from crying. "No biggie." I shrugged. "Maybe I can write another article or whatever, for another time."

"Yeah," Mr. Delgado said, but he didn't look at me. "I know how hard you must have worked."

I walked back into the room where Casey was still pretty happy about frogs. I didn't keep the door open.

"Why are you smiling?" I said. I pulled out my pillowcase and smoothed it on the table. "Do you have to smile at every little thing? Not everything is good and happy you know."

"I'm good at math," she said. She put her hand over my cards. "These are my good cards."

I slipped in a corner of my pillowcase. In what I'm pretty sure was a low voice I told Casey Blevins she wasn't that good at math. "And since you've got spit all over my flash cards, why don't you go ahead and keep them."

"These are my good cards," she said again. But different.

The laminator machine stopped. An orange light blinked.

Casey said, "That's not a smell I like."

My pillowcase seemed to be smoldering. I gave it a tug and felt the rollers lock up. There was a loud *clank-cachunk*! Definitely smoke. I pulled the plug out, walked quickly to the door, walked back to the machine, squeezed my bangs with both hands, and let out some girl sound that made Casey gather her cards in a pile.

"That is one broken thing," she said. "It's not a smell I like."

The fire alarm went off. Everyone had to shuffle outside onto the blacktop while Mr. D carried the laminator machine in his arms. Smoke purled from the back, my yellow pillowcase whipping in the wind as he walked. I stood next to Casey. She had her pinkies in her mouth. Other kids in different after-school programs came outside too. Heads turned looking for something.

"Was there like an explosion?"

"Sick. What's that smell?"

I watched the wind carry up the smoke from what I had broken. Not a lot, really, just little gray-white puffs and a dying spark or two. There was nothing to do but stand there. The covenant of hope that comes with spring and the promise of an emergency made me just like everyone else, and for a second I thought it wouldn't be so bad.

Someone said, "Rad. It's a bomb."

Across the blacktop Dale the Janitor ran toward us with a fire extin-guisher. Kids clapped and whistled. One of the Dig Its started to cry and had to be consoled. Through the cloudy murk of the fire extin-guisher I saw Mr. Delgado walking toward me. I looked around as if I didn't know what had caused the disturbance.

"I think it really is a bomb," I said and laughed. But by that time, no one was really laughing anymore.

9

this is how we stop, drop, and roll

We used to serve liquor, but now we serve the Lord.
—D. E. OPRAVA, *AMERICAN MEANS*

W*hat in the world do you want? God can get it for you.* That's what
Tammy Faye Bakker said on the record player. My mom said it too.
"God can get it for you. Whatever it is." So I lay on the sofa and cracked
my knuckles and wondered if God could make it so that my mom's
face wouldn't catch on fire if I stared at it too long.

I could do that now. I was in the seventh grade. I had that kind of
power.

"Don't you just love Tammy Faye's voice?" my mom asked. She did
this creepy little shimmy thing in the hallway that made me feel bad
for her.

"Let's put the Smiths back on," I said. "What happened to the
Smiths?" But I almost enjoyed looking at the cover of Jim and Tammy
Faye Bakker's albums, especially the one where they posed in the desert in front of a wagon wheel against a backdrop of rain clouds as black
as every demon ever thought of. No matter what angle you tried, there

was no clear way to distinguish the shadows of the cactus from Tammy Faye's mascara. But that poor woman's voice was the pointiest end of Lucifer's pitchfork.

"How can you listen to this bull?" I had been told I could put on whatever I wanted, but a minute into "How Soon Is Now" it was suggested I should be listening to something more uplifting.

"Why does everything you like have to be sad?" my mom asked. Often.

If I were more Drew Barrymore in *Firestarter*, and less Spastic Me with my new fears of spontaneous human combustion, I could've given my mother a hard and flammable look. Then there'd be the Smiths whenever I wanted.

The autumn before I turned thirteen the weather was bad. Bad as in nothing had really changed much since the summer except that everything was a little drier, a little browner, and susceptible to detonation. We hadn't had our first rain yet, and here it was late October. The sun came up white and went down like a contagious rash.

Fire was on my mind.

So were the diapered asses of old people. My grandmother's nursing home was in full swing, and that meant me, Kim, and Bryan spending our Saturdays with cleaning products and latex gloves while my mother sat on the back patio with the old people, spreading the good news of the Lord.

"I don't give a rat's ass how much it would be to hire a few maids." Kim walked down the long hallways of the Santa Ana Care Facility, her expression set firmly in annoyance. "This is the last time I waste a perfectly good weekend doing this shit." She held bundles of clothes and plastic trash bags with her arms so outstretched, she looked liked a resurrected mummy trying to find a way out of the museum. Though I had my own can of Lysol and surgical face masks, which I bought with my own money, I didn't believe anyone really expected me to do anything that would require getting upset over germs.

I wasn't right about that.

"Now, you've already been asked to put clean sheets on Mrs. Petersen's bed," my grandmother said. "Get off that damn phone and do as you're told."

This consisted of me going into Mrs. Petersen's room and convincing her she didn't need me to do anything with her entire bed.

"Hey, Mrs. Petersen," I said at her doorway, "your mattress is fine, huh? You don't want me to change anything about it, right?"

"What on Earth?" She fluttered a skeletal hand toward the ruffles of her bathrobe collar. "Who on Earth told you to change my mattress? Nothing's wrong with my mattress. You better leave my mattress alone."

So I went back to doing what I was doing before Mrs. Petersen became so uncooperative. I dialed my new friend's number. "Sorry about that," I said, "Okay, so, where was I?"

Leah Mateo and I were in practically every class together. She was the first kid in junior high to talk to me: "Hey, let me copy off your paper for the vocabulary quiz." And the first to insist that I talk to her: "You have to totally call me this weekend and come over to watch *Sixteen Candles*." She was full of eye makeup and stories about eager boys who reminded me of me: "So at first he said let's just talk, then he was all like wouldn't keep his hands off me. . . ."

But ever since the nursing home opened and my mother found Jesus, the only temptations I was allowed to give into on the weekends were the blood of the lamb and the diapers of old people.

I wrote in my journal: *My mother has contracted a sudden case of church*, but then I felt bad. That's not exactly how the Spirit had been moved.

Everyone knew my mom was always kind of a nervous person. If the *National Enquirer* ran a story about killer bees she'd keep the windows rolled up in the car and flinched if the shadow of a bird crossed the hood. If my brother was caught dousing his bedsheets with English Leather she'd appear in the doorway of his room asking if he knew how dangerous it was to pour alcohol-based products all over fabric.

Now she was more than nervous. Now she said she felt "unsettled" all the time. "Like I've been dancing nonstop." She had lost a lot of weight and almost every day she complained that her chest felt tight. My dad tried to make a joke and told me if I stopped acting like a girl possessed, my mother would ease up on all this praying nonsense. But really, we weren't so sure. Her anxiety had gotten to the point of half days at work and a psychiatrist all her own. At least twice a week she called my sister at her apartment and said she sure wished she could relax.

"Let's get Kim to come over and play some Yahtzee with us."

I sighed and slouched in the kitchen where I was about to begin a bag of microwave popcorn. "I thought it was just us watching *Hunter*?"

But in twenty minutes or less, there was my sister in her bathrobe, smelling of marijuana and Charlie cologne, holding a carton of my mother's cigarettes she'd picked up at Costco because that's where married people shopped.

Bryan spent more time than ever at the gym. Unlike at home, the Jazzercise and tanning-bed women of Vista Racquetball Club and Spa asked nothing more from him than a sit-up demonstration and his prettiness.

"I'm glad I got my hours changed at the store," he said one day while we both watched our mom write a check to someone on TV with miracles and a bad toupee. He'd been promoted from bag boy to checker at Lucky's, so between that, helping out at the nursing home, the gym, and his ROTC classes, he'd managed most Sundays to escape the embarrassment of watching our mother tearfully make her way to the pulpit, clutching a Kleenex and a new chance at a saved life.

Savior Cathedral was like nothing I'd ever seen. I knew from a handful of times with Theresa at Saint Julie's—falling asleep or trying not to giggle over cute altar boys—church was supposed to be quiet, deathlike. Not at my mother's new Pentecostal palace. I don't think I'd ever been inside a building *that* huge where someone didn't have to check your purse for weapons and tear your ticket stub. The noise was something else. Everyone shook and some even lurched. There was a lot of crying. A pendulum of hands like wizards drawing down the heavens swayed over tops of desperate faces while the full-on band with a drum set as big as Alex Van Halen's belted out songs that bordered on Elvis. In the halls and corridors people sold self-published books about Jesus equaling success. There was even a guy who made his own rap album on the subject of his life in prison until the Lord set him free. He didn't even mean it as a metaphor.

At first the place seemed jumping. Maybe a little threatening, but in a funky and exciting way, like how I felt at this one birthday party where the kids kept calling me honky but couldn't get enough of me doing backflips on the front lawn.

I had to admit this church was a lot more exciting than me and Theresa passing notes during Ten Commandment bingo.

But after a few weeks, well, you only had to not be in a full coma to realize the Stepfordness of the whole scene. I would've just come right out and said screw this, but it was getting harder and harder to tell my mother no. I mean, when your own mom calls you a sinner and a backslider (which you're not even really sure what the hell that word means), of course you're going to start thinking maybe you should want to feel as good as she professes the whole church thing is making her feel. At first glance the Holy Bible and highlighters and Wednesday nights in a dress would even look like something you think you might need, but if you keep taking harder looks—because you have to keep going back—because your mom says she is nervous about the direction you are headed, and she keeps saying, "Remember how we used to write instructions in your little books?" and you act like you don't know what she's talking about because every sentence lately starts with *remember when we used to* and it makes you feel like anything you do now or will do ten years from now will never be as good as the When You Used To time, then you'd see something totally different at Savior Cathedral. The view from redemption would burn your eyes like a witch on a piece of wood.

I started junior high with a constant stream of peroxide in my hair and an aching for the blood between my legs to begin. I had a new boldness toward boys who wouldn't talk to me or make the first move. Light hair seemed to suit my tanless skin, giving me a chameleon capacity to stand out, then disappear when I needed to. The confidence changing my looks (provided that and the cramps I was sure would any day now get me into the nurse's office acting annoyed to ask for a tampon) seemed like just the boost I needed. Leah Mateo and I showed up at school dances with ripped-up jeans and the pretension of boredom. Once I'd found my bird-of-prey abilities, I no longer waited for someone to move in slowly, to fill me with their Polo cologne and clumsiness. I didn't lean against the DJ's speakers with hope and *please, am I the one*? I said, "Dance with me," then took the hands of awkward boys and swayed along to Journey's "Open Arms" while we held each other's butts.

In my new classrooms I touched potential with both hands. I still sucked at math, but tried very hard to stop caring about the fractions I saw in my head as something that could kill us all. It was clear I was not going to grow up to be a physics professor, nor did I see any value of learning anything by heart that could be done with a calculator. In remedial math I sat at my desk and wrote skits for the drama class I couldn't wait to get to after lunch. In English I couldn't get enough of Mrs. Falhurst, who had more pictures of Paul Newman on her walls than anything educational. She said *crap* and *hell* and *damn*, wasn't overly concerned with people's feelings, and introduced us to Edgar Allan Poe.

> *From childhood's hour I have not been*
> *As others were; I have not seen*
> *As others saw; I could not bring*
> *My passions from a common spring.*

From the same source I have not taken
My sorrow; I could not awaken
My heart to joy at the same tone;
And all I loved, I loved alone.

The first time she read this poem to the class I had to look around and make sure I was still in seventh period, that the Earth had not melted, dripping me away from it. Sometimes I pretended Mrs. Falhurst was my mother. When it was her turn to sit with the detention bunch after school, I imagined us as equals like my mom and Kim: just waiting for the losers to leave the room and give up on themselves so we could get on with the business of cool.

The new school year at Bernal Intermediate was turning out to be not as bad as I had worked myself up to think/expect/kind of hope it would be.

Home was something else entirely, and I was someone else to match it. Almost every night I was too scared to go to bed. Obsessive thoughts made the nighttime excruciating. Only when I could no longer distinguish between the heaviness of my body and the murk of my mind would I allow myself to stop resisting and fall into a jerky trance, like a dog who sees his owner's car in his dream. All night I wrestled with these awful inferno visions of Jesus on the cross; then I'd wake up soaked in sweat over a documentary I'd watched about exploding people.

"Why the hell did you let her see that?" my mom yelled at Bryan. "You know how she is."

Unfair, I guess, since I was the one who had begged my brother to stay up late and check out the episode I'd taped of *Beyond Belief.* The subject was spontaneous human combustion, and together we ate a whole bag of Doritos while watching stories that all started out with old people in comfortable chairs and ended with someone's barbecued grandma—legs protruding from a black and scooped-out cavity where fast and mysterious flames had cooked up her insides.

No one was sure how it happened, or even if it was something else besides a strange phenomenon.

I couldn't not look.

And because I had no idea what was good for me, because I viewed my fascination with the morbid as simply looking into the heinous mirror of who I was and what I would end up being, scaring myself was as natural as breathing. The thought of life without the crippling fear of something seemed almost uncomfortable to me.

My fear of fire caused me to fill Tupperware containers with ice water and carry them around in my backpack until the muscles in my shoulders were so overworked and inflamed my PE teacher made me swear to God that no one had thrown me up against a wall.

When Theresa and I stood for an hour in line at the Santa Clara County Fair to be included in the first one hundred people for a free show of Barbara Mandrell and the Mandrell Sisters, I had to duck out early because I'd drunk all my water.

"We're not supposed to be running around separately," Theresa said, of course minding the warning my mother had given us before she dropped us off. "Stop exaggerating. You're not going to die if you don't get some water right this very second. I'm not waiting for you, Traci. I'll be stuck at the end of the line and have to pay for our tickets."

But she wasn't the one who had been up until two in the morning unplugging all the appliances and making the sign of the cross over all the outlets.

I took off in search of water. When I came back with the can of Sprite, I had to drink really fast, because I was embarrassed to have someone catch me pouring it into the trash, then say something about wasting or causing bees or whatever—then I had to fill the can with water in the bathroom then ask for a piece of aluminum foil from a hot dog vendor and convince him that I already did buy a hot dog but I just needed a new piece of foil so I could wad it up to block the opening of the Sprite can—by then it was too late. I could already hear cheering and the distant echo of "Sleeping Single in a Double Bed."

I found Theresa on a pay phone telling my mom to come and get us.

"And can you please just drop me off at home because I am definitely not spending the night."

Whatever demands came with my new obsession, someone was going to have to help us all through my agony.

"This is just a bunch of shit," Bryan said. He rolled out his sleeping bag on my bedroom floor and told me to keep my damn mouth shut so he could get some rest. "I've never heard of such a stupid thing as being afraid you're going to explode in your sleep."

My mother had sentenced my brother to almost every night in my room with me until I fell asleep. We (mostly me) figured if he could keep watch over me in my covers, if his presence had any power in it at all, maybe it could stop all this fire.

"Bryan? Bryan? Are you sleeping? Bryan? Bryan?" All night I pestered him about igniting. I came up with the idea that if he was looking at me, if his face was turned exactly toward me and his eyes stayed open in my direction, somehow this would counterbalance my powers of combusting. In the movie *Firestarter* (which of course was now the only movie I was interested in watching), all Drew Barrymore had to do was think hard and angry thoughts about who she hated and in seconds they were gone to cinders. I hated quite a number of people, including myself sometimes, and wasn't exactly known for keeping my anger in check.

"Bryan, are you looking at me?" I asked. "It's hard to tell in the dark. Are your eyes open?"

"Yes."

"Yes, you're looking at me, or yes your eyes are open?"

"If my eyes aren't open how can I be looking at you?"

"But like, *straight* at me, are you looking *straight* at me?"

Once he hit me so hard in the face with his balled-up tube socks the vision out of my right eye was blurry for two days.

"So you're looking right at me? Don't turn your head, okay? Don't stop looking at me. Bryan?"

In the cold sweat of myself I felt paralyzed. I shivered in my bed and held in my pee until I saw gnomes jumping on my bladder. The bloody red of half sleep. I tried to make mental images of Santa Cruz, tried my breathing exercises or focusing on hanging out with Leah the next day at school, but my mind was a Ferris wheel in a suspicious carnival.

Some nights when my brother just couldn't take it anymore he'd encourage me to type up a story. He'd put cotton in his ears and a dish towel over his eyes. If Leah was scheduled for a sleepover that night, he showed signs of happiness by going for an entire day without expressing his desire to find I had passed away in my sleep.

With Leah in my room I wasn't so afraid. We stayed up until way past the time any good shows came on. We talked about sex and God and sex. But when she told her mom I was reading her fortune with tarot cards, that was pretty much it for Saturday night sleepovers at my house.

"My mom says she thinks it would be better if you spent the night at our place. She's kind of not into stuff like that."

"How weird," I said. "Jesus is contagious."

When the shine of junior high began to wear off, the exhaustion set in. I spent at least two afternoons a week in detention for falling asleep in math or refusing to get off the bed in the nurse's office when I couldn't muster up a temperature or show any visible signs of a concussion. It happened so often I drew a little circle on my binder and wrote, *Place dribble here.* At the end of every wasted night I'd drag my wet-sand body from my sweaty sheets, setting my jaw to the intolerable ding, clank, ding, of spoons against cereal bowls.

Hey, missy, when someone says "good morning," you'd better remember your manners and answer them.

But I couldn't. My brain was like the time I jumped into my swimming pool with my roller skates on.

Leah and I tried our hardest to stay out of PE. We both came down with menstrual pains at the same time (hers were real), or we hid in the disgusting bathrooms behind the portables near the running track.

"God, it's rank in here," I said, then pulled out my imitation Giorgio body spray. But really, I didn't mind. Anything was better than running laps or watching *Brian's Song* for the twenty-seventh time. Plus, listening to Leah's true/false stories of boys with their hands up her shirt was food for the hunger that had begun to gnaw at me and all my stories. I spent a lot of time reading them to her.

"Okay, and then—listen okay, because here's where it gets really good." I explained the plot of my current tragedy about a poor girl who falls in love with this rich rock star who takes a lot of drugs and doesn't want anyone to really tie him down to a relationship, but then his bass guitarist flings his instrument all over the stage and accidentally hits the big star in the head and he ends up being paralyzed, causing his girlfriend to smoke a lot of cigarettes and think a lot about her life while she looks out of a lot of windows.

"God, that's so sad," Leah said. She pressed her finger to her cheek, pulled down her lower eyelid, and made her mouth all fish-circled to apply mascara. Leah was an obvious kind of pretty and looked older than everyone else. That alone was kind of a reason to hang around her, just to see what she knew to make her look like that. She feathered the top of her hair high and ratted it out like Sheila E. She wore rings on almost every finger and big hoops in her ears and said *what the fuck* to just about everything. I did/wore/said that too, but not with Leah's womanly ease. More often than not, I had to fake my girliness. I knew secret and sexual things about myself, like how watching a boy run his fingers through his bangs or the way his eyebrows turned down if he tried to understand something I knew he would never understand— those things were oxygen and water. But my own femininity was like those silver headless mannequins in the window of Wet Seal—the miniskirts were nice enough, but the missing body parts made the whole scene like a tacky magic trick.

I displayed what I thought people wanted to see.

Rules like, "laugh when his jokes aren't funny," "don't talk too much or say 'oh my god' or 'like' all the time," were almost the same as the rules you learn in drama class. Puberty was all lines and stage directions.

It was me missing my mark.

One Saturday night when I was supposed to be at the library I sat in Mike Hertz's hot tub and hated that he kept backing away from me and my all-consumingness.

"Don't you just want to swim and stuff?" he had asked.

I tried to get the point: thirteen-year-old boys weren't ready for me to stand in front of them with a knife and fork. But then neither was I ready for the way teenage girls in the seventh grade absorbed each other. The closeness of them freaked me out a little. I had never seen a group of people hug so much. Like every second they hugged. Walking to class, waiting in the lunch line, walking home, hug, hug, hug, as if one of them had been a missing person for ten years with no leads from law enforcement.

"Oh my God, sweetie!"

"Oh my God, call me!"

"Oh my God, I just saw you!"

Leah was a hugger. And a letter writer. That was another weird thing. Apparently girls in the seventh grade felt the need to write long, pastel-colored letters to each other, outlining every detail of everything they did at every second. Each morning Leah handed me a lavender envelope with stickers on the back and vital stuff written on pink paper sprayed with If You Like Poison, You'll Love Dark Passion.

Oh my God, I'm in Sanchez's class right now and I'm freaking out because you told me that Sean asked about me. We totally need to talk tonight. Do you have a plain black long-sleeved shirt? I need one. Oh my God, I just remembered my mom's boyfriend is coming over for dinner

tonight, he's a loser. He jacks off all day. I just need a plain
black shirt. Long sleeved.

Hug me.
Write me.
Be me.

Once Leah put a piece of a cookie in an envelope with a full report
about the baking experience she just had with her mom and how fun
it would be for us to bake cookies together. Seeing those crumbs and
melted chocolate chips was so bizarre to me, I thought long and hard
that having a new best friend was probably not something I should be
thinking long and hard about right now.

In a little office in our huge church I sat on a sofa with my mom waiting to be introduced to my new counselor. Dr. Schmidt was too big for
us now, too expensive. He'd moved his practice to Stanford and noti-
fied his patients via a form letter that wished them luck and said how
honored he had been to serve them as his patients, blah, blah.

"Yeah. Fine," I said when my mother told me. "Good for him." I
threw the letter in the trash. It was the same as every other letter. A
bunch of nothing words to fake you into feelings. Leah's letters said call
me, call me. Dr. Schmidt's letter said to call someone else.

"You're really going to like Glenda," my mom said. She balanced
her Bible on her knee and marked things with a yellow highlighter.

I looked at my mother and almost didn't want to. She had changed
so much in such a short amount of time. Now she was all about these
awful muumuus and big plastic beads hanging from her neck and
wrists. Not that her business pantsuits were anything I'd be interested
in, but at least when she was working full time she had the kind of pink
to her cheeks that suggested she'd been getting things done. Nowa-
days she wore her makeup like putty, like the televangelist wives she sat
mesmerized in front of every night. Also, she'd cut her hair above her

shoulders, bleached it strawberry blond, and started sporting this old-fashioned tight, permy bouffant thing. Sometimes it was hard for me to believe this was the same mom who let us turn off the fuse box so we could play hide-and-seek in complete and creepy darkness, the one who subscribed to *Cosmopolitan* and once helped me compose a letter to Dr. Joyce Brothers when I wanted to write an article on teen pregnancy. Where was the woman who saved her money to see psychics and chopped down the willow tree in front of our old house because she had a dream that bad spirits lived in the leaves? She had gone to the Lord, is where she was. "Finding home," she called it. Another place I wasn't.

"She's got a good way with teenagers," my mom said. I guess she meant my new counselor.

"What does that mean?" I asked.

"Well, what do you think it means? She's good with kids."

God, what was she highlighting in that Bible? Every word or what? "Is this Glenda like a pastor or something?" I asked, "Does she work here at the church?"

"I do," a voice said in the doorway. "I'm Dr. Glenda." She held her hand out to me. "But just call me Glenda."

"Oh. Uh . . . ok . . . I'll do that," I said. I picked up my backpack and began my familiar routine of following someone into their office. "So then, Glenda, I'm guessing that you're a good witch?"

"Right," she said. "And I'm guessing that you're not always so unoriginal."

I turned to my mom and mimicked a noose being pulled around my neck. I stuck my tongue to the side and rolled my eyes backwards. Usually she laughed when I did this little trick, but now she had Jesus.

And Glenda had Jesus too. Glenda had *a lot* of Jesus. She had country pink and country blue and ducks and little kids in bonnets praying and little ducks in bonnets praying and every picture of Jesus I had ever seen at the San Jose flea market. Jesus under a rainbow with one of just about every race of children. Jesus petting a baby lamb while a little girl picked flowers. And why the hell was he knocking on so many doors pestering people in the middle of the night?

"You just sit and make yourself right at home," she said.

"Were you in some kind of a show?" I pointed to a poster above her head. It was a picture of her in a bear costume holding her bear head in her bear paws. In the background was a row of fake trees.

Glenda had white hair and wore pink lipstick so bright and thick you could smell the machinery from the factory where it was made. "I sure was. The Carolina Bible Bears," she said. "Kind of an East Coast thing. It ran for eight years." When she sat down in her fifties-style swivel chair, her chubby butt in its light brown polyester skirt made the cushion whisper, *Nnnooo . . .*

"What did you do?" I asked. "Sing?"

She opened a file folder. Her very black painted eyebrows turned into a V. "Sing a little, dance a little, preach a little gospel."

"Ha. That sounds like that Cher song about the gypsies and the grandpa preaching while the men threw the money at the women."

She closed the folder, my folder, I guessed. "Did you see her in *Silkwood*? Not a huge part, but man, she was good. Oh, I just love, love, love Kurt Russell."

I could see that in her. The Kurt Russell love.

It wasn't as bad as I had originally thought there in the ugly Lord-infested room. When my mom told me I was going to see her counselor "friend," at first I thought she meant her own shrink who was now prescribing pills so my mother could stop feeling nervous and stop looking so aware. The day I waltzed in our front door at almost midnight from hanging out with Leah and some hoody guys in the neighborhood, she'd pulled my jacket until some of the shoulder ripped and threatened me with two choices: moving in with my dad or church counseling.

"And what in Christ's name is this?" She held up my backpack where the words *I ❤ Satan* had been written in silver glitter pen.

"So tell me what that was all about," Glenda said.

By now I had figured on my own that doctor/patient confidentiality did not apply to minors. Dr. Schmidt always seemed to magically know the details of each fit I had thrown prior to our visits or how many times I asked my mom to swear on her father's grave that I wouldn't awake in the morning with cancerous tumors under my armpits. It was so stupid how he would try to play it off like he'd guessed all that. At least Glenda came right out with it. I think there was something I appreciated about that.

"Oh, the backpack thing," I said, "that was just a joke. I seriously thought it would wash right off." Not true. "I didn't even do that, really, it was some guy." True. The boy I had caught tagging in the park last year, the one with the pentagram around his neck and the wavy brown hair and eyes the color of a poem you write in autumn, turns out he was Leah's brother. I had never seen him after that one time, because he'd been living with his dad on the east side. But one holy afternoon, after I convinced Leah of all the cute guys she'd meet in the youth group at Savior Cathedral, we picked her up at her house, and I noticed a bunch of ninja-clad boys hanging around the front porch. Right away I recognized him.

"Have fun being brainwashed," he teased Leah as she walked out the door. I stood there for a moment, finding my breath. Making sure. He walked up to me and cocked his head, recognizing me too. "Go in peace, child," he said, then made the sign of the cross in the air over my face.

The other boys laughed. I didn't think I'd be able to, but I forced myself not to stare at the dimples of his smile and the sprinkle of freckles across his nose. I climbed back into my mom's Monte Carlo with Leah and Kim and my mom's big chemical hair like the burning bush just seconds before Moses got there.

"But why did you let him write that on your backpack?" Glenda asked. "Can you understand why your mom would be a little concerned about this?"

I shrugged. "It was just a thing." And the thing was this: it took maybe a whole two weeks for me to become an official hanger-on of Leah's brother and his graffiti group. The night of the backpack and my mom crying and praying at the same time, he gave me a sketch he had drawn of my name wrapped around a fat comiclike heart with two chains breaking over it. That was also the night he held my hand and said to call him Goat. "Everyone who means anything to me calls me Goat," he said.

We sat on his skateboard under the streetlight and talked for three hours about aliens, art, and how no one seemed to care about asteroids colliding with the Earth. From what I already knew about being friends with teenage girls, I could tell it wouldn't be long before I'd have to decide between Leah and the boy with the five-pointed star.

"I think your mom just wants to make sure you're, you know—" Glenda folded her hands. Expensive manicured nails, not the plastic Sally Hansen dragon-style jobs my mother was so into. "She just wants to make sure you're on the right path and that you can come to her if you need to talk about anything. Have you thought about a future with the Lord?"

"We're okay," I said. But actually that *future with the Lord* bit threw me off. I thought Glenda and I were starting something cool here. Something close to normal. When were we going to get to the part where I talk about how scared I am of burning people up? I mean, right off I felt kind of different in front of a woman counselor. Glenda had an easiness about her. Even if her office somehow reminded me of that creepy movie *Southern Comfort*. I thought maybe I wouldn't have too hard of a time getting used to her.

Until this: "I'm just wondering if your fascination with tarot cards and your occult stuff isn't exactly helping you with your fears about fire," she said. "But it's important for you to understand that being overly concerned with so many things, you know, like uneven numbers and fears about fainting—well, that's perfectly normal for someone with OCD."

"Someone with what?" I leaned forward. "What is that? OCD?"

And how the hell did she know about my fear of uneven numbers and fainting?

She opened the folder again. "Oh, sorry, you're probably used to hearing it as obsessive-compulsive disorder. Didn't Dr. Schmidt ever call it OCD? It's easier." She reached her hand across the table and put it on mine. "And it's very common in girls who are bright and talented and have not yet started to menstruate. Have you been praying about it?"

I was crying. I was close to hysterical. If I'd known the correct way to execute a tuck and roll out of a moving car I would've hit the pavement on Santa Teresa Boulevard. "She had an entire folder on me," I sobbed. "You—you never said a thing about OCD—about obsessive-compulsive disorder . . ." In between words I sputtered on my breath. "And don't tell me it's not a big deal. It *is* a big deal. This is my life we're talking about here."

"Oh, for Pete's sake," my mom said, "we didn't just find out you have two weeks to live." At a red light she fished around in her purse—just a motion to do something other than what she was doing, and what she was doing was getting caught. It was so obvious that she—and probably Kim too—had read every single page in my journals and ledgers. There was no other explanation as to how Dr. Schmidt could've passed on so much information to Glenda. The way I thought uneven numbers had the power to make people sick; how I counted in my head the number of times I heard the word *you* on television between the hours of ten and eleven at night; the way the patterns in the plaster of my wall could turn to demon faces if you looked at them long enough; the way I constantly thought about that time I fainted into Kitty Thurman's arms. I had written all of this down. No one, not even Glenda with her God powers, could've just guessed at all this stuff.

In Glenda's office, while my mouth was still open, she said, "Now, we've already established that you don't have a paranoid personality disorder, so I think it's important you understand that a lot of OCDers find patterns in things like wall plaster or floor tiles. It's a way to make sense of the anxiety. A strategy of sorts to calm the panic."

Of course my mom claimed that everyone had come to this conclusion by observing my actions and *not just the things I wrote in my diaries*. But look at that—you can't lie to a grade A compulsive liar.

"What do you mean," I asked, trying to make myself sound clear, "not just the things I write in my diaries? How do you know the things I write in my diaries?"

She pulled into a gas station and put the car in park. "Now you look here. I'm not going to listen to your drama all the way home. I can barely drive with you in the car as it is."

I wouldn't look at her. All that makeup and her shaking cheeks. "You lied to me."

"No. No one lied to you," she said. "We read a few things in your books, okay, yes, but that's not the point here. The point is we've got a direction now, something we can go on."

"Well, how nice of you and Dr. Schmidt to sit around with *my* direction. And how extra nice to tell some crazy churchy woman, who I don't even know, about your mental daughter."

A service attendant in a blue jumpsuit headed our way. My mom waved him on and turned back toward the main road. "Look, Glenda gave you a lot of things to read. I know how much you like that. Everyone here is in your corner, Traci. This 'poor little me' attitude is getting so damn old. . . ."

I looked down at the brochures and booklets in my lap. *Anxiety: A New Approach for Teens; When Once Is Never Enough: The Hidden Shame of Obsessive Compulsive Disorder.*

"Just don't talk to me," I said and leaned my head against the window. Suddenly I felt so exhausted. I could barely even focus enough to watch the blur of buildings and yellow hills. Everything had turned into a slow and ignorant giant losing its ugly posture.

For the rest of the ride home I thought about *disorder*, rolled the word silently over my tongue. In my mind I repeated it, pulled it apart: The capital *D* like the sideways face of a devil or an empty cat. The way the middle letters hissed and snake charmed around the *O*. *Disorder*. Di*sssss*. Di. Die. Die from Order. Die from no order. Die-order. Sorder. So, find order. Sort her. There was no vibration in the thing. No whisper, zoom, and release like when I used to say the word *God* over and over and the soft *da* at the end of the word would float in front of me.

Disorder didn't float.

I tried to give the middle of my panic and anger some sort of balance by reading the stuff Glenda gave me. I copied all the stupid little affirmations in my notebooks: *Today is a single step. I am always on the journey into myself.* One of the things that struck me most about what I read was a part in one of the booklets where it said, *Imagine if you woke up one day and didn't care about what people thought of you.* The paragraph went on to explain about how people with anxiety problems, especially teens, spend at least 83 percent of their thought process time worrying about the way their actions will make them appear in the eyes of their friends and classmates.

Eighty-three percent of your time worrying what other people thought.

That seemed like a lot to me.

Under an outdated picture of a nineteen seventy–ish girl standing all nervous and upset in the foreground of a dance or party or something, the caption read: *Julie couldn't even speak to her own friends for fear of saying the wrong thing.*

I don't know. I never thought much about not talking to people. I mean, I couldn't really say I was ever shy or afraid to open my mouth. But I guess I understood why the girl in the picture looked so broken. I knew what it meant to be on the outside of normal people having a normal time. The last time I was at Leah's house, Goat had gotten upset because I wouldn't eat some pizza rolls he'd heated up just for me. People everywhere eat pizza rolls all the time. They sit in front of *Monday Night Football* or a scary movie they've been waiting to rent.

They bite into the processed cheese and iffy sausage, their thoughts focused only on touchdowns, or busty girls with meat hooks poking through their ribs.

Why couldn't I just be happy with what I'd been given?

"They don't smell cooked all the way," I said, trying not to make an obvious face.

He picked up the box and laughed a little. "Don't you know they're already cooked? Says it right here."

Plus there was a pile of dirty dishes in the sink where I had seen him only lightly rinse a plate and not even use steaming hot water.

"God, how rude," he said. "You just told me you were hungry. This was the last box. Are you always this annoying?"

The rest of the afternoon was spent with each of us on opposite sides of the sofa in front of MTV, him oblivious to how scared I was that salmonella would surely be lurking in the fake cheese and *maybe* cooked meat, me wondering if you could catch food poisoning by being too close to the breath of someone who may have just contracted a nasty case of it.

Unlike Seventies Julie from the brochure, when it came to being around groups of kids, my problem wasn't fear of talking, but my intense distress over the probability that I would never shut up. A few years back at Jenny Braden's tenth birthday party I got upset because everyone loved her huge fancy bedroom with her new pink canopy bed, and Jenny was looking like she was so annoyed about having all these great things in her room.

I told everyone to come and look at my cold sore.

I kept saying, "It's bad, huh? It could get worse." There was the clicking sound behind my eyes and I kind of split into two people. One Me said, *Traci, shut up. No one gives a damn about the scab on your lip.* The other Me (the one I usually listened to) just kept right on telling people to get real close and have a look, even when Jenny Braden said, "How grody to the max" because she thought she was Moon Unit Zappa, and led the party out toward her swimming pool so that the only kid left in the house with me was the one on the phone telling his mom about his stomachache. Even then, I would not stop talking about my cold sore.

I read everything Glenda gave me. Some stuff I read twice, three times. She had put everything in a manila envelope with my name on it. My name was spelled wrong. *For Tracey*, it said. I crossed it out and wrote *T-r-a-c-i*, then wondered if that even mattered. Underneath my correction I copied the last sentence from that interesting paragraph: *What if you didn't care what people thought about you?* It was kind of funny. My whole life seemed to be constructed out of what-ifs, and here I was purposely adding another brick to the uneven house.

Leah said it was all a bunch of boring crap. "Put those things away and tell me one of your cool stories." Lately I'd replaced my pregnant/ unwed teenage runaway tales with the hopes that Leah would be just as interested in a study of repetitive light-switch touching as she was in sex without a condom. But it was clear that with my interest in finding out as much as I could about OCD (that and the way I never stopped talking about her brother), we were both feeling the pull of a friendship coming to its end.

Though I didn't dare let Goat in on me washing my hands twenty-eight times a day or offer any real explanation as to why he never saw me eat anything at his house, I was curious to hear his opinion. I played it off like I'd seen a special on Phil Donahue about obsessive compulsives.

"Oh, yeah, I think I know what you're talking about," he said. "Like those people who are afraid they'll get cancer and shit if they touch a dollar bill or whatever?"

"Yeah. I guess. That's totally insane, huh?"

He shrugged, shook his spray can and pointed it toward the wall behind the video store. "I don't know. It's kind of funky, I think. Robotic. Like a broken microchip in someone's head. Maybe it's the military trying to fuck with people's minds."

Well, I didn't know about that, but I certainly did know that me raising my arms to praise the Lord in church wasn't going to fix a single thing in my head. I just couldn't get my mother to stop insisting it would.

"Then maybe I should move in with my father!" It was another yelling night. Another crying night. Another night I had picked the psoriasis on my knees until blood turned my shins into one of Goat's paintings.

"I hate it here anyway! I hate it here with you!" Sweat prickled my back, the air in my lungs so tight against my rib cage. "I just hate everything!"

When I was a toddler and didn't get my way, I used to open all the cabinets and drawers in the kitchen, then slam them shut as hard as I could. It was funny then. My mom would laugh and call me Vesuvius in a Pamper. I loved the way the sudden jangle of silverware made me think of myself at the sharp end of things. But the best part of those fits was my mother laughing.

It's funny to be bad.

People get in on the act when you make a scene. Until the day you're not Vesuvius in a Pamper anymore. The bells of silverware are no longer the music of you in control. And you're not funny. What you are is just a crazy bitch.

"You're not the only one who hates everything," my mom said. She sat on the edge of my bed. "But let's be realistic about moving in with your dad. You think your dad's going to drive you back and forth ten miles a day so you can stay in the same school? You think he's going to let Goat sit in your room and let you guys write all over each other's arms?" She was out-of-character calm. I knew it was from her evening tranquilizer. Fine by me. I didn't mind her highness when it was time for an argument.

"I don't really care," I said while I rubbed the sores on my knees. "I don't care about anything you say or do."

After a long silence of her on my bed and me on the floor pretending to be very engaged in my scabs, she finally spoke. "Wouldn't you agree that we can't go on like this?"

"Sure," I answered quickly.

"I know you're not happy, my dear. And you know I'm not happy."

"Uh-huh."

"Maybe a little break from each other would be just the thing to get us back into shape."

"Sure."

In the silence that followed I suddenly thought of my gay friend, Peter Veneko, how he told me his parents sent him away for the summer to live with his church-going relatives because his gayness needed fixing. I pictured myself being driven to a Jesus-y commune with snake charmers and rainbow kids in daisy pastures. Everyone loved oatmeal as much as dress smocks. "Like going to some kind of camp?" I blurted out. Goat talked a lot about cults and brainwashing. Once we rented a documentary on Jim Jones. "Can you believe that shit?" he said all the time. "People getting sucked into this crap like some sort of science experiment."

I stood up. "I'm not going to any Bible-beating loony farm."

"What?" My mom laughed. "That's funny. I don't really know of any Bible-beating loony farms around here." She reached out and rubbed my arm. "But I do know of a place that would love to have you."

She really wanted me to leave? I made a face like I couldn't believe it. But that face felt wrong. Inside I was flushed with the excitement of something—*anything*—new, and the promising comfort fear had always brought me.

"I've been talking to Grammie about letting you stay with her at the nursing home. I really can't think of a better place where you and I could just take a little breather."

"Grammie and the old people? I don't know."

"I've already talked with her about it. She understands that things are rough around here, Honey Bunny."

Now I was Honey Bunny. I wondered what I'd be if I said I didn't want to go.

"So like, you mean, live there? At the nursing home?"

I sat back down with my knees to my chest and ran my fingers over the parts where I'd made dramatic little maps of ugly places people didn't want to visit anymore.

"Well, not *live there* live there," she answered. "Just stay for a little bit. Maybe during the week or however you want it." My mother's face looked old from losing so much weight. "I mean, gosh, wouldn't it be great to have your grammie to help you with your math whenever you needed it? And she's way closer to the library than we are here. I bet you could walk there anytime you wanted."

"I know she's closer to the library," I said.

"Yeah, see? That and the fact that you'll be able—"

"Okay, I guess I'll think about it." That's what I said. But in my mind I had already started packing, moving in, taking better breaths with lungs that wouldn't burst from too much fire or too much Father.

"When would I be leaving?" I asked.

"As soon as you want," my mom said.

It would be a while before I realized (or convinced myself) she *did not* say, "The sooner the better."

part two

Everyone asked me, "How're you doing?"
And I said, "Well, I'm at the high end of low."

—MARILYN MANSON, INTERVIEW, *SPIN*

10

whore

We never actually cleaned but rather just turned on the
vacuum so it sounded like we were cleaning as we picked the
pubic hairs off the sheets and out of the tub . . .
—MAGGIE ESTEP, "SCAB MAIDS ON SPEED"

God didn't stop my dreams about fire. Just like he didn't stop me from crying and making a big thing in front of everyone on the first day I left my mother's house. The night before I put my suitcase and typewriter into the back of my dad's truck, I dreamed about my mother in flames. Jesus was in the dream too. He was on the cross in his underwear and wore a crown of metal spikes like the kind you use to stop a beast from entering a pretty garden. Blood ran down his cheeks and I could see my mom crouched underneath him. When the blood touched her skin it sizzled. Holes like empty eye sockets covered her face.

I don't remember doing a thing to help the situation.

"You leave and you'll die." It was my own quick voice in my ears. I couldn't stop shaking. Blue digital numbers blinked 3:15, *Amity-ville Horror* time. Without a second thought about it, I walked to the kitchen, sifted through my mother's purse, and stole one of her Halcyon pills. Sniffing it first, I broke a tiny piece off between my two front teeth and chewed it quickly. On the walk back to my bedroom I felt sick and dizzy, but that was just me turning the pictures of my head into something you have to purchase tickets for before you can watch.

Nothing really happened except that when I fell back asleep an opening unfastened itself behind my eyes. My mother was no longer caught in bloody fire. Jesus was gone.

I was grateful for that.

"You're only going to be like five miles away," Bryan said. He and my dad unloaded my stuff and brought it into my new home, the Santa Ana Care Facility for the Elderly. Watching my old and worn Strawberry Shortcake comforter hanging over my dad's shoulder gave me a pain like I missed myself.

"Just put it all in the living room," I said. I was embarrassed to tell my dad about not having my own room until the cement floors and cracked drywall of the back storage/office area could be converted into something a fourteen-year-old girl could call livable.

Only a half hour ago my head was at my mother's shoulder, all hot and snot-nosed in the candle ghost scent of the rouge on her cheeks. I wasn't the first to let go when we hugged. That had never happened before.

"We're being so silly," she said. "You've spent time away from home before."

But we both knew this was different. Bigger. From the last ugly toddler fit I threw over not being let in on my diagnosis of obsessive compulsive disorder to the few short weeks of planning what I'd take to my grandmother's, we had both changed. The edges of us were now precise, contoured according to what we were becoming—little ruptures of one another. It was all so grown up.

"It's going to be good for you here," my dad said. Though he was usually at odds with my grammie on just about everything—*even the sound of that bossy woman's voice makes me glad I'm not related to her anymore*—he was extra polite and almost friendly, telling her how fantastic it was that she'd come so far with her own business.

"Hell, Ted, that's just awful nice of you to say." She wiped her hands on the apron around her muumuu and gave him a hug. "But I'll tell you something, anyone can have whatever they want if they want it bad enough."

Bryan put down a box of my books and said he'd see me in a few.

"Saturday," Grammie said to him. "Early."

His hours had been cut back at Lucky's, so most weekends he worked at the nursing home. A sometimes-paid gig which was worth it, he said, for a dinner of Grammie's Southern fried chicken or a bowl of her potato-onion soup.

"So okay, then," I said to my brother. "Guess I'll be seeing you on Saturday."

He did this flick/touch/rub thing with my hair. I didn't think he would, but he ended up hugging me, hard.

When Bryan and my dad finally left, it was me on the porch with my grandmother, her arm around my shoulder, old people in rocking chairs. The sun was high, damn near immaculate. Just a few weeks ago a scene like that would've made my stomach churn in a green goo of Norman Rockwellness. Now it hurt in an entirely different way. It's a strange thing when you want to jump away from something and fold yourself into it at the same time. I waved to my brother and watched as my dad stood in the driveway with his hands on his hips, looking around like maybe he'd forgotten something.

I no longer have a mother.
I no longer have a home.
I went to go search for the truth
But it was all gone . . . baby gone.

"And you're going to send that song to who?" Glenda asked.
I closed my notebook. "I don't know. It's stupid, I guess." I was

almost sorry I had shared it with her. Glenda wasn't exactly my favorite person in the world right now. Her little *I know something you don't know* blurt about how she and my mother and Dr. Schmidt had such a friendly discussion about the things I wrote in my diaries—well, I hadn't forgotten that. My mom said to cut her some slack, couldn't I see how much our sessions were helping me, blah blah. Okay, yeah, the books she recommended and the ones she loaned to me, fine—reading those did help me to feel not so in the middle of the ocean (even if her sneaky little Bible tracts fell out when I opened them) and yeah, when Goat and I had fights and stopped speaking to each other—which was pretty often—and there was no one to talk to because Theresa was fifteen and I wasn't, I would make an excuse to return Glenda's books just so I could sit in her ugly, Jesus-infested office and listen to someone who wasn't a hundred and sixty years old and whistled through their gums.

I tried to talk to my mom, mostly about how I wanted Goat to stop being so immature and look at me as a serious girlfriend, but it was weird because she wasn't with Frank Ranaldo anymore. For reasons that had to do with her finding things I didn't understand, she ended her ten-year love affair with her married boyfriend. Now, she never really dated or even brought up the subject of men unless they were friends of Jesus or Jimmy Swaggart. When my mom and Glenda came to the nursing home for Wednesday night praise and worship, I watched the way my mother looked at Glenda for approval after every word. *Is it okay if I say this? You think this sounds all right? Did I do good?*

Gross.

Glenda played her guitar while my mom held up big cards with the words to "This Is the Day That the Lord Has Made." Once I heard her telling Glenda she'd always wanted to learn how to play the guitar.

"Since when?" I interrupted.

"Since . . . I don't know. I think it would be an abundance of learning."

An abundance of learning? What, was she a preacher now? I'd never once heard my mother voice any kind of interest in guitars. In fact, just the opposite. When Kim bought a used acoustic to groupie around with her old musician boyfriend, all my mother ever did was complain about the noise and the goddamn wailing.

Whenever my grandmother used to talk about her own mentally ill drug-addicted mother, she would say: "There are things we never know about our parents. Women got their own dreams and a lot of them don't involve any kids. That's just the way it is."

I tried to think of that when I watched my mother struggling to be anything other than what she was, what I wanted her to be.

I handed Glenda my sad little song and asked her if she thought it was salable. "Maybe John Fogerty could make a good ballad out of it," I said. "Or it kind of sounds like something Bruce Springsteen might sing. I don't know."

Lately I'd been into lyric writing and had even sent a few songs to places where I wasn't really sure where they were going.

I had no idea what I was doing.

I'd just pick a producer's name off the back of an album, dial information to New York or Los Angeles, ask for an address, then randomly mail things. Grammie said she'd be damned if I thought she was going to pay nine dollars in long-distance fees so I could call all over kingdom come looking for Cyndi Lauper's agent.

Glenda said she admired my persistence.

That, and of course there was the creepy picture of her in her singing bear costume. I thought maybe she could peddle my writing to some backsliding animal who was trying to make it in the industry without a felt-covered head. "Do *you* know anyone who'd be interested?" I asked.

She shrugged and leaned back in her chair. "I met Sissy Spacek once. My sister sat next to Merle Haggard on a plane, but to be honest, I was never a big fan of his." She squinted into my binder paper. "I think the subject matter is pretty interesting, though I feel like I should ask you: You don't *really* think you're without a mother and a home, do you?"

I did. And I didn't. Of course being in the soft steel embrace of my grammie and all the nonsense she didn't take from me was good for my temperament, but it wasn't always cuddly at the nursing home. First off, before I could move into a room of my own, before my grammie's budget allowed her to refurbish the back office, my bunking choices were limited to floors, rooms redolent of piss and Pine-Sol, or a sofa bed. Usually I'd drift off in front of the news or a midnight San Francisco talk show about loving diversity and gay rights. One of the perks of life with people over age seventy is you can leave a television on all night—*every* television if you want to. There aren't any good ears around to hear or care. Sometimes, in the middle of the night, I'd drag my blankets into the room that my grandmother shared with Mrs. Petersen, an eighty-five-year old combative who insisted Grammie was her sister. Mrs. Petersen knitted covers for wood hangers and wore a pink pillbox hat. Sweet. She was also a scratcher and a biter and would wake up from a sound sleep clawing and cussing. My grandmother was the only one strong enough to hold her wrists and talk her down.

Most of the time I wouldn't even bother with sleep. I'd run an extension cord from the kitchen to the back deck, sit outside in the chill of foggy pine trees and dew-covered patio chairs like almost-finished Popsicles. I'd put a couple of dinner mats under my typewriter to help absorb the sound of me trying to be something more.

To Mr. Quincy Jones,
Thank you in advance for considering my song, "Big Love on a
Big Train" . . .

Other nights I would get up and just walk around the house. When you're really old, the things you do in the day are basically the same things you do in the middle of the night, so it wasn't like I was really bothering anybody. I'd sneak a phone call to Goat, who was up late working on his line of comic books, or I'd peek into bedrooms at the spotted heads and opened mouths. If death had lips, this is what it would look like screaming.

Sometimes I'd unlock the big metal medicine cabinet and count everyone's pills.

As much as I loved my late-night rogue floats, not having a room to myself got old real fast.

"I'm just tired of that man calling me a whore," I told Grammie. She was showing me how to make hospital corners in the bed I'd slept in. The man who slept next to me was still lying in his own bed. I pointed to him. "He's disgusting," I said. "He coughs and gags all night and tells me to show him my tushy."

"Ah, hell, he's harmless," Grammie said. "He don't even have no legs."

The old man—we just called him Captain—grumbled under his stale sheets. We knew he couldn't understand a word we said without the help of his rabbit-squeal hearing aid.

He rolled over in his covers and farted.

"Oh God," I said, making a face. "He thinks I'm a prostitute he used to visit when he was stationed in Italy."

"That's bullshit. You just made that up."

"No, I didn't. I swear to God. He had this whole conversation with the air last night, he said, 'Oh when is my little signorina coming back?' and said he had some money for me and all this stuff."

"Well, it's just an old man going through the moments of a long life."

I sighed dramatically and tucked the edge of my pillow under my chin to pull on a fresh linen case. "Still, he doesn't need to call me a whore."

But I didn't hate that part as much as I was letting on. Lately I'd been thinking a lot about that word and the responsibilities that come with it. For a few months now I'd looked for sexy clues in the way Goat put his arm around me, but it was hard to believe he saw me as anything other than an old buddy who just got back into town and wanted to get together for drinks. The first time Goat kissed me was me kissing him. Behind the stage curtain in the gymnasium, on a day when the rain made nothing of PE but a bunch of bored kids who wouldn't stay put long enough to care about watching Winter Olympic ice-skating highlights on the television they'd rolled into the gymnasium for our enjoyment.

Leah seemed to do nothing when we were together but tease me about how I'd fried my hair by putting so much bleach in it. And, of course, the crush I had on her brother. "I don't know why you even bother calling my house anymore; all you ever do is ask me where the Idiot is."

On a dare, she and a bunch of other kids who were stuck in the gym for a rainy-day lunch period told Goat to stick his tongue in my mouth.

"You guys are totally gay," I said, then told Goat I wanted to talk to him about it privately. Goat wasn't that much older than me, and although he never really took the upper hand to make any romantic moves in my direction, I knew a lot of girls from the swarms of them that seemed to always be wherever he was. Most of them were *way* older than the both of us, and I figured someone in the bunch had to have taught him a thing or two.

It would take a long teenage time before I would understand just how carnally wrong I was in my guessing.

When I got him alone behind the stage curtain I said, "Let's just forget those jackoffs are even here, okay?" I put my hands on his face and closed my eyes. In seconds too fast to take in all the way, his breath was my breath. When I felt his lips, everything about me became outlined in a fluid that filled the spaces between my stomach and my heart.

I had never really had a flying dream before. I knew what they were from hearing about other people with their arms spread out over city lights and purple hills. But mine were always me running in a football field or an open meadow, jumping through the gray syrup of dream gravity, feeling like I could take off at any moment if I just wanted it bad enough.

That's what this kiss was.

You're at school, I had to say in my mind. When I could feel him pull back just a little, his hand like a soft secret against the small of my back, I blurted out, "I guess that wasn't so bad."

He said nothing. I looked for the dimples in his smile, maybe one of his corny jokes about my mom's church, something to tell me it was still okay, that I was still me and we were still whatever it was we were.

When the bell rang he asked if I wanted to watch *Terminator* with him on Saturday. "That movie is so crazy," he said. "The special effects are insane."

"That's cool," I answered. "Insane is good. I like insane." I folded my hands and brought them to my face. The breath I took up was his Polo cologne and warm rubber from a ball I was bouncing earlier.

It's hard to find symmetry in a place where a lot of people and a lot of loneliness exist at the same time. Everything cancels out every other thing. It pushes you away from proportion, crawls under the skin of your throat where it wails out as an unearthly noise in the shower, in a blanket over your head—any place where it's safe to ignore people who keep calling your name.

I missed my mother.

The care facility was only a thirty-minute bus ride to my mom's house, but it may as well have been on the other side of the world. In the busyness of what was going on around me, I had to find an ease to remove me from my loneliness. Even if I was determined not to.

"Are you sick?" my grandmother asked me. She buzzed around like the place was on fire.

"Huh? Sick? No. I'm fine."

"Because I sure see you standing around an awful lot. That's what sick people do. Now I don't know much, but I sure as hell know there's three people waiting to get helped into the bathtub and get their hair washed." She handed me a stack of folded towels. "But I'm not sure how you're a-gonna do all that staying in one place, sighing and a-looking so damn bored."

Most of the time I could exchange my dislike for rubbing skin-fold cream into elephant seams by just hanging out and watching television with the residents. (My God, how many times can one person misplace their remote and have you look for it for something like an hour only to find it right there under a knee or an elbow or a wad of tissues?)

Some of the residents wanted me to take them to the store. Some of them wanted me to take them to their old houses.

Everyone wanted more cigarettes.

"I don't have a license, Mr. Gray." He needed to get to his ice-fishing cabin in Anchorage.

"I don't really know how to drive, Mrs. Petersen." She had a son graduating high school every Friday. It was important to get good seats.

"I don't think I'm interested in rubbing you down there, Captain." He just wanted his signorina whore. Every night he said I took his money.

"I saw you take it, whore. I can give you more if you want, but just tell me that you took it. Come here and tell me that you took it. Hey, whore, I'm talking to you."

Actually, most of them thought I was stealing their money. Or their Kleenex or their socks. A couple of times I'd been accused of taking children that didn't belong to me. This one woman with a dent in her skull from brain surgery and a metal cap that Medicaid wouldn't pay for told my grandmother that she saw me giving birth to a baby, then hiding it in the basement.

Only a handful of them weren't too disgusting to hang around. Marisol Hertz was a German-born, South American–raised high-priced call girl, an erotic artist with thick gray braids she coiled on top of her head. Her eyes were the same color as the cartoon leaves on a pack of spearmint gum. The story was she had serviced diplomats and dictators like Benito Mussolini and Juan Perón, and though my grandmother insisted those stories were things Marisol read in books and never really happened, there was no explanation for the framed picture of her on some beach smiling in the arms of the Dominican Republic's bloodthirsty dictator Rafael Trujillo.

One day she put her veiny blue hand on my arm and spoke about Frida Kahlo. "Miss Traci, I want to tell joo somesing." Her other hand shook a little as she brought her cigarette to her lips. "I knew a vedee good painter. She vas called Frida Kahlo. You remind me of her."

"Really?" I asked. I couldn't believe it. Just months ago I had begun a new fixation with the painting *Henry Ford Hospital*, which I'd come across in a book about women artists who had dedicated sketches and paintings to their dead fetuses. Frida Kahlo crafted the piece after her second miscarriage. The pooling blood behind her naked body and the dead baby still attached to its umbilical cord floating above her head conjured nothing short of a sad and holy beauty. Things that couldn't carry on anymore interrupted things in jars with angry time bunched in their fists, and paper eyelids had always appealed to me. Like the snakes in formaldehyde at school, like Kitty Thurman's ear, or the math problems that danced out of their columns and suspended their typefaced bodies in front of my mind if I thought about them too much. Touch it and you screw it all up. Let it die from a safe distance and watch how beautiful it all is.

"You were so lucky to be friends with her," I said.

Marisol loved for me to read to her. There were many nights of us just talking about books rather than actually opening one. Once a month I made a library run for the old people. If you didn't bring your own stash with you to the nursing home, your choices were limited to the Bible, *The Watchtower*, or *Reader's Digest*. Large-print romance novels always made my list of what I was supposed to bring back. Military history or anything Louis L'Amour were also hot among people who really didn't care about what they read as long as they didn't have to get out of bed to read it.

For Marisol I checked out Spanish-language books and some Hispanic authors she thought I'd be interested in. The poetry of Juana Inés de la Cruz and a few poorly translated pieces from Rosalia de Castro were totally over my head and language barrier. Still, I tried not to be too uninterested when she talked forever and showed me the important people who had shaped her life. But when she showed me a book of poems by Pablo Neruda, I almost lost my breath: *Death is drawn to a sound / . . . and its clothes echo, hushed like a tree.* She promised me I would like it. She had no idea what that promise would mean. Time and time again I would go back to Neruda in desperation for the perfect sentence, the one word that would rescue me from a day with too many uneven numbers, contaminated doorknobs, sleep in the colors of a bad flu.

Years later I would be crouched in the corner of a cold eastern city, two weeks of skies like the inside of a witch's hat, an aftertaste in my mouth of the boy who didn't want me anymore. I would read my worn copy of Neruda's *Isla Negra* over and over again. I thought of Marisol who got paid for sex and her friend Frida Kahlo who seemed to have had enough for all three of us.

There was so much comfort in our collective rotten choices.

"Everyone loved that girl," Marisol said, "but no one could stand her."

I will always wonder if that's what she meant when she made the comparison.

When I worked with the Dig It kids I didn't want to get too close to them for fear of catching crooked chromosomes. But I did it anyway on account of my agenda of needing Mr. Delgado's approval and the laminator machine.

It was different with the old people. You can't catch senility. It's a worn-down, tired-of-life-so-I'll-just-be-crazy-now type of thing. Also, having Bryan there at the nursing home kind of helped to remind me that my reasons for moving out of my mother's house were peaceful ones. We cracked jokes about how adult diapers were like pictures of us at the beach in Santa Cruz when we were little and we'd come out of the surf with our rumps overflowing with the seaweed muck of the shoreline. When I horsed around with my brother it helped the space in my chest shrink from empty womb to tiny umbilical cord. It also made me jealous. I'd see my brother walk in through the front door of the nursing home, and sometimes I couldn't get over the bizarreness of it, him coming from the house that I technically didn't live in anymore.

I tried to smell my mother on him, search his expression and the air around his steps for her stupid church shows, the too much pepper in her turkey soup, the not enough Real Her in her new, hard hugs. It was the same when I talked to her on the phone: long pauses with me listening to her breath. The noises in the background became things I could see.

"What does Sprinkles want?" I asked. "He's crying at the door."

"Oh, I think your kitty just wants his mama."

And the rest of the conversation gashed and gnarled its animal teeth until I never wanted to speak to her again and never wanted to hang up.

At Grammie's there were nights of Don Ho with fabric leis and bingo with prizes to help your bath time be the best it could be. Fun, I guess, but it sure takes a lot of calming bubbles to make you forget how you live in a nursing home.

"I don't want to smell like strawberries," Mr. Pacheco said. He was our youngest resident, sent to live at the home on a kind of post-drying-out sabbatical, fresh from a month in an expensive Saratoga rehab. One bingo night, with I-27 and B-8 in Mr. Pacheco's favor, he handed me the Calgon Creamy Essence he'd won and motioned for me to lean toward his face. "You get your brother to take me to a bar on Friday, okay?" he whispered. "You can keep the bubble bath. I'll give you both fifty bucks to make up a good story."

He was seventy-one, with both a wife and a girlfriend, who came to visit on their respective days; a full head of white hair; and skin the color of my favorite Jamoca Almond Fudge ice cream. You could tell he used to be a fox.

By the time the weekend rolled around Mr. Pacheco had developed a sudden interest in Friday night church services at Saint Julie's and would appreciate a ride. A little past midnight he and my brother returned from the Royal Morocco with cheap chardonnay on their breaths and tales of belly dancers who wouldn't give out their phone numbers.

It took all of forty seconds for my grandmother to catch on.

She cornered my brother in the hallway. "Now, I'm gonna tell you this just once."

I slipped into the bathroom to listen near the door.

"You ever take that man out drinking again and that will be the last time you come here."

"Okay, God," Bryan answered. "I was only trying to—"

"It don't make no difference what you was only trying. I've worked too damn hard for licensing to come around and say we're putting residents in danger. Now that man is an alcoholic. If I ever catch you runnin' him around to bars again you're gonna have a heap of trouble to deal with. You got it?"

He did. But I don't think he cared much anyway. In nine months he'd be leaving for basic training in Georgia. The whole time my grandma was chewing him out he had a look on his face like he knew he was going to see a whole lot worse than Grammie with a Salem Light in her hand and hush puppies on her breath.

Not that the warning mattered. Three days later we wouldn't be able to rouse Mr. Pacheco from his sleep. He was the first dead body I ever saw. A person I had touched and talked to. A man who wore expensive cologne and Polo shirts in the colors of a life that had a little more living to do. The last thing I would know of him would be crossed eyes and feces smeared all the way up his back.

It was real. His liver had burst, turning parts of his skin the shade of a neglected plum. It wasn't one of my poems.

They wheeled him out on a plain black gurney. I was on the sofa, half-asleep, when I smelled an odor that didn't belong to a Saturday morning.

"Traci, come on." Grammie nudged my shoulder and said she had to fill out paperwork with the coroner so I was in charge of breakfast.

For days I babbled in run-on sentences to Goat about the scary stains on the sheets and the girlfriend who wouldn't stop crying and the wife who didn't cry at all.

"That's crazy," he said and tried not to sound too impressed. "Just fucking crazy." On a walk around my old neighborhood we held hands while I confessed that maybe my brother and I helped soak a recovering alcoholic right into the dirt of his grave. "But I wouldn't worry about it too much," he said. "If he was that much of a boozer he would've died soon anyway."

I prattled on about how tragic and disgusting the whole thing was, but what I was really thinking is how lucky for me to have witnessed such an important thing as death. I wanted to tell Goat that, but I wanted to say it in the true and easy way I was feeling it. Like a sudden burst of love for Mr. Pacheco had opened up inside of me when the after-death silence filled his room and mixed with the sweet, sweaty smells of a life going away. But the best connection I could form between my clogged heart and my fat mouth was, "Oh well. Maybe it's all for the best."

There were other parts of that morning Goat would never know. Like how I'd pretty much thrown myself at the cute guy who assisted the coroner and how my grammie yanked me by my arm into the foyer and said she was as embarrassed as all hell. "We got us a resident who died in our care and you're a-hanging all over the guy who takes away the dead bodies?"

A seriously pathetic little show: me leaning around in my Garfield pajamas, no bra, arching my back so my belly button showed to a black-haired Sly Stallone type old enough to be an uncle with whiskey on his breath and a bad idea. He said his name was Edmund but yeah, sure, he had no problem with me calling him Eddie. While we waited for the coroner to call an official death time, I twirled my hair around my finger and asked Body Van Man if he enjoyed his job.

"I guess," he said, then asked me if I wanted to learn how to fill out incident reports. "You're about what, eighteen? Nineteen?"

Hanging around my old neighborhood so I could be with Goat and his graffiti gang was weird in a spectral way. Being close to my house without actually going inside it turned me all wrong. From a comfortable/uncomfortable distance across the street I walked by the windows and wondered what everyone was doing in there. My mom in her room with *M*A*S*H* on her little TV, a cigarette burning in her Pea Soup Andersen's ashtray while she highlighted the splendor of all those angels and demons in her Bible. Sometimes I thought I could even see my brother in my room—on the floor in his blue sleeping bag keeping watch over me so I wouldn't explode.

Was I in there too? Was I sitting at my desk with my typewriter and the street-lit view that made me feel like an almost-smart girl in an almost-smart city? Was I in there counting, crying, worrying about burning bodies and uneven numbers, hating the real girl at the desk who wasn't an almost-anything but a spaz who couldn't even live with her own mother?

I stared at my house for a long time. Goat sat on the curb tagging our names. I could feel him looking up at me, waiting for me to finish thinking. I wanted it all back. The missing knob on the drawer where I kept my pencils, my Ramones poster, clumps of my cat's fur on the corner of my pillow where he slept. Even the cold night scent of Ajax, which hadn't touched my toothbrush in over three years but still gave me a tickling pain whenever I saw a can of it, like a clean heroin addict taking a blood test.

I wanted that too because it went with the other stuff.

I wanted Goat to stop waiting for me.

"Let's just go," I finally said, because it was all a waste of time. Or a trick of it. It felt the same as how turning the clocks back in autumn fools you into a sudden darkness—that instant you realize five o'clock has deceived the whole sky.

"Let's head to my house and lie down," Goat said. It was our thing we did a lot in the late afternoon when Leah and his mom weren't home.

"See you guys." I waved to my old house. *I'm leaving now to get in bed with a boy.*

Away from his street followers and permanent seat in sixth-period detention, Goat was a gentle and shy boy. He never really asked me to climb into bed with him but rather scooted just enough to the side so I would have room to place my head so our cheeks could touch. With the blacktop heat of school still clinging to our skin, we listened to the train whistle and felt the room vibrate softly from the railroad tracks near his house. On the busy throughway that was his street, cars honked and bus brakes made sounds like children without parents.

Sometimes we kissed. Sometimes we lined up our hands and commented about whose fingers were longer, whose were stained more with marker and spray paint. Goat's house was always cool, with the shades pulled down and the fluid whir of ceiling fans and a refrigerator motor that made cooing noises like doves on a gray roof. At first it felt bad being there for reasons other than Leah. I took it upon myself to close her bedroom door so I wouldn't have to feel like a slutty traitor when I walked down the hall. Then I'd go back to my boyfriend, close my eyes, and listen to the doves. I pretended we were in a loft in New York City or an artsy little apartment in Los Angeles with Spanish tile and arched doorways. I would write. He would paint. No one would call him a stupid hood or tell me I wasn't good in my heart if I didn't go to church.

Even when I wasn't in the relief of Goat's arms and room, there was something easy and comfortable happening to me. What had begun as a place of earning my keep at the nursing home was slowly developing into something else. Something better. You had to step back and look at it in between the Thorazine and insulin rounds, just a little beyond being called the name of someone's dead child and getting mistaken for someone's whore, but it was there.

It was calmness. A curious peace from being so damn busy. Though it wasn't obvious, wasn't in my face, it was still as true as anything I could feel or see: many of my compulsions were slowly coming to an end. There were many nights I fell asleep in front of the television, no problem. The exhaustion I felt at the end of a full workday overshadowed the worry I felt about not being able to relax at the end of the day.

At the nursing home there was an abundance of just about everything I had ever been afraid of. Hey, you want an overload of germs? We've got smeared feces from angry folks whose ungrateful kids haven't visited them in months. Thinking about fire too much? Wait until you see the mounds of Kleenex and newspapers eighty-year-olds leave so carelessly behind their bedside tables or the floor where the electrical outlets are. Glenda explained it to me in the analogy of someone who thinks about food all the time. "Then they get a job working at a restaurant and after a while they've had it up to here with the smell of french fries and chicken nuggets."

I could totally see that.

"But I want to warn you. Don't think it's all gone away for good," she said. "Remember how we talked about OCD and anxiety problems all coming in waves and retreats?"

I shrugged. I seriously didn't want to hear how you may have a few good months, then a few weeks of torture.

Of course my compulsive behavior wasn't *entirely* gone—I still rinsed with peroxide and had developed a new thing about clicking my tongue whenever I heard a long *a* sound. I think journaling helped that a lot. Not my usual blah, blah, black sheep in my ledgers. Glenda made me follow a specific daily exercise. I hated it at first, maybe because she called it the Expect and Accept diary, and I thought, I can't believe I'm actually going to name my journal entries, but after a week or so of questions like *what is the underlying fear that is making me act out* or *is this thought helping me to be productive,* I started to get the idea.

Glenda said that the point of it all was to find a connection between what I was doing and feeling just before a compulsive act. For instance, I'd developed a thing about tracing Marisol's name with my finger in her books while I read to her. I tried to see if I could go a few nights without sweating over loopy *m*'s and perfectly straight *l*'s, but I would wake up in a panic, hating myself for dreaming that I killed poor Marisol in her sleep.

When I journaled about it and wrote down what I was doing just before the urge to trace her name hit me, I realized I had been looking at the framed pictures she kept on her dresser. It made me feel so bad—those snapshots of a woman who had led such a wild and exciting life; now here she was in a tiny room with paranoid me in charge of her beautiful books.

"Guilty," I said to Glenda. "I feel so incredibly guilty. I mean, here is this totally interesting woman at my grandmother's nursing home. *My* grandma. Like, I don't know. It's like my fault somehow."

She didn't say anything back. She just looked at me.

"What? Is that right?"

"Well, we're not looking for right or wrong here," Glenda answered. "But I really like the way you're picking this all apart. That's the way you should be doing it."

The main objective to the Expect and Accept exercise was to understand that if I could see a predictable pattern to my compulsive behavior, then when whacked-out thoughts would show up, say about a math test that kept me up all night worrying over numbers, or me feeling bad about not living with my mom, which made me want to scrub my hands, then maybe I could ride through the compulsions, *expect* that they're going to come up, and *accept* that they are there.

"It really doesn't matter if the connecting thought to the event is super clear or not," Glenda said. "Just the act of trying to string the two together will get you to train your brain to understand that compulsive behavior is always triggered by something else. Something that you consider stressful."

I kind of got that. "And then there'll be a day when I will never think those retarded things again, right?"

But she would never answer yes or no to this question. Instead she told me not to think along those lines, and that people who start out having compulsions at a very early age may have the personality types that will always struggle in some way or another with them. "Now that's not a for-sure thing," she said. "It's not a solid study or anything. But I'm telling you theories here and facts from my own experiences because I know it makes you feel better if the truth is laid out on the table."

It did. Things like that were why I stopped making a fuss about seeing Glenda, why I couldn't dislike her as much as I wanted to sometimes. Even with the bear costume and the songs about salvation. Plus, it felt so right when she said life in the nursing home, a life of taking care of other people, was helping to bring me out of my own head. I'd even thought of that on my own. It just made a lot of sense: the people I lived with were so much worse off than I was. Sure, I had to sometimes walk down the hallway and touch all the doorknobs and count to three while I placed my index finger on the left side of the knob, and yeah, I knew that human spontaneous combustion could very well be a real thing and maybe it wasn't always a good idea to look at the old people for too long on account of their skin was so brittle and flammable, but at least I had all my teeth and didn't awake in the middle of the night screaming for someone to shoot me.

"When you start thinking about how bad you have it," Grammie said just about every day, "there's someone right next to you got it ten times worse."

I told Glenda it made me feel better to think of that dumb cliché.

She smiled her cakey-pink-lipstick smile. "Feeling sorry for yourself gets boring real quick, huh? Maybe you should write a song about being grateful. I'm sure we could find a lot of places that would love to hear something as upbeat as that."

But instead of wasting time in the flowers of happy songs, I should've been paying attention to the music in the background.

"Don't get real excited over the compulsions slowing down," Glenda warned.

I already knew if you stay too long in the fiction of bliss, the menacing crescendo of violins will turn into something you won't even be able to hear.

"You've got to keep in mind there are times when you'll just have to expect periods of high anxiety," she told me, "because it's those times when the OCD and depression may start to spiral out of control."

And the angel harp song you thought you knew by heart was really just a hard hand against your shoulder blades, as swift and fiery as Armageddon.

11

i am the world

A mess like this is kind of a talent.
—THOMAS BELLER, "THE MINTS FROM FRANK E. CAMPBELL"

I'll tell you one thing, you don't have to consult your Bible or a pack of tarot cards to know when your family has pretty much run out of money.

It was never a huge secret that we struggled. I knew we were surface spenders. Nothing really saved, new things as soon as we got new money. But at least we used to pretend we could pay bills and see therapists and stay in our vacation rental in Santa Cruz and no one would ever feel the crunch of living under the stuff that in a million years we could never reach.

In the summer before I entered high school, we stopped pretending. The weight of the real world was a quicksand certainty, a little piece of swampland up for sale. The real world was all we could afford.

My mother needed her pills. She had bad nerves. She'd also had some serious complications from routine gall bladder surgery that left her in excruciating pain most of the day.

"Pain is free," she said. "Pain pills aren't."

Plus, you can't work or help anyone with algebra or stop yourself from napping when you're on them. You can still get dressed up for church and spend all day watching *This Is Your Hour of Power!*, and you can manically shop at Mervyns and max out credit cards, and you can make a scene in line at the pharmacy because a refill hasn't been authorized—you just can't work.

"So I don't get to see Glenda anymore?" I asked. We were making a Sunday dinner. It was good to be around her spinach manicotti, the one my father said wasn't authentic. Sunday nights at the "other" house. We still had that.

I stirred sautéed garlic into ricotta cheese while she smoked and said she wouldn't be able to pay for my sessions with Glenda anymore but maybe one day all three of us could travel around Africa spreading the news of the Lord.

"I'm not saying you can't see her at all," she said. "It just won't be in regular sessions in her office."

In between too much olive oil and a hunk of paper towels to soak up my too much olive oil, but dammit, not too many paper towels, because paper towels should really be considered a luxury, she tried to explain how things were going to change. And how they were also going to stay the same.

Soon I would be in the ninth grade. I knew gibberish when I heard it.

"You're still going to be seeing Glenda at the nursing home when we're there for our Sing and Worship nights," my mom said.

"But she's not going to like, be my regular person anymore?"

My mom was careful not let her ashes spill into a bowl of diced tomatoes. "Well, sweetie, you know, that's costing us a lot of money. I mean, Glenda's my friend and all, but she's still a therapist. She's not free, and since your dad's not helping with any of this—it's just me floating out here, you know."

And something else I knew: secretly, I wasn't doing a whole lot of floating. My grammie was giving me close to eighty dollars a week for helping with the old people, all the while paying half of my mother's bill for her visits to her own psychiatrist. (Sneaking into unopened mail is another interesting thing to do late at night in a nursing home when you can't sleep.)

"I guess," I said, shrugging. But I knew there'd be some mighty limits to what I could tell Glenda at the nursing home with my mom standing right there. Like last week when I saw Goat pushing some skanky girl on his skateboard and then I had dreams about stabbing the little tramp. No way was I going to let that one leak out in front of my mom; she was worse than Glenda when it came to telling me to pray about my problems. Plus, there was another thing I kind of wanted to get off my chest and I was hoping to tell Glenda at our next session. My stealing habit had advanced from the occasional pack of hair ribbons and lip gloss to something that could have landed me in the *real* Bad Kid Jail. Though most of the time I didn't give a rat's ass what the Good Word said regarding much of anything, I thought maybe I should ask Glenda if there were ratio guidelines for bad move : good deed. Like say you swipe stuff about three times a week, then the other days you're reading to old people and riding your bike in the rain to pick up the eczema cream your grandmother forgot for Mr. Shields who broke out into a rash that was so exaggerated you could not stop yourself from saying the word *stegosaurus* out loud when you saw him picking at the big welts and radish patches on his head.

Did stuff like that even out bad karma?

I had bumped it up from cosmetics at Thrifty's to a leather jacket from Macy's. There was also a bracelet and some tank tops from Wet Seal. At Aaron Brothers, Goat showed me how to slip expensive art pens and colored pencils up my sleeves.

I just had to have a fat marker in a color called Angry Baby.

Taking stuff without paying for it helped to replace a capable part of me that seemed to disappear each time my mom said, "I'll drive you back to Grammie's." When I pulled off the tags of that leather jacket and walked out of Macy's with it wrapped around my body, that was me having the say. *I'll decide when you'll drive me back.*

It didn't matter that I almost always had money. I spent a lot of it on crap like beef jerky and Vicks and new toenail clippers every week for cleanliness. I bought notebooks by the dozen and more magazines than I would ever read in my life.

"*Modern Archaeology?*" Grammie asked. A tile floor of the back office had just been installed and she was helping me organize my stuff in a new dresser. "Why the hell do you need this big ol' stack of *Modern Archaeology?*"

For nothing. But a Crown Books had just opened up near the Tower Records on Blossom Hill Road.

Besides my grandmother, I never saw anyone else in my family save a penny for anything. When we had it, we spent it. From my dad we learned how not to ask for any money; from my mom we learned an urgency to acquire and how to make it look necessary.

That part was getting worse.

It seemed the more my mother stayed home from work, the more her back hurt, the more she slept, the more she woke up at one in the afternoon to shop.

When I was in the first grade, I came home from school to a packed suitcase. The trunk to my Mom's Monte Carlo was open.

"We're moving to Santa Barbara." That was all she said. A dark curl stuck to the dewy skin of her forehead as she rushed around with luggage on rollers. The whole scene reminded me of a hospital show where bodies on gurneys could stop living if you didn't get them where they needed to be.

During the nine-hour trip from San Jose to Southern California my brother and I caught bits of conversation in between our backseat hatred for each other and Connect Four. From what we could make out over Rod Stewart and the profile of my sister's moving mouth, it seemed my mother had been offered a job as an executive secretary to a big movie mogul. I heard *better life* and something about appreciating women. Frank Ranaldo's name was in there too.

"I wonder why Frank's a no-good son of a bitch?" I whispered to Bryan.

He shrugged. "Beats me. Maybe he loves his wife again."

We ended up not staying more than a few hours in our new home. In a secondhand furnished two-bedroom apartment right on the beach that would later be declared by my mom a Beach for Lowlifes, we found a note under a vase of flowers that welcomed my mother to her *new position and paradise!*

While Bryan got his feet wet in sand that didn't feel like the rough northern grains we were used to, all I could think of was that this paradise was *way* too far from my dad. How would he be able to take me to Dairy Queen on Saturdays or to see a scary movie that I wasn't supposed to watch? I knew the evening's orange glow on the water was supposed to feel like the symbolic exhale of arriving, but it only exhausted me with sadness. The air was warmer than the beach air at home. Thicker. Everyone on the street and shore seemed so relaxed. I didn't like that one bit.

"Hey!" I yelled toward some rocks where Bryan had started climbing. "We should call Grammie." That was all I could think to do.

But before he could answer, Kim came down to the water and said we were all going back home.

"Why?" Bryan asked. "This place is cool."

"They lied," Kim said. "They don't want to pay Mom what she's worth."

On the long ride home there was a feeling in the car that made me keep checking to see if my seat belt was fastened. In a halfway nap against the window my head kept repeating what my sister had said, about mom not being paid what she was worth. I had seen my mother crying on a wicker chair in the kitchenette just before we left, and though my knowledge of moms in tears was usually derived from ex-husbands and bad daughters, I somehow understood that this time, it was all tied into money that we weren't going to have.

Now, eight years later, there weren't any more jobs, no sad twilights or notes under vases. There would never be another position of work for my mother. Only church and couch beds still open in the middle of the living room at four in the afternoon.

If I understood anything about what Kim had said that day in Santa Barbara, if money defined a person's place in the world, now that we had none I guess that meant our places didn't exist anymore. Or maybe they did, but they just weren't as paradisey as we were all supposed to be pretending they were. Just like that unfamiliar Southern California sand beneath my feet, why get used to soft and nice when you know damn well it won't make as great a mark as the harder stuff?

It seemed the only person whose life was going according to plan was my dad. He had fallen in love with a woman named Sarah. Sarah had huge boobs and cooked like one of those fancy waterfront places in the city where raw baby squid coiled around chopsticks passed for appetizers. She was so nice to me it almost seemed like a trick in a horror movie to divert your attention from the guy with the hatchet behind the door.

Sarah said: "I love to read your poems, Traci." "I love the way you wear your eyeliner, Traci." She sent me "just because" cards with cartoon animals doing human things like baking cobbler and driving. On all the cards my name was spelled wrong. They made me think of that packet of brochures on anxiety and OCD Glenda gave me on our first visit, and how I had corrected the misspelling of my name and I was so pissed off at first because I had just spent an hour with this counselor who seemed to know so much about me, and here she couldn't even spell my name right.

Sarah's cards also reminded me of how it was okay to get over all that.

Often she would call and ask, "Did you get my gift?" "Did you get my message?" "Did you get my card? Those little penguins were so cute. I saw that and thought of you."

Why? I never once said I had any feelings for penguins. "Yeah, thanks. You spelled my name wrong, though. I don't spell it with an *e* at the end anymore. My dad does because that's what's on my birth certificate, but I don't. But yeah, the card is nice."

Nothing ever came out of my mouth the way I wanted it to.

Poor Sarah. I imagined her in a low-cut blouse in the kitchen with my father, preparing authentic spinach manicotti and wondering what was his take on penguins?

My dad was happy (though I guess it's easy to be happy when you're only looking one way). Once when I threw my purse in the back of his truck a bunch of Glenda's OCD pamphlets fell out, along with all those secret Bible tracts.

"What the hell are these things?" But he wasn't talking about *What to Count On When You Can't Stop Counting*. He meant the God stuff.

"Oh, Mom's friend gave me some junk to read about being saved or whatever." I quickly scooped the tracts into my bag. The OCD stuff I waited on. I just thought maybe he'd want to know.

"I guess your mom is still on her God thing," he finally said. Then he told me not to act up, to get my ass in shape, and maybe the church stuff would get better. "You need to be nice and do what you're told," he said. "Maybe your mom is just trying to find her way. Whatever weird way that is."

When the back room of the nursing home was finished and all mine, I painted the walls purple and bought the biggest poster of Madonna I could find for above my bed. But when you're in a place where the spaces between three in the afternoon and five in the evening have to be filled with games/words/pills so that everyone stays alive, there isn't a whole lot of time to spend with the Material Girl and your purple walls.

Every Wednesday night, like divine clockwork, my mom and Glenda showed up and tried to convince a sleepy audience to eat their dinner quickly because fun and holiness began promptly at seven.

See, the thing about the Lord is you can pretend you're not listening when his shepherds tell you things, like when the third seal is open a black horse will come prancing out of the sky and a great hand will open up in the clouds. Even when those shepherds adorn themselves in prairie-style dresses and wear as much makeup as Jezebel but with less money or status—and as painful as that is to look at—well, sometimes you just can't escape the Word. Especially if you have to stick around and listen to it or your mom will make a comment about how come every time she comes over you run off and disappear into your room and don't you know what that does to her heart? Plus, the book of Revelations talks about things like fireballs dropping down from the sky and dead people popping out of their graves and you've always kind of liked stuff like that.

And something like a great mountain burning with fire was hurled into the sea. And a third of the sea became blood. . . .

Every week for a month the subject of Wednesday night Bible group at the nursing home was themed around trumpets in the sky and holes in the ground spewing forth toxic smoke. There were also scantily clad women riding horned beasts.

How could anyone ignore this stuff?

My mom and Glenda passed around a small book called *Questions About the Second Coming ANSWERED!* I took one too. Tanks shooting missiles at robed and sandaled children while a bowl of something like lava dripped down from huge hands in the sky sure were intriguing, but of course the paragraph that captured my interest the most was headed "Harlotry Today: Be Aware of Modern Temptations."

It all reminded me of what Goat said when we watched *Helter Skelter,* about how Charles Manson interpreted the whole book of Revelations to match all the Beatles songs.

"I don't know if I believe all this crap," he had said. "Those Holy Rollers think pretty much all music is from the devil or has some sort of evil message in it." And he was right. Since my mother began hanging out with Jesus, it was brought to our attention that several of my favorite rock groups not only carried subliminal messages in their lyrics urging listeners to do things like have unnatural sex with dogs and kill all parents, but their very names were dangerous acronyms understood clearly by prophets and evildoers alike. (And Pentecostal preachers.) AC/DC = Against Christ, Devil's Children; RUSH = Running Under Satan's Hand; KISS = Knights in Satan's Service; W.A.S.P. = We Are Satan's People and/or Worshipping All of Satan's Powers.

I'm serious about this.

Of course it was all a total load of crap (Goat and I even made up our own nefariously clever ideas and laughed until we couldn't breathe at how stupid you can make any acronym if you're nefariously clever and/or stupid enough): ELVIS = Evil Lives Vicariously in Scrotums.

Ha-ha. Everything's funny until your mom won't stop reading Bible verses to you and you're kind of starting to maybe wonder about God and Jesus, like you know none of it is true, but what if your mom knows something you don't and you wake up at two in the morning with stampeding dreams of fireballs and screaming sinners.

The clicking in my brain started up again. That's when I got all weird about song lyrics. In my pretty purple room with Madonna and her crucifixes, I locked my door and turned on my new favorite song: USA for Africa's "We Are the World." With images of skeleton people, their pupils the color of a kidney infection, blazed into my brain, I couldn't stop thinking about the children of Africa. God, those kids. They were starving. Their whole existence was a bloated belly with tree limbs after a forest fire. I opened my notebook and wrote down every single lyric to that sad and hopeful song.

Seven times I did this.

Mom and Glenda said seven was the Lord's number. Seven could save you if you had it imprinted on your head when Christ came back for the people who weren't misbehaving. Did anyone in Africa know about seven? Even if there wasn't a smidgen of holy truth in that uneven digit, writing down the lyrics seven times just felt like a good enough amount to help those dying people.

Way into night, until the first string of pink threaded down the gray dawn, I scribbled in my notebook as fast as I could for those unfortunate, disgusting kids who had nothing but flies in their faces and air under their ribs.

Listening to that song, watching that video, all of it made me sick to my stomach about the times I let my mom take me shopping and spend the money we didn't have on junk I didn't need. The thought of those kids going to bed hungry, of living under the hot sun without a drink of water while I pissed around Red Eye looking for a belt to go with the pink cords I would only wear once, made me physically ill.

And don't think for a second when I closed my eyes and saw those people under all that blazing heat it didn't remind me of Misty Salvano, the little girl I locked in my grandmother's car. I couldn't *stop* thinking about her. I had dreams about her red face screaming in the window as I ran away and left her sweaty little body there to evaporate.

What if she had ended up like those starved and sunburnt babies?

There's a choice we're making. / We're saving our own lives.

Okay, so how was my buying stacks of magazines I would never read helping out the situation in Africa? Or stealing jackets from places when I was always too hot to even wear a jacket?

Down the great dragon was hurled, the original serpent, the one called Devil, Satan, who is misleading the entire inhabitants of Earth. . . .

Seven times.

Every line.

I really wanted to talk to Glenda about it, but this was just—God. I thought I was getting so much better. I knew she said I might have these issues for the rest of my life, that there would be periods when compulsions went away and new ones came to take their place. I thought about that when my alarm clock went off at six thirty in the morning and all I wanted to do was cry because I'd only just shut my eyes a half hour ago. Living like this forever? Maybe I'd rather have the Son of God come down and strike me dead.

I tried to do my Expect and Accept exercise to find the trigger as to what could be causing my panics over Ethiopia and lyric writing.

But the more I journaled about it, the more lyrics I wanted to write down, the more I saw letters on my binder paper as hungry people begging to die. The fancy girl loops and curves that came from my right hand were stomachs full of space and rigor-mortis bodies curling up in the hot sands. The straight-spined cursive from my left hand were the people who judged the starving ones. The taller ones pointed to the smaller ones on my binder paper and said, "See how our heads touch the top of the blue line? We will say when you get your water."

I even filled up my books with my frantic obsession at school and on the bus ride home.

Okay, so if I write one line before we reach the stoplight no one on this bus will die of starvation. Four periods and two line breaks before we get to the crosswalk and one baby's heart in that sad country will not cave into the nothingness of its chest.

If Theresa or Goat wanted to stop at McDonald's before the walk from the bus stop to our houses, the swell of a panic attack rose into my limbs and shook me into not going.

"I don't feel very well," I said if it was just me and Theresa. "Let's go to the library and chill on the sofas."

If Goat was there I just walked in the opposite direction, my breath short, my hands sweaty. I didn't say anything at all.

"Uh, okay, so, 'bye Traci. What, you can't even walk home with me anymore or what?"

Fuck it.

Oh, I wanted to so, so much. I wanted to take advantage of the times when my first real—and slipping away—boyfriend wasn't acting like an idiot in front of his graffiti followers. Once at Aloha Roller

Palace I saw a very skinny girl faint on the rink. A boy skated over and picked her up and they were kind of laughing and he said, "Now, no more of that. If you feel weird you just lean on me." I wanted that too, but it had only taken a few weeks to advance my lyric writing from one song that could save one country to more than five songs that could potentially save the whole world.

How was I supposed to explain that to Goat or anyone else? *You see, Goat, last night I didn't get to finish writing down all the words to Nena's "99 Luftballons." I stopped just before she sings, "This is what we've waited for, this is it boys, this is war . . ." and although there's nothing I'd like more than to hang out with you now, I'm sure you know that we're presently having some issues with Russia and what if I can stop the cold war by writing down that line? Or what if I can stop all wars by writing down all songs with the word war in them?*

Right.

Plus, honestly, I barely had time to really care that Goat was always pissed off at the way I acted. All I could think about was songs and sleep and the F's that were now filling up my binder papers.

Mr. Clark, my second-period English teacher gave me back my poetry assignment. "I have no idea what this is even supposed to be?" A red question mark and a sad face you would write for a first grader with social limits sat in the top right corner. "I asked for an example of a dactyl poem. Is this supposed to be a haiku? Because it's not."

I was too tired to even argue. "I don't know what it's supposed to be," I said and took back the hurried piece of crap I'd scribbled out on the bus that I almost didn't catch.

Dear Pillow. I hate you.

On Wednesday nights I'd find myself barely crawling over the end of Hump Day, spiraling toward a weeklong tally of about twelve hours' sleep. I was more than just a little cranky. A zero-tolerance approach was all I could offer when I had to assist the old people for my mom and Glenda's God time.

"I'm supposed to be wheeling you out there now, Mr. Gray. Do you want to go or not?"

Mr. Gray held up these hideous Day-Glo things and told me he had new socks. "But they don't fit," he said. He pointed his magenta-gray foot in my direction. "You put them on."

I bent down to the smells of crotch ammonia and tried not to gag. "Men's socks are one size fits all," I insisted, and okay, so I wasn't all that gentle as I yanked and tugged and he was so right about them not fitting. I guess the daughter that hardly came to see him and sent ridiculous juvenile presents in the mail like a ten piece Chubby Board puzzle or a package of Krazy Straws figured since she was already in the kids' department of Sears picking out another gift for her dad she might as well stock up on Garanimals.

When Grammie caught sight of what I had done as I wheeled Mr. Gray to the Praise and Worship circle, she went nuts. "That's dangerous! Now you know better than to let socks just a-hang off these people." She blocked me from going any farther, then tried to pull up the hot pink and fluorescent green stripes dangling from Mr. Gray's limp toes. "Now I'll be goddamned if this isn't an accident waiting to happen, Traci." Mr. Gray's crusty heels kept hitting the footrests of his wheelchair. He yelped while Grammie spat about the goddamn socks being so goddamn small. I think right about then I just stopped caring.

At dinner that evening I was assigned to what Bryan and I called the mouth breathers' table, but I couldn't even keep my eyes open long enough to check if the pockets of dribble/catchall bibs were reaching their maximum mashed carrot and Tater Tot capacity.

It didn't matter though. Evelyn with the Glasses was watching, keeping track of everything with her incessant staring.

"Evelyn, please eat," I said. "There'll be plenty of time to stare after dinner."

This was an every-night thing.

"Evelyn? You better listen to me and quit it with the staring."

She was actually a pretty woman with big white curls springing from her pink scalp like flowers in a children's book. She had captivating Susan Sarandon eyes, but with her dirty-fingerprint glasses the thickness of the bulletproof drive-thru window at the Wendy's on Monterey Highway, her whole face turned into something you wanted to spray with Raid or Windex.

"Evelyn? I'm going to get my grandmother to set you straight," I said. "You're being very rude. You really need to stop staring at people." My whole head was clogged in a haze of exhaustion and frustration. My eyes burned. I almost slammed my fist against the table. "It's not polite to stare!"

Captain looked up from his chicken patty and asked, "Who's staring at you, whore?"

It's hard to say what happened first, me tossing a Jell-O square right into Captain's face or me screaming that both Captain and Evelyn could kiss my ass.

"I hate everyone at this table!" I yelled. "All of you are disgusting and rude!" If it was possible for Evelyn's eyes to get any bigger, they did.

"I just can't take this anymore," I started crying as I ran through the day room like a B-movie girl into the forest, fleeing from geriatric monsters.

In the hallway my mom held me while I sobbed. "I'm just so tired," I said. "I can't sleep, Mom. I'm so tired you can't even believe how tired I am."

I felt Glenda's hand on my back.

"She's not feeling well—I don't know," my mom whispered to her. "Something's wrong."

"What's all this about?" Grammie joined our circle of Woe Is Me and told my mom she was worried about my insomnia. "She's awake at all hours writing down poems," she said. "I try to make her hot toddies but she won't drink them."

My mom said she didn't know if she liked the idea of me drinking alcohol. "Maybe half a Halcion would help."

Sleeping pills. I knew some of the residents had them in the locked metal cabinet from all the times I took out everyone's medication and counted the bottles. I also knew my mother liked them almost as much as *M*A*S*H* and Christ. That one time I snuck one from her purse, it did help me, I couldn't deny that. But now it was being discussed as something that wouldn't have to be kept secret. That felt weird. If it wasn't a secret, how would I handle it? Secret things were all I knew. The embarrassment I would die from if anyone found out about my thoughts on Ethiopian hunger trickling down from Africa into my own family; how Gorbachev would let loose his missiles if I didn't keep writing down lyrics of songs with *war* in them. My new way of shaving my legs hard and fast so that each scrape along my shinbone was one person in the world who wouldn't succumb to disease or famine.

Now the 8 P.M. med round would include me and my sleeping pills. I'd wait like everyone else, ticking off the minutes until peace would float in like changelings through the window. I would get excited about shows that came on at six because that meant I only had two hours left—the evening news meant one hour. I would never be able to associate the opening music to *Punky Brewster* with anything else but T-minus thirty minutes to blastoff.

At first it was easy. At first Halcion was gorgeous, all warm eclipses and moon breath. I would lie in my bed and wait for sleep to cover me. These weren't the Bible flames I was used to, no devil bombs being cast down to crush the skulls of nonbelievers. These were candle flowers. Slow-blooming candle flowers.

My pills actually gave me three days of rest. I took a shower like a regular person and did a math ditto. Only got a 46 percent but I did it. And in class, too.

Then, just like that, the pills stopped working. I would take my half at eight o'clock, lie in my bed with some Edgar Allan Poe or a rerun of *Bewitched* and wait for my fading. Nothing happened.

"Sometimes they do that," my mom said, but more than half a pill was never offered.

One night while I was waiting to see if my half a pill—and the extra whole pill I snuck—would work, Marisol caught me coming out of the bathroom with my eyes all puffy after a familiar when-will-this-end cry. "Joo come here, honey." She clutched my arm, sat me down in her room, and told me what I needed was to take a giant gulp of NyQuil with my sleeping pills.

"I never in my life had good sleep without somesing to help me." She opened her nightstand drawer and pulled out an econo-size bottle of dark green slush. The light caught the liquid inside and made me think of magic trees and enchanted bugs. I took a big swig. Tinkerbell was all lit up in my mouth.

Under my Strawberry Shortcake comforter with the pink bellies of newborn puppies in my veins I was a little flying thing, then a great big flying thing with my own set of wings and ambitions. Whenever sparkly leaves floated down from the ceiling I caught them between my eyelashes and collected them on my cheeks until I was so smart and shiny you could've made a clever woodland poem out of me. One that you would eventually know by heart and want to hear again and again.

12

of paper bags and porta-potties

The human body falls fast.
—JEFFREY EUGENIDES, *THE VIRGIN SUICIDES*

Pretty soon, the only thing I needed was NyQuil. Four tablespoons. Every night. Eight o'clock. I promised myself that this much gorgeous would stay at four tablespoons and only before bedtime, and even if I can divide fractions better when I've swallowed my tablespoons than when I haven't, I made myself say it out loud: "Only when it's bedtime."

And then I got a lead role in my theater class's presentation of *The Matchmaker* and couldn't stop my hands from shaking or my stomach from turning or my throat from tightening every time I thought about passing out onstage. My only really bad panic attacks since I fainted that day with Kitty Thurman had been limited to a sharing circle in the sixth grade when someone threw a Lando Calrissian action figure at my face while I read a poem about my cat, and the Burger Pit with Mom and Grammie after I realized I had already eaten half my cheeseburger before noticing the middle of the meat patty was so undercooked even a zombie wouldn't be okay with it. Running to the bathroom with Lando's body indentation still on my forehead, scampering under the restaurant table because Grammie couldn't get out fast enough to let me free of the booth—it didn't matter where I was or what circumstances caused me to hyperventilate and cry. The attacks always began the same way: everything dark and shrinking, shadow gnomes laughing through the filthy periscope lens of my peripheral vision. Sometimes my whole body would tingle, sometimes only my chest, but each time, the tightness never let go. Like the whole of me had been wrapped in an Ace bandage. I could actually feel the valves in my heart open and close, my pulse spewing out my blood, taking it back.

In and out.

Hiss and growl.

They're going to see you faint. They'll know what a loser you are.

When my dad found me in the downstairs bathroom of the condo he now shared with Sarah, I was sniffing air from the paper bag I carried around in my purse.

"What is this all about?"

"I feel so sick," I answered. "My burrito tasted funny. Did your burrito taste funny?"

Ask questions. Take the eyes off you. Say something clever.

"I think Mexicans are involved in some sort of a conspiracy to spread diarrhea to everyone in all bordering states."

He looked like maybe he believed me.

You get really good at that sort of acting. When you're trying so hard to cover up the fact that you know your lungs are going to burst and you'll just die right where you are and your body will crumple to the floor, not unlike the way they found your dead great-grandmother after she lit her eyeballs on fire but you're not cool or brave enough to do something that bold, so all they will find is your skinny body like a ten-year-old boy with bad armpit odor due to your inability to remember that you need more deodorant than most people. Maybe it will be that guy who drove the coroner's van who finds you, the one you totally flirted with after a man you maybe helped kill had passed away because most of the time you possess no ability to think of anyone but yourself, and the coroner guy will see how disgusting your limbs are in the early stages of rigor mortis and he will smell your smell then he'll go home and hold his girlfriend extra tight and thank God he never got involved with you because what kind of basket case drops dead on the floor with her face in a paper bag?

Everyone will see you this way. So you're just going to have to teach yourself how to make the world think you're almost the same as them.

That's exactly what I did.

If my hands shook because I needed to run outside for some breathable air, I looked around and said, "I knew I shouldn't have had that coffee bean milk shake." (If I was able to get myself together enough, I'd insert a joke and compare myself to an alcoholic with the DTs, ha-ha.) If my eyes started to tear up from the nervous crying I tried to hold in, I'd pat my face with my shirtsleeve and ask, "Was your taco salad as spicy as mine?" or "I wish it would rain and clear up some of this ragweed. My allergies are working overtime."

If I needed to find an easy way to get to my paper bag, the one I could no longer leave the house without, I would first think about where the exits and/or bathrooms were so I'd have a decent spot in which to fall apart. I also found that cupping my hands over my mouth, acting like I was cold, and blowing into them helped to disguise a hyperventilating fit.

In drama class I used the fear of the stage for any excuse to be nervous. But that was a hard one to take. It felt as if I was betraying the one thing that *didn't* make me spaz out. I had never been anxious performing in front of crowds; in fact, all those eyes on me at once just seemed to blur into one collective eye that wasn't even real. Being in front of an audience felt almost the same as when I used to prop up my stuffed animals and pretend they were Ponyboy Curtis and the rest of the Outsiders watching me do a sexy dance to "Little Red Corvette." Lots of attention and invisibility at the same time. They like what they see of you. They'll never know the rest. In that kind of easy love, I was normal.

But now it seemed no amount of journaling or deep breathing could get me back to that. Over and over again, with each little twinge I felt in my spine, each jump of my stomach, all I could think of was the time I passed out into Kitty Thurman's arms. I relived that whole scene whenever I felt the crinkle of a butterfly's cocoon trying to give itself life in my lungs. I was sure I would float away from my body, from the ground, or I'd fall headfirst into it and my brains would turn into one of those spinning-flower fireworks on a hot July sidewalk. That this was now happening on and around a theater setting made disgust and shame grow inside of me like I'd never felt before.

That's when I broke my only-before-bed NyQuil rule.

For my role as Minnie Fay in our tenth-grade production of *The Matchmaker,* I played the busty, ditzy sidekick to the confident, business-minded Mrs. Molloy. The shine of "busty" wore off super fast when I experienced the horrors of corsets and bustles and balloons filled with hair gel in a push-up bra. I also had to squeeze my size-eight feet into size-seven turn-of-the-century lace-up boots.

The confinement was nauseating. I couldn't have been more pan-icky about such discomfort if I'd wrapped myself up in electrical tape and jumped into Glenda's old bear costume. Worse, Goat and I had been bickering for weeks about how time-consuming the rehearsals were. He said if I really wanted to be with him I would try to at least find a way on the weekends. I thought about that all the time. It's hard not to put the blame of selfishness on your shoulders when you've always been the cause of so much distress.

"But why don't *you* ever take the bus to the nursing home to come see *me*?" I asked him. "It's just as easy for you as it is for me, you know."

"I know," he answered. "But I'm not the one who moved like six hundred miles away."

"Oh my God, are you serious? Why are you acting like this?" So many of our conversations were full of these push/pull sparring matches. Most of the time it was impossible to say why exactly we fought. I had something he wanted, he had something I wanted. Maybe neither of us knew how to give these things unless a little torture went along in the asking.

"As if I had a choice," I said. "I had to move."

"Everyone has a choice."

"Well, I'm not everyone."

"Yes you are." He didn't even pause before his response. "Oh yes you are."

Most of the time, when it got like this, I'd just hang up, convincing myself he was either high from paint fumes or looking for a way out. Afterward, I'd spend a good portion of the next day analyzing every word I had said. It felt like the time after Theresa and I beat up that boy, when Dr. Schmidt made me write down those three questions to ask myself how my actions made people feel. Sometimes I missed easy conversation with Leah, when all I had to do was give my input about which shade of nail polish went better with her pink Converse shoes. Goat wore me out. I wished we could go back to the quiet times in his room, the awkward silences on the telephone, when our sentences didn't feel like part of my therapy. When I asked if he could please promise me that he'd be there on opening night, he answered by reminding me what I had called him during out last argument: "I'd love to be there," he said, "but I probably won't be able to find the right bus stop, you know—being the knuckle-dragging caveman asshole that I am."

In the days before opening night (appropriately named Hell Week), we practiced nonstop from 3 to 10 P.M. When the white cold sun cast its crumbling bones into the evening fog that surrounded the school, the theater became a sacred place, a perfect religion with just the right amount of scary and beautiful. Every footstep in the wings, every movement of props on the stage's hardwood floors echoed like a lonely phantom only I could love and understand. In the warm antique spice of Goodwill furniture and velvet curtains, I was who I was supposed to be.

Sometimes it really did feel as if everything was going to be all right in that building, with my fellow actors who were weird and faggy and looked at themselves a hundred times a day in anything that reflected. But almost every day, my constant fear of fainting blocked that lovely supernatural.

I worried about being sick onstage: *If you shake too much you're going to have a heart attack.* I worried about feeling good onstage: *The reason you don't feel shaky right now is because you have a blood clot that is preventing your circulatory system from working correctly.* I tried to think about that one booklet Glenda gave me where it said teenagers spend 83 percent of their time worrying about what people think of them. When I first read that I thought, how stupid to waste so much of your life obsessed with other people's opinions—and now I was a sweaty girl waiting for the NyQuil to kick in.

I thought it would help if I strategically placed some paper bags in the dressing room in case I needed them. Also, we had a medicine cabinet in the prop closet and I took it upon myself—spending close to twenty dollars—to make sure it was well stocked with every cold medicine that carried a *caution: may cause drowsiness* warning label. Come opening night, I'd be ready with the supplies that would calm me down if I really needed them.

I really needed them.

After squeezing into my dreaded costume, I bent down to pull my stocking feet into those hateful shoes. Suddenly I felt a stabbing pain in my side. The NyQuil I'd sipped on earlier had just begun to take effect as a hot swirling sensation in my torso. I thought my appendix was trying to dislodge itself from my insides. I shot up out of my chair. I couldn't catch my breath.

Fuck it. I'm sick with something. I've got appendicitis. This is it. I knew it. My fists clenched and that familiar lava hurried into my forearms toward my fingertips. A searing headache and stiff neck would soon follow. *So not appendicitis, then, but certainly the onset of meningitis.* I stood and began pacing. *Congratulations, you've also just fucked*

it up for everyone else in the play who has worked so hard to make every-
thing perfect.

Those sentences became alive things in front of my eyes. Thick mag-
got squiggles and fat black lines. Chains around dead bodies. Exclama-
tion points floated, then burst over the lights of the dressing room mirrors
before settling into the graveyard dust of rouge and pancake makeup.
Goat had a friend of his deliver a pretty bouquet of autumn flowers to the
dressing room with a card that read, *I'm here.* And now I couldn't even
look at all that orange and yellow without hating myself. I was going to let
him down too. Outside the door someone laughed. *See that, they know.* I
covered my face with sticky hands. My stomach tightened, hard and flip-
floppy like those sledgehammer minutes just before puke.

One of the stage guys popped his head in the dressing room and
asked if I could check to make sure all the clothing irons and hot curlers were turned off before I left.

"Okay, will do," I said, wishing him the hell away from the door, the
stage, the world. For some reason I also thought I'd like his parents to be
dead. I had to force myself to keep my fingers from squeezing my hair
and messing up my Gibson Girl bun while I tried to remember where
the hell I put those paper bags. Did I have one in my purse? Where
was my purse? I knew I hid three of them last week. Three. I should've
brought four. Three used to be okay, but four would've been smoother.
So maybe that was why my heart was going to stop beating any minute
now, a lesson about how you should always keep everything even.

I cupped my hands over my mouth and nose and took up deep
breaths while counting backward from ten to one. A rush like a speed-
ing train filled my skull—not my ears, they always plugged up at the
beginning of these episodes as if my head had been submerged in
water—I mean a coal black train so evil there wasn't any room for pas-
sengers just sped right through the hard pieces that encased my brain,
the soft tissue that covered my mind.

Check the curling irons. I breathed and managed that, but you can't
be around dangerous electrical appliances or water or fire or the side-

walk curb while you're in the middle of a panic attack, because what if you're standing next to one of those things at the exact moment you pass out and then you fall into, say, a curling iron and singe the skin right off your forehead or burn your eyes like your crazy great-grand-mother did on purpose before she died, but you, who would never possesses the courage to do something so cool, wouldn't be all singed and pretty and tragic. On you it would just be stupid.

There was one curling iron that had been left on. I picked it up, wrapped my hand around the hot metal, and squeezed. I push my palm into it until I felt nothing. Then something. Then I let it drop to the floor, where I stepped on it with the soles of both feet.

Here is your diversion. This is your exit door. Now, if I fell down in a panicky seizure onstage, if I started crying because I couldn't breathe, I had invented a way out.

"Someone left a hot iron on the floor," I said as I limped toward a bench in the wings where we waited for our entrance cues.

Heads turned. Mouths opened. The assistant director wanted to have a look, wanted to make sure I was okay to go on.

"No. No. I'm fine," I said, already feeling the heat of anxiety lowering itself into a shady corner you turn when you're almost home from a bad day at school. "Really," I said. "It was just an accident. I'm sure I'll be okay."

According to everyone else I was going onstage despite the pain in my feet and hand. I wasn't the incapable girl floating around in a medicine bottle. I wasn't the nervous spaz who would now worry for two weeks about a deadly infection crawling into my burn wounds. I was simply doing what any good actor would do.

———

On a sort of a free visit that doubled as Glenda coming to the nursing home to see who'd be interested in riding a bus to a healing revival, I managed to get her alone and let her in on my revelation about why I was having so many of these panic attacks.

"I'm going to die soon," I said. "See, that's what all the fainting feelings are about. Because I'm being shown what it will be like when the time finally comes. You know, like being prepared so I won't be so scared when it happens."

At first she said nothing. We sat on the back patio sipping iced tea and watching a chess match between Marisol and Evelyn with the Glasses who was watching everything but the chess game.

Finally, after crossing and uncrossing her legs a bunch of times, Glenda said, "Okay, I'm thinking if—well, this certainly is a new thing, isn't it?"

I knew it sounded crazy when I put it out there, but that's what I really thought. Whenever I would get to the whirling tail end of a panic attack I would tell myself, *Keep steady and wait.* Blood would recede from my limbs and my pulse would slow quietly in my eardrums—I'm not entirely sure how I came up with the idea, but I started to think all of it was a sign. Each attack left me feeling so drained I could barely keep my eyes open in the minutes that followed the adrenaline peak. But when the heaviness went away, something weird began to happen. I felt this sort of power like I could do anything. Like I'd been to a place no one else had been and knew things no one else knew. It was as if my panicky episodes were little death previews, and when each one finished, it was a perk to go out there and live and live and live.

"You hear about people surviving plane crashes or being attacked by polar bears," I told Glenda, "and then they spend the rest of their lives skydiving or wrestling wombats or whatever because now they feel like since they've made it through all that danger they've probably cut their odds of early death considerably." I tried to explain this as non crazily as I could, but from the way Glenda's stenciled-in eyebrows bent down almost into her eyelashes and the way she kept saying "uh-huh," I knew I was failing. "I mean, even the Bible talks about that one guy Lazmund being raised from the dead, right?"

"Lazarus." Glenda laughed, then went back to looking worried.

"I bet he felt just really awesome after that whole experience."

"Um, well—I don't know if a biblical resurrection is what's going on here," she said. "I don't think Lazarus was into wrestling wombats."

One Friday night while in line at the Capitol Drive-In with Theresa and her boyfriend, I literally leaped out of her boyfriend's car as it slowed toward the ticket booth and dashed into the porta-potty of a construction zone. A radio report of a bad accident involving a fiery big rig and a school bus set my mind reeling as I imagined the "two confirmed dead in the explosion" were probably on account of earlier that morning I did not turn down the part of AC/DC's "Highway to Hell" where it says *no stop signs, speed limit*, even though I felt very strongly something bad would happen if I didn't. In the stinking darkness of the outhouse I breathed into my paper bag and ripped out strands of hair until I felt enough pain to go back into the car and get normal.

Theresa laughed and accused me of having the runs. But when that near-death excitement kicked in, I talked nonstop through the entire movie, then proceeded to skip around the drive-in playground singing, "A wonderful thing is a Tigger, yes, Tiggers are wonderful things." Her boyfriend asked if I had any more crank.

You know what really helped? Antihistamines. Lots and lots of antihistamines. In the evening I would take my spoons of NyQuil—which nobody really said I couldn't due to the peace it gave everyone—but it wasn't until I came down with a nasty sinus infection that I would discover the beauty of Benadryl.

Two tablets as pink as Molly Ringwald. If my chest was extra super tight or an algebra quiz reared its surprise head toward the end of the week, I took three pills. The first time I took three and combined it with the NyQuil nothing really kicked in until I was standing in front of the bathroom mirror looking at my hair. I had cut it short. Really short. Quite a feat, since a panic attack ensued the minute the hairstyle woman Velcroed her vinyl noose around my neck and started pumping up the barber's chair. I was afraid she would pump me up where there wasn't any breathable atmosphere. I was also afraid I might stab her with her own scissors.

When I could feel the pills loosen in my veins, the heat started in my arms like the beginning of a panic attack. Except this fire was lovely. Shiny dripping tinsel. I stared at my reflection and ran my fingers through my short do. To the hovering girl in the mirror I said, "How stupid of you. Why on Earth would you do that to your hair?" Then I laughed and thought about my feet and how much we take our ankles for granted. I walked to my room, crawled into bed, and vowed to love my ankles for the rest of my life.

The Benadryl helped me not flip out on the school bus and allowed me to take that much-needed nap during fourth-period history. With antihistamines you can pop them in front of people and the allergy lie totally holds up. Plus, the forty-five-minute bus ride from South San Jose to my high school in Morgan Hill made it easy to be just like everyone else, because practically everyone was asleep.

God, those drugs made me sleepier than I'd ever been. In the mornings I was water and sand; by the afternoon, the water part had settled into concrete, and I had to lie down in the backseat of a car or fake an illness to get to the nurse's office. On Friday afternoons Jorge Silva would park at the McDonald's up the street from the school and sell pirated rap tapes from the back of his mother's car. I paid him two dollars for the use of a spot to lay my head.

How stupid and weak to rely on cold medication to get me through the day. How loserish.

I was always going on about people who do drugs being soft-minded robots of ignorance. If someone offered a joint or a drink I was the first to say no. "Believe me, I'm crazy enough without any help," was my usual answer. And yet there I was. Three o'clock in the afternoon, half passed out in a Chevy Astro van between stacks of *Lowrider* magazines and illegal extended remixes of "Egyptian Lover."

It didn't take long for everything besides sleep and not fainting to lose its appeal. First to go: anyplace that interrupted my afternoon naps and required concentration.

"I didn't say I was quitting," I said to my mother. "But I think I'm finished worrying so much about going to school." I had just come home from distributing flyers with Goat in the parking lot of the Alpha Beta shopping center. A Xeroxed copy of our middle fingers now stuck to the windshield of every unsuspecting midday shopper. On the walk home I came up with the idea that school wasn't something I really needed at this point in my life. "Plus I've already missed like three weeks straight so I'm probably not even registered anymore."

The missing three weeks had come from a horrible case of pneumonia. (Well, weeks one and two were being sick. Week three was my lack of motivation to accept the fact that I wasn't sick anymore.)

"First off, that's illegal," my mom answered. "Second, there's no way in hell I'm letting you quit school!"

But she wouldn't have a choice. I was so done with these yelling and pleading matches. I couldn't stand to look at her anymore. Her hodgepodge moods and apathetic face made me think of how I felt that whole three weeks I stayed in bed. Except my mom's anguish didn't include Lucky Charms and *Gilligan's Island.*

While she yelled and threatened, I quietly decided that no matter what she said, nothing was going to change my mind.

"If you really think for one second I would even consider letting your schooling end at the tenth grade—" She pulled her pack of Merit 100's from her muumuu pocket and sat down at my desk. "Well, I guess you think you have all the answers, isn't that right? You just don't care a damn thing about anyone but yourself." She rolled the tip of her cigarette inside the mouth of an empty Mountain Dew can on my desk.

"Godammit!" I yelled. "You know I don't want anyone smoking in my room. Talk about not caring about people." I waved my hands in the filthy air around my face, then leaned across the top of my desk to open my window. Suddenly, there was a snap at the back of my neck like a wet towel with a rock rolled inside it. My mother's fist had swung and met its mark just below my head. I flinched and tried to turn, but all at once her hands were full of my hair. She yanked hard until the top of me bent like a backwards *C*.

"You sit your fucking ass down now."

For a second I thought I should scream, or hit her. Instead I plopped into my chair and wept. "You're nuts," I said. "You don't even know what goes on half the time—"

She was so close to my face, pointing, smoke purling from her nostrils. "Oh I know what goes on all the time, little girl. You think your grandmother is best secret friends with you?"

Huh? What kind of stupid thing was that to say? *Best secret friends?* I was even beginning to hate the way she spoke.

"Well, she lets me know everything, all the mornings you're late for school, all the times you've been in the medicine cabinets fooling around with the old people's medication."

"What? That's a damn lie!" I could feel my fists ball up. Yeah, a few times I took out pills and just counted them. I wasn't really sure how Grammie found this out, but still. "I never fooled around with anyone's pills. You're a liar. I wonder what Jesus would say right now if he could see how you lie?" For a split second I wondered if I should tell her about the Benadryl. How I'd been buying and taking so much of it. How when I ran out of NyQuil I'd go to Marisol and put on a big show so she'd give me what was left of hers. In my desk chair with the pitiful gravity of my mother hovering over me I wanted to hit and hug and scream and confess. But all I did was cry.

For three days I would beg my mother to let me finish the tenth grade through a program my high school offered called Independent Studies. I would keep on and on until one night with her tongue thick and her eyelids heavy under the cozy pillows of Xanax, she broke down at the nursing home dinner table and yelled, "Holy Mary, mother of God! This child will see me dead before she shuts up!"

Evelyn with the Glasses had been staring at me since we sat down. Without breaking her glare into my face she said, "Carole, I believe you are right."

Independent Studies was an early homeschooling idea before home-schooling was for kids with hunting rifles and forty-eight siblings. It basically consisted of a packet of vocabulary words that a toddler could use in a sentence, a cut 'n' paste about the Alamo or some other fun historical event, and a math ditto that I usually just threw away. Once a week I had to report to a small trailer behind the running track of the high school and wait in line with pregnant girls and gangbangers. I turned in my Name That Dictator dot-to-dot, got my packet checked off, and went home. But by the second or third week of me learning absolutely nothing except that the story line to *General Hospital* was much more fascinating with a bowl of Top Ramen on a TV tray, my mom came to the conclusion that it was time to bring my afternoon lounge act to an end. The compromise was that I could continue Independent Studies if I went to her church.

"I'm not going to your stupid church!" Here we were again in my room. That little no-yelling promise I made to myself because it just wasn't worth the time or energy—well, that wasn't holding up very well with the Bible in my face and a hideous new plaid skirt she'd bought special at Nordstrom just for me so I'd look "ladylike yet fashionable" for the youth group.

"Then you're leaving me no choice but to call your dad and tell him all about your attitude and you being in Reject School."

With my dad's new marriage to Sarah and their new life that very much included monogrammed duvet covers but very much did not include paying for my visits to the orthodontist, it wasn't exactly hard to keep him away from the fact that in the course of about nine months I'd gone from a straight-D student with poems and potential to a housebound flunkee with the motivation of a coma patient.

My mother was sure she had me cornered.

I called her stupid and brainwashed. "You don't even live with me! What makes you think you know what's best for me?"

That was the first and last time she hit me with her closed fist.

Sometimes people with OCD think they are responsible for everyone's happiness and peace—sometimes they think those words don't really exist. But do you know what I was thinking when I threw my backpack from my window, then climbed out into the dark street below and ran like hell to the nearest bus stop? Baby turtles. The saltwater kind that hatch all over the beach all at the same time and have to find their own destined path to the water or else they'll get eaten by seagulls or trampled on by surfers or whatever. When I was little and my father and I watched his Mutual of Omaha nature shows together, I remember how he explained to me that this night journey into the sea was the turtles' one shot, their big chance to make it to the water and begin their lives. I remember thinking, How could they even know where to go without their mothers? How could they even think about such a brave journey if a grown-up wasn't there to help them?

As I waited for the bus and rinsed my mouth with the pink powdered hand soap in the bathroom of the Greyhound station, I was still thinking of those turtles and wondering about their paths. Maybe it wasn't so scary for them to get to where they were supposed to be because it was pure instinct they were following. Maybe they just needed to do it by themselves and let their senses feel the way for them. I paid for my ticket and sat alone on a metal bench with my backpack double-knotted around my waist for safety. Maybe those turtles just needed everything else out of the way.

13

nipple daisies

Your goal in this experiment is to sense an object that your target person has concealed on himself.
—PAUL HUSON, *HOW TO TEST AND DEVELOP YOUR ESP*

The first thing I did when the bus let me out on Front Street was take the cold ocean air deep into my lungs. The fish salt smells of Santa Cruz beach hovered in the fog as travelers peered through it for the people they came to meet.

In the Greyhound station with my backpack and a pretty good idea of where I wanted to be, I had looked into the safety-glass mirror of the bathroom and been overcome with fun-house waves of nausea, of sadness and exhilaration. Crawling out of my window and running away into the night—I guess that's just about as bad as you can be.

Maybe it's also a little brave.

"I am here now," I said under my breath, but the statement didn't make me feel as clean as I thought it would. People waved or squinted off into the distance. They embraced. None of that was for me. The gritty steel of late-night travel was still on my clothes. I thought I'd like that more than I did.

This is what it's like to chase something good. I repeated this until the words flowed into one another and held hands. But even as I tried to remind myself that I didn't have to go back to a place with disgusting old people and disgusting cigarette smoke in my room and the disgusting people who blew that disgusting smoke in my room without a single care for anyone but themselves, I couldn't get my heart to settle down.

I found a pay phone and called an adult. Lisa Crane had worked for my grandmother when the nursing home first opened. She was twenty-six with jet-black hair she kept in a punky spike cut with one thick glob of spiked bang hanging over her left eye. She wore flowy linen pants and boy's Converse shoes. Every chance I got I'd corner her somewhere and ask about boyfriends or French kissing or was John Taylor really as cute in person when she won backstage passes to a Duran Duran concert. When she was offered a permanent and great-paying job at a fancy-schmancy old folks' home in Monte Soreno, she handed in her resignation and said she was moving to Santa Cruz. I pestered her about it almost every day:

"And the mountains are so pretty. I bet you'll go hiking all the time. You've just got to let me come and visit you so I can show you some hiking tips I learned in Indian Princesses." "You know you've got to start surfing now, right?" "When I come to visit, we'll double-date with our boyfriends and camp out on the beach."

It was way past midnight when she picked me up at the bust depot. Her little yellow Toyota with the gray mismatched door and Depeche Mode bumper sticker had been traded in for a Volkswagen Passat. When she got out to hug me I could smell the fading Giorgio in her now shoulder-length bleach-blond hair.

She said, "Oh boy, here you are I guess." Instantly I knew she had already spoken to my mother.

As we drove up the mountain pathway to her house, the air in my lungs rippled with excitement and emptiness. There was a silence in the car that I didn't expect or really know what to do with. *How fun,*

I said to myself, and hoped that would help my stomach stop feeling like when you're at a birthday party and all of a sudden you're totally covered in this inexplicable sadness.

I wondered about NyQuil.

"Now when we get to my place," Lisa said, "I want you to call your mom, tell her you're okay. Then we'll talk about what your next step is going to be." We rounded a corner where a brightly lit driveway opened up to white condos. It was hard to tell where one little twin house ended and the other began. "We have to have some kind of strategy here to get you on the right track."

Strategy? On the right track? These aren't phrases you use when you're about to host a slumber party. What happened to the girl who let me keep her first-run copy of *The Bell Jar* and took me to see my first indie film downtown at Camera One?

Inside Lisa's place my disenchantment deepened. Where were all her books and the framed pictures of each individual Thompson Twin? When I tossed my backpack into a leather recliner, she sucked in air through her teeth and said, "Whoops, not there. That was just delivered this morning."

While I placed two T-shirts and one pair of jeans into a black lacquer dresser in a room that was nice in one way because it was kind of like a doctor's office but bad in another way because it was kind of like a doctor's office, Lisa stood near the bed with an Evian water in her hand and asked if I was getting all settled.

"Just about," I answered. Couldn't she see I didn't have anything to get settled with?

"Ah, honey." She came up behind me and put her arms around my shoulders. "I'm sorry that things are gross for you right now, but running away isn't what it's all about, Traci."

I turned into her hug. All at once I was so tired. "Hey, you know what? Let's take a ride to Walgreens for some medicine."

When I was heavy into gymnastics I wanted to be Nadia Comaneci. I'd watched that made-for-TV movie about her and read a few books about her life until I had enough information to thoroughly convince myself that we had so much in common. Sure, okay, I didn't have a communist sports scout pluck me from my school yard to join his tumbling team, but I still managed to recognize/invent our similarities.

Want it like her. Want it like Nadia. That's what I would tell myself before a scary back walkover on the balance beam or a parallel bar spin that I couldn't manage for fear of heights. In the movie, that big-eyed ponytailed girl who portrayed the gymnast would stare at the obstacles in front of her, while a cut to Memory Cam showed gauzy images of Nadia's grim childhood. In the grip of my fear about following through with a double flip dismount from the pommel horse, I'd conjure up Nadia's visions and make myself overcome in the face of her borrowed tragedy. I imagined my father showing up in a butterfly-collar shirt with a Donna Summerish girl on his arm while my mom sat smoking and upset in the audience, glaring every so often at my dad before strolling up to him and demanding the child-support check.

Oh, Papa, please don't fight with Mama on my special day.

In my little scenes of misfortune, I flew. I jumped into my routine and pulled the gravity away from my spine. My landings like fallen bricks on the blue mats. For about five minutes I was everything. No one was better or smarter or prettier or more normal. The morning I awoke in Lisa's perfect spare bedroom, I almost had the same feeling.

Then I called my mother.

"Juvenile hall?" I asked. "But I'm not on the streets. I'm here with a responsible adult."

My mom's voice quivered in a choky mixture of cigarette smoke and tears. In the background I heard Tammy Faye Bakker screeching about salvation. "It doesn't matter," she said. "I called a private police officer and he gave me all the information I need for when it's time to lock you up."

I laughed a little. "A *private* police officer? I'm so sure. Do you think I'm like, super retarded or what, Mom?" It was her made-up story of Bad Kid Jail all over again. Only this time with Xanax and Jesus— much less creative.

"Your brother and sister are here," she said. "Your grandmother's having to use her inhaler—you've got the whole house stirred up into such a frenzy."

But when everyone passed the phone around to speak to me, it was clear that the frenzy part seemed limited to just her.

"This is real bullshit," Kim said, then asked me if I was okay and had I packed a sweatshirt. She covered the phone and I heard, "Yes, I'm telling her that—hold on," then back into the receiver, "Um, so Mom's having really bad chest pains. If you want me to come and get you, just call and say when, okay?"

When it was my brother's turn to talk he said, "Look, Big Head, just come on home. It's not cool to make everyone's life like a soap opera," then asked me if Lisa was still hot.

Grammie was the only one I asked how Mom *really* was. "Holding up," she said, "but let me tell you something, I got medications in this place and you really did a number on that damn screen and now it don't fit right."

"Has she really been having chest pains?"

"Not that I've seen," Grammie answered. "But you come on back now and we'll get this whole thing a-worked out, honey. You're a-gonna pay me back for that screen, too."

Three weeks. That was what my mother and Lisa agreed on before I told everyone I loved them and hung up without apologizing. Three weeks to get my head cleared, my mind made up about whether I wanted to tell my dad where I was, and to finish all the incomplete homework packets my mom was going to send to Lisa's.

Three weeks to get normal.

The last time I placed my tarot cards into the shape of a cross and asked which direction I should go in my life, I'd been given a direct order from the card of Death: Do something new and drastic, or die old and unchanged.

I figured the kitchen junk drawer where Lisa kept a bunch of quarter rolls and dollar bills could help me buy daily bus tickets into town, getting me the hell out of the seclusion of her gated mountain community—taking care of the parts that were unchanged.

Benadryl and NyQuil would stop the dying.

I told Lisa that my time spent downtown was at the library finishing the homework packets my mother had sent in the mail. But really, I was hanging out with homeless vets and hippies who tried to convince the patchouli-doused wanna-bes that there really wasn't anything cool about a leftover life of too much LSD and Jim Morrison. In the evenings Lisa was with her boyfriend working on a solid foundation of trust and security for their soon-to-be marriage. I took my notebook of poems to any place that offered free day-old scones and an open mic.

One night, a very cute and very gay guy said he loved the way I compared the castles in Poe's "Annabel Lee" to crumbling dreams made from sand. He said his name was Carrington, but he reminded me so much of my old friend Peter Veneko I sometimes had to tell myself to stop being angry with him for the time Peter said he was coming back into town to visit me but left me waiting in the driveway with his Irene Cara tape.

Me and Carrington spent our afternoons cruising the boardwalk or hanging around Beach Street talking for hours about how unsatisfactory our lives were. While he played his banjo, I rhymed words and prattled on about how someday I was going to own one of the million-dollar homes we passed while trekking around the high bluffs of Sea Cliff Drive.

"I'd like to have an Alice too," I said. The brown-green ice plant crunched under our bare feet like zombie snails who wouldn't know how to get out of the way if you showed them. "Alice Nelson from *The Brady Bunch*. Man, she kept everything in tip-top shape."

For a guy so tall yet slight of build, Carrington had a laugh like a cow. "Oh, wow, I could totally see you and Alice cruising around town in that stupid green station wagon." We climbed out past the Danger: Unstable Foundation signs on the cliffs at Steamer's to watch the little black dots of cold water surfers. "Now give me a house with *Greg Brady*," he said, "and it don't have to be no mansion for me to be happy."

Carrington had a car and always enough money for cigarettes, gas, and an endless supply of tacos from Jack in the Box. I never watched him go to a job or even try to panhandle money when he played his banjo.

"What other songs do you know besides 'Rainbow Connection'?" I asked. "And how is it you always have money?"

For the song part he said, "It's just something I do." For the money question he answered the same. He also had a boyfriend who knew every line to every *Miami Vice* episode and worked in the theater.

"It's one of those nature productions," Carrington said.

"Oh, cool, like Shakespeare in the Park?"

"Kind of," he answered, "but not really."

One afternoon when the sky above the sea was a distracted kid shaking an Etch A Sketch, we ducked into the hallway of a ramshackle twenties Victorian apartment convert to get out of the rain and pick up Carrington's boyfriend for lunch.

The gigantic house stood between a row of motels and an alley of time-share condos. My family's old place was so close, I could see the terra-cotta rooftop and the pink stucco porch from the hill where we stood.

I told Carrington, "Let's hurry up, okay?" My stomach was in knots. I thought, *What the hell am I doing here?* My family hadn't been able to afford a Santa Cruz vacation in over two years, and like the bitch I was turning out to be, I just had to mention this to my mother during our last phone conversation when she threatened to sic my father on me.

"You want me to send you money so you can ride the goddamn rides at the boardwalk?"

"Yeah," I said, and then proceeded to lie about how boring it was just to stay inside Lisa's house doing homework all day.

"Are you living in outer space, little girl? How about I tell your dad to send you some money? I mean, for how long do you think I can lie to him about you spending the night at Theresa's?"

Part of me wanted her to; part of me wanted to shake my father from his new happy little family tree, with his new happy little wife, and make him look at what I had turned into. The last real time we had gotten together was almost a year ago when he moved me into the nursing home. Since then, he and Sarah were in Tahoe. He and Sarah were in Monterey. He and Sarah were in Vegas. He and Sarah were entitled to a life, goddammit, without a bunch of drama.

Carrington shouted for his boyfriend, Robbie, to come on now, while I couldn't believe the ghastly mess we had walked into. The apartment reminded me of a report I once saw on *20/20* about people who live in their cars because they can't throw anything away in their houses and have a hard time grasping the idea that a roach-free place to eat your breakfast might be just as important as collecting one more kitty-scratching post. Pizza boxes everywhere, clothes strung all over, a sleeping body wrapped in blankets on a futon. When the covers moved I smelled pot and cold carpet.

"God," I said.

Carrington didn't ask why I said that.

"Oh, people are here." But it wasn't Carrington's boyfriend who suddenly manifested from behind the shadows in the kitchenette. A tall man in nothing but a Speedo recognized me almost immediately. "Am I seeing who I think I'm seeing?" he said.

And before I found the sense to back away, the steam of sweat filled the air as the space between us became smaller.

"Traci?" He stepped closer until my field of vision was only gray and brown chest hair. I had to make a conscious effort not to look at his unit.

"Yeah, God. Mr. Mark? Jeez, how weird." I tried just sticking out my hand, but suddenly his arms were around me.

"Well, I guess the sun finally came out after all," he said. Suddenly I was aware that I hadn't combed my hair in over a week.

Warren Mark was a teacher who helped my brother through some rough patches in high school. He'd been to our house several times for dinners and meetings; he had served on the board of education and even let my grandmother use him for an upstanding-citizen reference when she applied for a business license.

He didn't look as upstanding as I remembered him.

"How weird that you live here," I said.

"Well, you know I left San Jose when I quit teaching."

I nodded, but how would I have known this?

With his eyes still on me, Mr. Mark backed up a bit. "Yeah, I just had to get the hell out of that horrible city." He pulled on a pair of ripped-up jeans while I tried to pick a different spot to look. "I had no idea you were friends with Carrington and the gang," he said. "These guys work for my theater, you know?" He zipped up his pants. "You still into acting, Traci?"

"Traci?" Carrington said, his nose all wrinkled. "I thought you said your name was Alex?"

I pretended to look for something in my purse. "Ha-ha—yeah. I'm technically Traci, but I kind of, well, like on a spur-of-the-moment type of thing, just decided that Alex is, you know—not so bad."

Mr. Mark cocked his head and ran his hand through his hair. Shoulder length, the same deep brown I remembered. "Why Alex?"

I shrugged and giggled. Suddenly, I wanted to be somewhere else. I certainly wasn't going to explain that I'd fashioned my new name after Jennifer Beals's character in *Flashdance*.

Mr. Mark picked up some car keys and tucked them in his jean pocket. "Well, it's very cool. Very Frances Farmer," he said. "I also changed my name. The kids on my production team call me Question Mark."

Carrington's boyfriend appeared at my side and said, "Don't listen to him, Alex. It's completely insane, choosing punctuation as identity."

"Oh, hi," I said. "It's good to finally meet you." Good Lord, was Carrington right about the *Miami Vice* thing. This boy was Don Johnson all the way, if Don had been more elfin and had pimples. "You coming to Alive with us?" he asked me. "We're making plans for the next play."

"Come on," Mr. Mark said. "You want to ride with me, Traci, or you want to ride with Carrington?"

A grumbly voice from the marijuana blankets on the futon called out, "We're leaving already? Shit."

"Yeah, loverboy!" Mr. Mark answered. "Give a kiss good-bye to whoever's under you and get your ass in my car."

My seat belt was snapped before Carrington even started the engine.

We followed Mr. Mark's van up the winding and uneven streets where the San Andreas had given itself a little elbow room in the pavement.

A caravan of freaks.

The whole scene reminded me of that part in the *Rudolph* Christmas special when all those ugly orphaned dolls from the Island of Misfit Toys suddenly make friends with the Abominable Snowman and then they're all happy, traveling though the cold, cruel world to find their place in it. Me and Carrington in his car with the mystery sofa surfer in the backseat, who I now understood was called Ringo. Carrington's boyfriend, Robbie, rode his bike alongside us, turning every so often to wave and tip his white fedora.

"Why isn't Robbie riding with us?" I asked.

"He can't," said Ringo. "He's got a thing about vinyl."

Later, when I pumped Carrington for details, he told me that Robbie had worked at an illegal bathhouse in San Francisco where the Wednesday night theme was Sexy Sports Figures Throughout History. Part of his job description included vinyl wrestling suits, taking care of the towels, and performing certain maneuvers on clients and/or parts of his own body.

"No kidding?" I said, "That's completely nuts." I tried to imagine how you would execute a half nelson on yourself.

In the restaurant, we all sat on beanbag chairs next to a small bamboo table. Aside from a vegan bagel shop in Berkeley, it was the first meat-free place I'd ever been to.

"Get it?" Mr. Mark asked as he scooted as close to me as the little space allowed. "*Alive*? No dead animals."

But from the looks of the people inside, the "alive" part stopped at the menu. Half-asleep patrons melted in mismatched chairs or slugged around by the hookah room in the back, separated from the dining room by beads and a naked mannequin wearing a gas mask.

A nasty redhead came up to our table to hug Mr. Mark. After that, I couldn't hold it in any longer. "So what kind of theater do you own?" I asked.

He turned to me and smiled. I guess there was a kind of Jack Nicholson *One Flew Over the Cuckoo's Nest* aura around him. His teeth were nice, anyway.

"The Santa Cruz Forest Players," he said.

Ringo looked up from his tomato soup and smiled. "At least that's what we're calling ourselves to keep the juvenile courts off our backs."

Mr. Mark put his hand up, "Okay, come on now—" He turned to me. "What I want to know is why you're here in town, sweet cheeks."

I would really like to tell you that I tried to stop myself as this enormous string of lies began flying out my mouth. "I'm staying with my aunt," I answered. "Actually, my mother kicked me out. I was kind of staying with my grandma at the nursing home. I don't know. It's pretty much all fucked right now."

Robbie and Carrington leaned in with genuine concern. "Kicked you out?" Robbie said, "That's total bullshit."

Carrington agreed. "What did you do to get kicked out?"

Mr. Mark was quiet.

"I don't know, really," I said. "I was kind of involved with an older man and I guess my mom just couldn't handle it." I took a sip of my water. That had to hang there for a while. The only image I could summons was that one guy—Eddie. Greasy Eddie who drove the van for the coroner and peeked down my pajama shirt when I hovered over him as we filled out poor Mr. Pacheco's death report.

Eddie this and Eddie that. Oh, I went on and on. Sure, it wasn't vinyl wrestling suits and contortions, but at least it was something more than, *Oh, I just didn't want to go to church.* By the time the tortilla-and-tofu platter arrived, I'd thrown in a locked cellar, someone robbing me on the Greyhound, and being forced to see a psychiatrist. Not for obsessive-compulsive disorder. You think me telling everyone about dousing myself with water bottles so I wouldn't ignite in line at a Barbara Mandrell concert was going to get me a lead role with whatever production company Mr. Mark owned?

"It was for a sex addiction," I said. "An addiction to older men."

Robbie and Carrington were the only ones who thought that was funny.

That night at Lisa's I felt jittery and nervous. The Benadryl was trying to work but I couldn't get out of my mind what a total ass I'd made of myself at the restaurant. In a borrowed nightgown that very much wasn't my Garfield pajamas, I stood on Lisa's back patio and watched the fog drizzle out little messages across the tops of the redwoods. One of them, I'm sure, said *idiot in the cold.* I thought about everyone at the nursing home, wondered if Marisol had asked where I'd disappeared to. I even laughed a little when I imagined Captain's crinkly old face calling me *whore*. I wondered if my mom was over there, playing Yahtzee with Grammie or maybe writing checks to Jesus Christ via Billy Graham in exchange for her youngest kid to come back and act the way a good daughter should. I wondered if Goat missed me. I had tried to call him when I first got to Lisa's, but Leah answered the phone and I heard him in the background saying, "Tell her I'm in bed with another one of your friends."

Every day I told Lisa I was going to the library to do my homework packets. I'd walk through the woods and wait at the end of Lisa's street for Carrington to come and get me. Then we'd spend all afternoon with his banjo and my poems looking for spots where we could perform our work. On the boardwalk this tourist who looked an awful lot like my father with the thick mustache and poufy dark hair said he'd give me ten bucks if I lay on my back and read my poem.

"Do it," Carrington said. "Ten bucks is ten bucks."

So I frumped against the damp grass with the gray clouds and moon-colored sun in my eyes and talked about a place where I had a leading role in my own life. The man was kind of laughing, but he did end up giving me the money. The next time I would lie down for a man that old would be without my clothes on.

One night when the cable went out at Lisa's and I was sick of hearing owls hoot and frogs croak, I called a taxi and headed to Mr. Mark's place.

Everyone was outside in the cold, on the little common patio. Kids I didn't know shuffled in and out of the back door—some asking where Mark went off to (some actually using the words *Question Mark*). I stuck close to Carrington and pestered him about everything I didn't know: "Does Robbie live here or what?" "It's kind of weird here, huh?" "So what's up with that Ringo guy? He looks awfully young."

As I garnered information on the patio, I learned that Ringo was

Mr. Mark's son, but he didn't call him Dad, and yes, Robbie lived there most of the time because his rich parents who both worked in set design preferred Los Angeles over their own kid.

"Yeah, it's kind of weird here."

Later, when everyone wandered off and all that was left were a few sleepy couples making out/breaking up, Mr. Mark showed me the script to the play he was working on. Fourteen cast members dancing in the caves of Hidden Beach. Not a whole lot of speaking parts. Mostly jiggling.

"I remember you in that performance when you were with South Bay Dance Academy," he said.

I had totally forgotten that my mom invited him to my recital when I was twelve.

"Oh. Yeah."

Carrington and Robbie fell asleep in a huge cat-scratched papasan. Me and Mr. Mark sat on the futon well past midnight. We talked about my career.

"I just think with the right guidance, your talent could be channeled into something so successful," Mr. Mark said. Our outstretched arms draped across the back of the futon, my hand on top of his. "Think about the things you could do if you had the right person to guide you. You could be a professional dancer or a writer. You could be a real actress."

I was already a real actress. "Carrington said you knew a lot of people in the publishing business."

The writing was what I really wanted to talk about.

When I couldn't get ahold of Lisa on account of Mr. Mark couldn't find his very new space-agey phone that didn't have any wires, I decided to just crash at the apartment. I knew that wouldn't be too big of a thing. I'd stayed out pretty much all night a few times—me and Carrington driving around with Robbie, doing nothing but keeping away from bedtime. As far as Lisa knew, Carrington's parents were these very sweet country club types who gave just as much money to charity as they did to their church.

"So fill me in just in case she asks," Carrington had said. "And tell me about this youth revival meeting we're supposed to be at. It has to do with God, right? 'Cause I've been to something kind of like what you are saying except it involved nitrous oxide tanks and a whole lot of acid. I just want to be clear." He laughed his big laugh. "This isn't that, right?"

Every step in Mr. Mark's place was a thing with its own pulse. That's how much crap was in that apartment. You always hear stories about condemned buildings in downtown Santa Cruz, cockroaches in wall cracks, earthquakes causing the masonry to crack, abandoned corridors attracting lovers of crack—how did I keep it together under the weight of all those germs? How did I lay my body down in a place with all that mold? But hadn't I wanted something like that all along? The grime of running away wasn't supposed to be Lisa's spotless tile countertops and her bottles of Neutrogena Rainbath. If this is what I was writing about all those years, all my stories of teen love on the run from parents and cops and unwanted pregnancies, well, here it was, this life of wild 'n' reckless I'd always wanted. I was smack-dab in the middle of it. Alex the actress. Alex the writer. Alex the girl who had cut her hair super short and bleached it such a washed-out fake blond any makeup I wore made me look like a corpse at a wake.

So is it any wonder that first night in the dark and dirt of Mr. Mark's apartment some of my obsessive compulsions came crawling back? I thought about scrubbing with Ajax. I bet there wasn't a can to be had in the place. SOS pads? No, wait . . . hadn't I seen a can of paint thinner somewhere?

"Who are all these girls?" I asked Mr. Mark when he came back in from a beer run with his son. Both he and Ringo smelled like steel and some sort of animal. On the floor near my feet was a girl who I'd been talking to earlier but never answered my questions of what exactly she did in the play/apartment/futon.

"They're all in my next production," Mr. Mark said. He handed me a Dr Pepper in a bottle with the lid already off.

"Thanks, I don't want any, though. So you've really got to tell me more about your play. Can I be in it?"

He sat down in front of me on the floor. "I need to look at you from a different point of view, if that's okay."

I laughed, but I still wasn't drinking that already-opened Dr Pepper.

"Look, I'd really like for you to get in on that, with my play and all," he said. "It's a musical. If I remember, you had a big poster in your room from *Godspell.*"

I remembered that poster. I don't remember Mr. Mark ever being in my room.

"But aside from all the fun stuff going on in my life," he said, "I first think I should tell you that it hurt my heart the other day to hear all that crap you're going through at home." He picked up my hand and put it on his chest. "See how it hurts?" He wasn't kidding, either.

"Nah, it's really no big deal," I said. The sides of my eyes started to burn. I giggled when I didn't want to. "I've been talking a lot to my mom on the phone and stuff." I stood. I had to make a little room; my arms were starting to feel hot like just before a panic attack. "Plus I'm staying with a really nice girl so it's not so bad." And then, for reasons that were nothing more than to create a distraction to keep from falling apart right there in front of a man who maybe thought I had it all together (that and stopping yourself isn't a strong point with obsessive-compulsives), I said, "It'd be cool to stay here with you, Mr. Mark. I'd sure like to be in that play."

Generally, people who are overly fascinated with the evenness of patterns, the comfort of repetitive flow and the swiftness of things that *go!* find it pretty damn near impossible to put the brakes on bad ideas. Mr. Mark was a bad idea. Mr. Mark was an unmade bed. I thought maybe if I just changed the sheets, smoothed out the wrinkles, tucked in the corners, fluffed the pillows, maybe even hung up a set of matching drapes to go with the comforter, things wouldn't be so gross. But then there's that time between midnight and Mr. Mark in his Speedo and the way everyone has always accused you of being mean, of not understanding about other people's feelings. So you just have to force yourself to accept the fingers and tongues, the easy sound of *please*. . . .

If those things weren't there to pose some kind of beautiful threat, you'd probably just end up inventing something else to sabotage the unfamiliar feeling of ordinary.

———————

I threw a glass ashtray right at my sister's head when I was five and she wasn't paying attention to me. She blocked it with her hand, but not before it shattered onto our yellow kitchen linoleum and gnashed into the meat of my calf. My first stitches. I watched the doctor when it was time to get my skin sewn up—the way the black thread opened and closed the bright red flap of meaty tissue until the last stitch shut me out completely—until I could no longer see the inside of myself.

The emergency room doctor told me, "Now maybe you'll think twice before being so naughty." I didn't understand that at all. I liked the string in my skin. I liked the way my mom kept touching my arm in the car. All they way home I couldn't help thinking it was the pull of the stitches in my leg I loved more than the breaking of the glass at my feet.

———————

Mr. Mark called all the girls in the production Sweet Cheeks. To my new friends and my new life, I was Alex. Now that I was officially one of the Santa Cruz Forest Players, I expected to be addressed as such. But Mr. Mark/ Question Mark/ Quest refused to call me anything other than Sweet Cheeks. Or Traci.

"All you have to do is put a little rubbing alcohol on your nipples before you put on the tape, then the daisies stick right on there." Sweet Cheeks Kelly bounced up and down to demonstrate.

Robbie bounced too. "I feel like mine are the best here." He arched his back and rubbed his chest.

I kind of had to agree with him. His daisies were pink and big and the inside part was like a carpet for fairy royalty. Robbie was the leading man for Mark's untitled play interpreting various Jan Hammer pieces. So why not the nicest nipple daisies?

For the bottom half everyone was allowed a pair of plain white shorts, which seemed to have been bought in bulk. Mr. Mark presented us with our costumes and we all changed right there in the middle of the redwoods. I slipped out of my jeans and put on my shorts. For the boob flowers, though, that was a little harder. Just a few miles up the road, near that very spot where I was standing half-naked with girls and boys I hardly knew, with a man who thought he should know us all, was where my father and I did our play at Indian Princess camp. I dabbed my nipples with alcohol like Sweet Cheeks Kelly showed me. When the sharp fumes surged through my nostrils I lifted my face toward the sun to make myself sneeze. Those things together, the medicine smells and the two seconds of heavenly satisfaction a good sneeze can bring, brought me to the edge of a memory: me in the forest with my father when we first arrived at camp, unloading our backpacks and sleeping bags. He'd tossed my pillow across the hood of the car, and I caught it close to my chest like a boy at football practice. My dad asked me if I was ready to become a real Indian Princess. Kelly held her hand out and told me to come on. I don't remember if I told my father yes I was ready or no I wasn't ready.

"I think we're going to start now," Kelly said.

Were there little Indian Princess girls up there with their fathers right now? I stuck on my flowers.

"I am here. I am invisible. I am everywhere." These were my lines as I spun with arms outstretched, twirled, and pointed my toes. I lifted my legs in those very short shorts. The girls had been asked not to wear underwear. Kelly and I locked fingers and spun together like best friends in a mental hospital. We took our direction and leaned against the walls of the caves that hung below the high bluffs of Hidden Beach. Kelly's tanned skin was smooth with lust and art. When I looked down at my stomach all I could see was the arc of my ribs poking out. I couldn't stop shivering.

On the phone I lied to my mother and told her I was in a very special production.

"At the university, but we're doing some of it outside," I said. "I was really lucky, I just happened to be in the library studying when I saw the flyer for the audition. . . . You don't sound so excited."

My mom said to come home. "I really thought by now you'd be back."

But *by now* had only been two weeks. How was that supposed to be long enough to see if this play was really going to take off? We were to have three full rehearsals. A choreographer from the city was to come in and help us point our toes and straighten our spines. If I was going to be something more than a *failed* runaway, I'd have to figure out a way to stay here long enough to prove I could at least be a *normal* runaway.

"I like it at Lisa's," I said.

"Well, she tells me you're out all day."

But not all night? I guess my old friend wasn't all A through Z and left to right. That or she just didn't give a damn.

"Well, duh, I mean, I need to study to finish my packets and a few times I've been watching her neighbor's kids."

"Really? That sounds like a lie." She started crying.

"I ran into Mr. Mark. Bryan's old teacher. Remember him?"

She said she did. Her voice was little. Something wanted me to talk about Mr. Mark, to tell her he was a big theater producer now, and how the other night he looked so deep into my eyes and told me I could really be a good actress if I wanted and how much talent

I had, and how he was telling me these things while he was rubbing my shoulders in between my dance scene and how when he was rubbing my shoulders his hands went down to where the fake flowers were almost falling off and how I know that I'm smart enough not to be letting a forty-four-year-old man do these things but at the same time, I kind of didn't care.

"I'm just so thankful," my mom continued, "thankful that I have some doctor's appointments lined up for next week, because I'm having such bad chest pains."

And how I let him get on top of me and push my legs open with his knee.

While Carrington and I waited for our pita chip platter at Alive, I told him that I knew Mr. Mark had to use something stronger than just pot. "My sister smokes a lot of it," I said. "Mr. Mark shakes too much for someone who's just into reefer."

Mr. Mark was in the back room picking out a new pipe with Ringo and Kelly.

"It's barbiturates," Carrington said. He pointed to where the beaded curtain separated the people who wanted their food from the people who needed their food. "Ludes, blues, yellow jackets—whatever the hell he can get his hands on."

A few nights back, I had held Mr. Mark on his bathroom floor while he trembled and threw up green blubber. I rubbed his back as his lungs and chest heaved against my lap. I told him I was quitting the play. That was also the night Carrington and Robbie told me Kelly was expecting a baby.

When Carrington and I finished eating we walked outside the restaurant. The sky showed little openings of aquamarine. Somehow I knew that would be my last day in Santa Cruz.

I guessed after that night I probably wouldn't see Kelly again either. My plan was to try and be nice—and to get her to talk. I wanted her to confide in me about the pregnancy. In so many ways she reminded me of Leah. I tried to imagine what I would do if it were me sitting out in the cold on some shitty patio with a kid in my belly. I couldn't even wrap a single thought around something like that.

"God, aren't you freezing out here?" I sat down next to her in a rusted metal chair.

"Nope." She pulled her legs up into the little tent she'd made over her lap with her UCSC hoodie. "I'm never really cold," she said. "I don't know. It's always been weird like that with me—never feeling the cold."

We watched the neighbor's wet suits whip in the frosty wind. I made some stupid comment about cold men with no hearts or heads. She squinted at me through her cigarette smoke, a look like she knew I was just trying not to be clumsy.

"Cool jacket," I said.

There was a weird silence—to which she answered, "Fuck it all anyway, right? I don't give a shit whose it is; it'll be taken care of next week."

How easily little broken things can be fixed. The thread of my stitches had been the only thing I needed to hold me together when I threw that ashtray at my sister. I could see how dark Kelly's eyes were when she spoke about her own shattered things. Like those lines in my legs after I couldn't make my sister see me the way I wanted her to.

"Yep," Kelly said, "exit stage left, take your final fucking bow." She flicked her cigarette into a planter where a sorry shriveled cactus reminded me of both of us.

That night I sat for a long time in Mr. Mark's cockroach kitchenette while he slept in a sleeping bag on the floor. I had been in that sleeping bag too. The downtown sounds from the open window—the skaters and the tourists, the shouts of kids on the boardwalk for the first time without a parent—they poured over me in places where I didn't even have to listen. I knew them all from memory. It was just two years ago

Theresa and I were allowed to walk around this town on our own. We waited in line for the roller coasters. We screamed and dared each other to jump out of the cart on the haunted house ride. We pegged our jeans, feathered our hair, and held hands with boys from other towns. When you're a little girl you get your ideas from watching older girls. The trick is to know when it's time to watch in a different way. There in the dark, I finally confessed to myself, this wasn't me. This kind of filth. I couldn't take all that cigarette and bong smoke. I was always so light-headed. So much in fact that looking at Mr. Mark on the floor where we'd been sleeping, I actually felt bad knowing I was going to leave him. When he caught me with my hand on the pizza-grease doorknob he squinted and asked where I was going. I lied and said, "Just to the coin op to do a quick load of clothes." Those words made my chest open. I could feel myself leaving just by standing there. I also felt the movement of body lice under my clothes.

Breaking into the Happy Flower Laundromat felt natural. Sort of. Like taking things that weren't mine. I remembered how easy it was for me to waltz into the dressing room at Millers Outpost, pull the tags off clothes, and help myself to everything I was entitled to.

But this wasn't an Esprit jacket or a cute top—this was an emergency. Filth on filth. I itched all over and had to get myself halfway straight. Yeah, I guess I could have walked the four miles through the woods back to Lisa's or just waited until morning for Carrington to give me a ride. The problem was I had called my mother from a pay phone earlier that evening and told her that I thought it was time for me to come back. I could hear in her voice that I had called well after med time. She told me to sit tight, said she would call Kim and the two of them would drive up together. But when she asked to speak to Lisa, I panicked. It was way past midnight. "She's not here." I said, "I mean she's here, but she's asleep."

"I want to know what the hell is going on, Traci. You sound like you're on a street corner or something."

And now the *or something* was me folded up into a big washbasin with the hottest of hot water scorching the infested hair on my private parts. I poured my stolen bottle of Prell shampoo over the places where I could see the white bugs. They looked like they were moving, or it could've been the beginning of me finishing the last of my drugs. My skin had felt hot and crawly for two days now, like something was under it. But it wasn't until Mr. Mark scratched himself and announced that his eczema was coming back again that I realized I had better get into a place where there was a way for me to get clean. It was well known that this Laundromat had no security and a barely functioning lock. There was also plenty of streetlight pouring in through the window. Under the glory and salvation of that scorching water, I picked the lice off my pubic hair with my fingers. I tried to cry, but I was just too tired.

I pulled on a pair of sweatpants I had taken from Lisa's. In the near distance I heard the same muffled radio sounds like that other time I hid out in a Laundrymat—when I was ten and I tried to kill that girl. "Oh man, you've got to be kidding me," I said out loud when I saw the police car. Only this time I wasn't ten. I was almost sixteen. And my mother's face in the window with the flashing lights behind her was a reality I had not quite expected.

"Is that your stuff there?" One of the cops pointed to an open dryer with my clothes hanging out of it.

"Oh. Yeah. Those are my clothes. Let me get them out." I was polite, I was chirpy. There was a sideways kind of happiness about my mother's worried look, her coming to get me. That and the drugs.

Outside I could see Mom and Kim talking to the police officers as I sat half in/half out of the police car. I tried to ask questions, maybe even answer some. God, it was so hard to keep my eyes open. Kim made some desperate hand gestures while my mother lit a cigarette, then clutched her housecoat. The one police officer who was in charge of writing stuff down kept asking what I was doing there. "I'm just so tired," I answered. "I thought I could wash."

They didn't take me in or even slap on handcuffs. In my mom's car I sat on my wrists with my arms pressed behind me. It felt like the right thing to do.

14

playing the part of god is tony montana

She was cute, but what was the deal with her fingernails?
—MICHAEL CERA, "PINECONE"

The story was this: my mom told my dad that I had in fact run off, but only for a few days and only to Theresa's where we, according to her, had a big neutral meeting and decided that homeschooling was the best way for me to finish off the year.

On the phone my dad said the only kids he knew of who were homeschooled were criminals. "I had a neighbor whose mother had to teach him division and stuff at home because he was a hoodlum. Fought all the time, a total disrespect for authority. Is that what you want people to think—you're just too cool for school?"

I tried not to giggle at his dumb fifties metaphor, but he just kept going on. In my head I switched channels to the sad scene of my mother talking to the police and how Lisa was wringing her hands all big-eyed when we came back to her place to collect my things. That stopped me from laughing.

My mom said to keep my mouth shut to my dad on damn near everything. "He's changed the information on his health insurance," she said. "All the bills and statements are going to go to his house now."

"And?"

"What *and*? He's going to see that you and I both will be visiting the new therapist. So I don't want you flapping your mouth all over and making it so that we can't get the help we need."

What *we*? In the car, during the most uncomfortable hour of my life, I had made a promise—and not because anyone asked me to or anything, this was something I did entirely on my own—that I would complete and turn in all my homework packets, then, come next semester, start my junior year back at regular school without acting up.

I meant that. The whole time with Carrington and Robbie and my poems that hardly anyone clapped for on open mic night, I'd carried around this feeling about school. A panic, really. Maybe it was seeing all those homeless people on the beach. Maybe it was Mr. Mark's apartment and his hands that gave me a glimpse of what my future was going to be like if I didn't start caring about education.

"Real writers don't need all that technical crap to stop their creativity." Carrington said this when I mentioned about how cool it would be to just skip out on high school altogether and go straight into some sort of creative writing program. Even when I asked Mr. Mark if he ever missed teaching, his answer always matched his pill bottles and throw up.

But this thing about seeing a new therapist with my mother? I don't remember that even coming up.

"I told you on the drive home," she insisted. "It's a guy Glenda recommended to me. She says he's helped so many young people get their lives together."

"Shit," I said as quietly as I could. I just didn't want to picture it. "Is he all Pat Robertsoned out?"

"I have no idea. All I know is we need to get on board with some *very* serious home repairs, if you know what I mean." The cigarette in her hand shook a little. "I told you all of this in the car and you were fine with it then, so I don't want any attitude now."

If that was true, which I don't think it was but it could've been—maybe I just forgot on account of the Benadryl and NyQuil and the way my mom hugged the curves up Summit Road like the passage into reincarnation.

"You almost killed me," she had said in the car. "You realize I could've died because of you? The whole time you were gone I had such bad chest pains."

That much I remember.

That first night back in my own room at the nursing home, I wrote a letter to Carrington saying I missed him and how weird it felt to be back. *Weird in a good way*, I wrote. But that kind of didn't feel right. I stuffed the letter in my desk drawer and called Goat.

"Okay, so let me get this straight," he said. "I'm supposed to just drop everything and come over because you got bored in Santa Cruz and now you're missing things the way they were?"

I breathed in hard, but I had already started crying before I picked up the phone. I knew he would be like this. "I guess," I answered. "I don't know, but—yeah, maybe. I mean, it's just so sad here now. If you're not too busy could you just—"

I heard the Velcro tear as he opened his wallet, checking to see if he had bus fare. "I don't think I can," he said. We were both quiet until I said, "All right then. Guess I'll see you when I see you."

Kind of fast, as if he didn't want me to hang up just yet, he said, "You should come over tomorrow and watch movies." The edge of his voice made the offer into an almost command. I didn't care.

"Yeah? What movies?"

"My mom rented *The NeverEnding Story* so you should come by and check it out. I watched it last night. It's pretty gay but kind of cool." Then he laughed a little and my stomach felt like those few seconds just before the last bell of the school day rings. The beginning of thinking about home. "That sounds cool." I answered. "I'd love that."

But when I hung up that sense of native belonging just wasn't there. It was like the lens on a movie camera closing slowly until everything was smaller, tighter, like in a dollhouse. I was now the big scary monster at the front door in a place where small people lived. I'd have to knock over a lot of furniture to make room for myself.

Adding to the grip around my air was the fact that my mother and I were acting like strangers who had once been friends but maybe wanted to be strangers again. In the just under three weeks I'd been gone everything was different. Little things that you couldn't put your finger on but nonetheless so very there. Like how you walk into your bedroom and you know someone's been reading your journals and going through your stuff but you can't really tell what exactly has been touched because clearly, *everything* has been touched.

We were small and we were big. All at the same time.

Every so often were the glimpses of what we could have been, used to be. She put her arm around me a lot more instead of always having to touch my face. I liked the close distance of that. When we got into the glass elevator to Dr. Harvey Benette's high-rise office, she said, "Wait till you see this guy. He's such a fox."

Dr. Benette shook our hands. "I'm so happy to finally meet the both of you." His Rob Lowe looks helped me not to be too upset about being there. But it was that same chiseled chin and those tanned forearms under white rolled-up sleeves that made me upset about being there with my mother. Besides, wasn't I an old mental patient pro? Meeting and making nice with contestant number three.

"You can call me Dr. B if you guys want to," he said. His pretty blue eyes with girl lashes helped me not care one way or the other.

I tried not to look too bored while he and my mom went over the prospect of the billing statements not going to my dad's house. I sat in my chair and looked around Dr. B's room and made comparisons with Dr. Schmidt and Glenda. I pointed to the things I recognized. "Ah yes, *Cognitive Therapy and The Troubled Teen,* I think that's mandatory reading for all kid shrinks, huh?"

My mom glared at me through her cigarette smoke.

"Oh, and the proverbial family vacation at the beach." I lifted an expensive-looking frame with a picture of three towheaded boys loving their life against a backdrop as perfect as when you're first born. "Now was this Bermuda or Florida? Dr. Schmidt went to Florida a lot—he was the first guy who helped me with my crazies." But then I saw a weird bumper sticker tucked away half in and half out of the bookshelves toward the side of his desk. "Hey, we have that sticker," I said.

"Oh, this embarrassing thing?" Dr. Benette handed it to me.

"You've got to be kidding," I said. It had been a long time since I felt the urge to laugh out of relief.

"Cute," my mom said.

But I know she didn't think there was anything cute about someone defacing the very first bumper sticker she had put on her car after she discovered the Lord: *Christians aren't perfect, just forgiven!* But on this one, someone with a red marker had crossed out the *just forgiven* part and replaced it with: *so they should stop acting like they are!*

"Yeah, that's my son's rebellion against his first girlfriend breaking up with him last month," Dr. B said. "She was really into Church, but— my son kind of—isn't. I meant to throw it away. Let me just get that out of here. I'm sorry. He's been in my office doing some filing for me."

After that it was easier to relax.

Just in case you've never been in therapy, you should know the basic start-up questions. They're something like one of those goal-setting sheets they used to make us fill out for that waste-of-time day at school where a bunch of adults we didn't know asked us what we wanted to do for a living but then it really didn't matter because all the boys ended up milling around the police officers or the army guys while the girls walked right toward the booth with the giant comb and golden scissors.

What would you say is your main reason for coming to therapy?

What do you hope to accomplish from your visits?

What do you expect out of me as your therapist?

And I guess because of the Rob Lowe thing or the fact that Dr. B was sort of obvious when he held in his laugh about the bumper sticker, I answered all my questions the same: "I just want to get normal."

"Well, that's pretty straightforward," Dr. B said.

My mom lit another cigarette in a way that said I was trying to smart off.

Dr. Benette sent me to a place called "group." Group therapy, but everyone just said *group*. The term brought up images from that movie where Carrie Snodgress hates her life because her husband calls her a cheap whore for wearing seductive clothes just for him, so she sits in a circle with a bunch of people she's never met and confesses that her childhood was harder than most and that she's having an extramarital affair with a man who said the exact same thing about her clothes only with better words because he's a writer. The people in the room do a lot of nodding and crying.

I said I would try it. The promise I had made to stay in therapy had actually been easy. There was no denying the tools Glenda had given me, back when I was seeing her regularly, helped me to look at things in a way that made me feel sort of like an adult. But in group—a bunch of strangers sitting around talking about their OCD—that was going to be something theaterish. Hopefully.

Dr. B didn't screw around. "I have to put you on a sign-up sheet for the Wednesday night meetings. So you need to tell me how serious you are about getting better."

"Very serious." That one was to just say something quick. "I really am serious." That one was the truth.

He smiled. "You're very serious about what?"

I knew he wanted me to say serious about getting with the program or serious about getting on board or serious about stopping my stinking thinking. Goddammit. I said all three.

I'm sorry, but do you know how hard it is not to laugh at people who cry when they see a gum wrapper on the floor or have to pop a Valium when someone wears mismatched socks? I walked into the medical arts building near the old Santa Teresa hospital expecting something close to the same scene as in *The Exorcist* when the priest goes to visit his ailing mother in a mental institution and a crowd of unshowered people grope and cling to him. The prospect of salvation you can find only in a new person from the outside. But it wasn't like that at all. There was a circle of folding chairs arranged in the center of a pastel mauve room with decent oil paintings of beach scenes on each wall. A huge chalkboard with a half-erased schedule of some sort took up the main wall behind a fancy beverage-snack cart that looked as if a rented bartender in a tuxedo should've been standing behind its dark wood counter. Except for the fact that there may have been just as many throw pillows on the floor as people milling around before the meeting, nothing about the scene was odd. Until everyone started talking. Amy with the Ben-Gay was a hypochondriac who always said she was probably going to be too weak to come to the next meeting, but would show up anyway because, thank Mother God, she found the strength in the Universe to keep going and hopefully someday her sick body would catch up with her healing mind. Alison and Spencer, a soft-spoken yuppie couple who wore a lot of yellow and aquamarine, had been married for just under a year when Alison began pulling out her hair until her scalp was like one of those vinyl bonnets you wear when you're getting highlights. There were people who looked doped-up and people who looked like they needed to be. This one guy, Troy, who looked like Lurch from the Addams Family, talked so much that Dr. B had to actually point to his watch when it was time to wind down the story about how he couldn't have any envelopes in his house because he'd be up all night checking and rechecking them to make sure he hadn't accidentally stuffed his teenage daughter into one and suffocated her.

That first time, my mother was with me. She wore a bright pink muumuu and pink plastic bracelets almost up to her elbow. I had on a black T-shirt with a big alien head on it and the word BELIEVE spray painted across it's sci-fi eyes. My acid-washed ripped-up 501s had also been decorated with writing, a poem about geometrics and love gone wrong I had penned myself in purple marker. Most of it was faded save for the line that explained the feeling of a heart being trapped inside a Rubik's Cube. *The only way to solve this puzzle is to peel the stickers off.* The whole time I kept thinking my mother and I sitting together must have looked like a couple of circus sideshow freaks. Troy got up and made a speech about how his parents drove down from Flagstaff for his birthday. "I was so worked up," he said, and kept rubbing his hands against his jeans; they looked red and rashy. "But I tried very hard *not to let my irrational thoughts anticipate the outcome*" Shrink talk for stop worrying about all the little crap we can't control. And even though he had to do a little extra journaling and ask for an emergency counseling session with his own therapist because the thought that he might stuff his daughter into an envelope was stronger than it ever had been, the visit with his folks had gone surprisingly well. "As well as it can go for a week alone with my parents," he said, almost laughing.

My mom was shifty in her chair. She fiddled with her ugly bracelets and made one of those faces like I used to make in church when I was stuck listening to a bunch of nonsense I didn't believe in. "Good Lord," she whispered to me, "all that anxiety just because his parents came for a visit? Nowhere else to lay the blame, I guess."

During cookie and coffee time she asked if I had irrational thoughts about envelopes and stuffing daughters into them.

"I don't have a daughter," I said. "I have a mother and a sister, but no daughter."

That night she stayed late at the nursing home. We went to the Taco Bell drive through, then ate our mushy burritos in my room and watched reruns of *The Jeffersons.*

"If I hadn't been there tonight," she said, "would you bad-mouth me like that guy did?"

At first I had to think of what she meant because I couldn't remember a single bad-mouthy thing Troy had said. "Of course I wouldn't," I answered, then I shoved my face with a huge bite of meat and beans. I just wanted to eat and watch George and Weezie in peace. It was way too late to talk about the truth.

On the second group night Dr. Benette lit up a cigarette, passed his pack around, and talked about exposure therapy. We first watched a movie on how it was going to be, on how certain phobias were going to be addressed directly by, say, getting personally involved with germs or being in the same room with a pack of envelopes. We were all going to support each other while this was being done. Though I was the youngest in the whole group, save for a twelve-year-old girl who came once with her dad and did nothing but hold a Monchhichi and snap her fingers, there were three people who shared my phobias: germs, checking locks, uneven numbers: A fortyish woman, Annie, had a thing about digging in her ears for parasites; Bill, with a bright gray comb-over on his pink head and bad facial tics, had to touch everyone's eyebrows for fear that if he didn't they would go blind. Also he couldn't be around anything aluminum or his grandkids would fall out of their bunk beds and die in their sleep. There was also Barry. I know he had something going on about phones and Atari joysticks but on account of his being about twenty with Ralph Macchio eyes and perfect square fingernails, he was the one whose testimony I listened to the least. It's hard to care about catching hand, foot, and mouth disease from playing too much Space Invaders when everyone's talking and you're trying to find a line that rhymes with *hold you until the dawn*. We called our little clique the Germies. The first order of getting well in exposure therapy was for all of us to touch the outside of a garbage can, then talk to one another about how it made us feel.

Bill did the best. He lasted fifteen minutes without heading to the bathroom to wash his hands. Dr. Benette asked me to share with the group what I was thinking when I reached for my pack of baby wipes right off the bat.

"Well, first off," I said, "I didn't want to catch anything. I've got a bunch of crap I have to keep up with so I don't flunk out of school. Hepatitis is the last thing I need right now."

Amy blurted out, "Oh, I've had hepatitis!" like she was totally proud of her accomplishment. I'm so sure. To be proud of being sick—how stupid is that?

Dr. B put his hand up. "Hold on, guys, let's wait now. We want Traci to organize her thoughts and tell us exactly what she's thinking."

"I just told you what I'm thinking."

He turned to me. "So is it just about *you* getting sick?"

"Huh, what do you mean?"

"Well, you said you couldn't afford to get sick right now. So here's a good chance to find the underlying cause of your anxiety."

I scanned the circle for potential allies. "Actually, no. It's the cross-contamination that I'm worried about." I think that's what I meant. Everybody nodded. Yeah, that's what I meant. Still, such a big non-crazy part of me felt like I had to assure Dr. Benette that I couldn't be as nuts as the other people in the group.

I said on a private visit, "I mean, come on. Look at poor Alison's head from ripping out her hair."

He asked me to put my hand in front of my face and tell him what I saw. My mother was there. We looked at scars from old sores, scabs from new ones. The past few weeks I'd fallen in love with Ajax again, but not like when you first meet someone and you keep having to write down your last name next to his last name to see if it looks better with the hyphen.

My mother rubbed my pinky where some of my nail was coming off. "It's not always going to be like this," she said.

I pulled my hand away and sat on it. "It might. Glenda said it might. All the books say it might." Plus, how would she really know anyway?

Neither she nor my father ever bothered to read any of the literature I purposely placed in obvious areas.

Once in the fourth grade I'd come in from roller-skating in my driveway and pretending I was in that movie *Xanadu*, but not really being Olivia Newton-John because I had fallen facedown in some gravel—at the exact same moment that Olivia's song "Magic" blasted from a parked car somewhere, the part where she goes, "I've always been in your mind." I was sure that such synchronicity would result in Ms. Newton-John also falling down, but her crash would be somewhere in the Australian Outback and both her ankles would be broken and no one would be able to find her. And she would have to wait for three days for someone in a Jeep to bring her water, but they'd never show up, so all her beauty and talent would just singe and char into nothing under the heat of the crocodilian sun. Newspapers from Sydney and Melbourne would talk about the mysterious death of their star citizen: *Could there be some sort of American cover-up?* "Is there someplace we can call to make sure she's okay?" I had asked.

My mom was in her nightgown heating up some Rice-A-Roni. She looked at the ceiling and said, "Jesus, how long is this going to go on?" I guess she meant for me not to hear that.

Dr. B mentioned the sores on my hands again. "I don't want you to set yourself apart too much from the others in the group," he said. "When you start separating yourself from folks who have the same problems as you do, you're going to fall back onto that high horse of not being able to relate to your peers."

I didn't really understand. I was saying what I felt. I wasn't trying to be separate or anything, I just wanted it to be clear, I wasn't really like *them*. Was I being mean? Is that what he meant? Sarcastic. Was I acting the way I'd acted in Mr. Delgado's special-education class, when he told me that my positive attitude and me calling his students "special" was transparent and fake?

"I can relate to my peers," I said to my mother and the doctor. "I mean, I'd like to think I can." I wasn't looking at anyone in particular when I said, "I'd like for you to think I can too."

The summer before my junior year, I kept myself as busy as possible. Dr. B and most everyone in group said that when you're idle the OCD will do something to busy itself. I did a lot of journaling. I checked out books about psychotic behavior and even though Dr. B said he didn't think it was a good idea (also because of this) I read Plath's *Ariel* and *Go Ask Alice*. I also spent many afternoons in Goat's room, writing poems while he painted, melting through the air with words and toxins and home.

My sister was at the nursing home a lot. She tried to make it look like she was just popping in because the fertility specialist she was now seeing was in the area. I don't know, really. It felt like she just wanted to spend more time with me. She had been so upset in the car the day she and Mom picked me up in Santa Cruz. I know my sister had been waiting and wanting so much to feel a baby inside of her, I was sometimes jealous of how much she talked about it. I tried to feel bad as I watched her running errands for both my mom and grandmother, taking over a lot of my chores while I stayed in my room reading. *Not being able to relate to my peers.* It was also weird that Grammie kind of left me alone, said it was okay if I didn't want to sit at the mouth breathers' table with Evelyn and Marisol, and even told Captain to shut his goddamn mouth one day when I'd counted four even times he said, "Come here, whore."

Breath felt held.

By the time school started up again I still couldn't fully exhale. Though exposure therapy and all that ridiculous journaling was doing for the OCD what it was supposed to be doing (I actually sat through a whole dinner at Denny's without wiping off the table and arranging my french fries, worrying if the cooks had washed their hands)— something else was there. Something not smooth. I felt like a tight blanket had been wrapped around me, and I struggled to move in rooms where everything was so small. I spent a lot of time wanting that feeling from when I ran away (inserting glitter where needed). I bragged/exaggerated/preached about it every chance I got.

"Sure, I can lend you some lunch money this one time, but it would really help to build your character if you knew what it's like to go without food." "Yeah, beach weather is nice, if you don't have to sleep in the sand." "There's a great prejudice in our society against the homeless."

Goat was the first one to tell me to shut the hell up. The day he just upped and left Jack in the Box midtaco, because I was going on and on about how easy it is to score free fast food from a drive through if you have enough courage and street smarts, I said to Theresa, "What a predictable baby. What can you expect from someone who thinks drawing cartoons on brick walls qualifies as the real world?"

One afternoon a very large chunk of the real world waited for me just outside the parking lot of the school. In the sixth grade, "Cheryl Cheryl Built like a Barrel" was my ha-ha funny little song for the shy Samoan girl who thought she was better at math than everyone, even the boys, because she won an E.T. penny bank during a rainy day recess game of Division Wars.

"I don't know what the fuck your problem is, Foust." She stepped closer to me. "You think you're better than everyone or what?"

What a fat-ass. What a lowlife.

"You're fucking around with Ashley's boyfriend, aren't you?"

"Who's Ashley's boyfriend?" I knew she was talking about her cousin's ugly man who walked all stupid from one leg being something like fifty-five inches longer than the other or whatever. The one who I couple-skated with only once because I felt sorry for him. Plus there was this bet. "No. What the hell are you talking about, Cheryl?"

I was all dressed in Robert Smith black, my notebook opened to show a few girls who weren't interested in the A I got in English for writing about the time I spent eating out of trash cans and fighting off muggers.

"You know what I'm talking about." She made so much shadow and my heart beat so fast it was like there wasn't any light at all and very little air. "Someone needs to fuck you up."

She clamped her fat fingers on my shoulder. Before I could flinch or piss my pants, she punched me in the jaw. I heard/felt/tasted a noise like a building blowing up. I bent down to see blood dripping from my chin. People left. People came. I bled a lot. I made some sort of grumbling noise like in a voice-over karate flick. Every sound was one loud voice jumbled into the same scream, "Fight! Fight! Fight!" I swung a punch, but It landed nowhere. All at once my shirt was torn off, clear plastic buttons springing up through the air like chunks of pollen. I bent even farther to see what I could see. Then I heard the tear. The liquid down the side of my head was the hottest blood I had ever felt or will ever feel again. It's unbelievable—the rushing sear of pain that a quarter-size patch of scalp in someone's hand can inflict. And then came the icy wind of no longer having any scalp on my temple. The last thing I watched before all those shoes without legs walked away from me, was Cheryl Cheryl Built like a Barrel tossing the chunk of my head onto the pavement.

Someone said, "That's fucking gross."

Someone else said, "Traci, I picked up your buttons." Her hand was almost in mine. "That's a totally cute top. You should totally keep these buttons. You know, to like, sew back on." It was Roxanne Chetta from my seventh-period history class. Roxanne was a cheerleader, a member of the pep squad, super tan, teeth like a vacation. Everybody loved Roxanne, but there was something worse than that—she saw to it that she loved everyone too. Some of the blood from my head dripped into my mouth.

Aside from the occasional *hey, what's up* in the halls, Roxy Rah-Rah wasn't anyone I would have spoken to unless I needed a ride somewhere. "Are you going to be okay?" she asked. Her voice reminded me of the people in group whenever they said, "We're all here to help one another," almost as if they meant it.

I hadn't been close with many females. My cousin, yeah. Then Leah.

Being friends with Goat was easy; most of the time we had no expectations of or for each other. When I finally got past the idea of him as a serious boyfriend, we closed the gap of what we would never be and just *were*. But it seemed the older I got, the harder it was to relate to anything that wasn't hard. Roxy's parents were still married, they went to church sometimes but not always, her two brothers played football and wore braces. There was also a family movie night.

At first she started calling me. At first just to see if my head was okay. Then . . . for what? It was hard to tell. One day she grabbed my arm in front of Nordstrom and said, "Oh my God, you *have* to see this cute guy in here!"

The two friends that were with her looked at me the same way most of all the girls looked at me, but there was something in the way Roxy leaned in close when she laughed, the way she teased and yelled, "You're such a liar!" at most of my stories, the way she threw her head back and put her arm around my shoulder whenever she said, "you're like the funniest person I know," that helped me to look those other girls dead in the eye when I spoke and when I chose to ignore them.

One rainy day of doing nothing but renting movies at my house, Roxy blurted out, "Oh my God, Al Pacino would totally be the awesomest boyfriend *ever*. I love his eyes. Don't you love his awesome eyes?"

As we watched the most gruesome scene of *Scarface*, the part where Tony Montana and his friend are tied up in a motel shower about to meet their demise via an angry Colombian drug lord and a chain saw, I agreed about Al Pacino's awesome eyes and let myself relax in the comfort of this cheerleader who surprised me with her adoration of such a violent flick. I thought for sure she'd be covering her face as blood splattered against ugly bath tiles and Al Pacino's awesome eyes, but when I glanced over, Roxy was giggling. "Oh my God," she said, "isn't that *totally* the most disgusting thing you've ever seen? Thank God they didn't get Tony. We should declare this day to be Thank God They Didn't Get Tony Montana Day."

I laughed and said the only thing you could say to a statement like that. "Yeah, I guess we should."

Together we screamed out lines, voiced our discontent when Tony chose Michelle Pfeiffer for his skinny coked-out bride, and jumped up, pointing our fingers and machine-gunning the walls, yelling, "Say hello to my little friend!" That night I asked Roxy to sleep over. We stayed up talking about boys, about Goat and cute Barry from my therapy group. I even told her about Mr. Mark.

"Forty-four! That's like completely disgusting."

She never asked what kind of therapy.

I knew things were going to be different, being so close to a girl, especially someone like Roxy. Someone almost famous, halfway to heaven. I sometimes felt like any day she could turn into another thing I would just screw up. More than Theresa or Leah or Goat, I worried what would happen if she saw me with my paper bag; if she caught me sweating out a panic attack at the movies, checking all the locks in her house whenever I spent the night. But the more time I spent with her, letting her drag me off to jock parties, watching her cheer and insisting that we buy matching neon green jellies, the more I wondered how much she would care that her new best friend was insane.

One night Roxy showed up at group. I was walking down the steps to my mom's car and there she was in a Frankie Says Relax T-shirt and her cheerleading skirt. "I totally get to spend the night on a school night," she said. "My parents got held up at the airport." She jumped into the splits right there on the lawn, the same spot where once we all had to sit outside and support Troy from group when part of his exposure therapy included rubbing his hands in the grass blades.

"I can do the splits all the way now," Roxy said. "Check it out!" She looked up at Dr. B's office building, then, making a squishy face, asked, "So this is where you go for therapy? That's totally insane. But can you believe I'm totally doing the splits like one hundred percent right now?"

15

special forces of nature

Clouds pile up at the horizon, plum colored and full of shoulders.

—ANTHONY DOERR, "PROCREATE, GENERATE"

The day my brother left, the morning was full of September as his army recruiter came to take him to the airport. The night before, we had a big farewell dinner at the nursing home in honor of the newly enlisted Private Bryan Foust. My dad and Sarah kept going on about how smart you have to be to get into the Green Berets.

"But you don't have anything to worry about," my dad said. "You've always been smart." He said that in front of everyone. I had never in my life heard my father call any of us kids smart. A twisted breath in my solar plexus made me jealous and sad at the same time.

Grammie made Bryan's favorite fried chicken. Through greasy drumsticks and the honey in her hush puppies, I was able to completely ignore Evelyn with the Glasses at the smaller table in the dining room. Captain too, for that matter. I wanted to look at my brother for as long as I could without anyone getting in the way. The sight of him across from me already felt distant. There were other sad things at that table. Like my dad and Sarah all polite and lovebuggy to each other, Kim and Gil finishing each other's sentences—but my mother had no one since Christ superseded Frank Ranaldo. I looked at the way my parents spoke to each other, short sentences, manners, convenience. Kind of the same as when we all first separated. Back then everything was waiting for potential. I looked at my mother now, her long nails around her water glass, how the flab under her chin moved in a way she couldn't do anything about. I wondered if my dad felt sorry for her. I did. Over the past year my mother had been coming to the nursing home, sleeping on the couch bed, and staying up all night watching TV. She spent half the night smoking and eating. In one year she must have gained seventy-five pounds. I wondered what my dad thought, sitting there with Sarah who had a body like sculpted ice.

I sat on the driveway hoping Goat would show up.

"You could've stayed with me, you know?" Theresa joined me outside. There'd been this weirdness between us since I got back. A sad inaccuracy where sureness use to be. "I mean, you could've stayed with me for reals, Traci, instead of running off and having me lie to your dad."

I watched the way my cousin's dark blond hair shimmered in the dim porch light. So saintly. In the house across the street a toddler cried and wouldn't stop. I felt sorry for Theresa. She didn't get to see what I'd seen.

"Well, you don't have to make a big thing about it now," I said. "Plus my dad didn't even call you, so—"

"Yeah, but he could've."

"But he didn't."

She clicked her tongue, then jumped from the porch step to get to my level—kind of in my face. "I'm just saying—God, do you have to be so annoying? You could at least say *thank you*."

She used to be so much taller than me.

When morning came, we all stood outside in the break of a murky dawn. We said good-bye to my brother. I was the last one to give him a kiss before he ducked into his recruiter's station wagon. I watched his face in the window of the car as it pulled away, his high brown cheeks that framed his smile—his teeth were always so white against his dark skin. He still had those upper canines that crowded his smile. We never did manage the money to get those pulled. So my brother went into the army with his fangs.

After good-bye, the sadness came. But I could almost tell this round was going to be different. Thinner than when my sister left home five years ago, not as immense as when my father and brother carried my Strawberry Shortcake comforter and my suitcases into the nursing home. I didn't feel that hard flow of dark water pushing down through my mind. Even though I knew it would be at least three months before I would see him again, I couldn't help but think of what Glenda always told me: "Depression and anxiety is a wave. A wave and a retreat," she said. "You have to ride out the whole thing. Forcing it not to come is like trying to stop the ocean from doing what it's supposed to do."

I'd written that (or dim-witted poetic variations) so many times in the pages of my journals:

A wave and retreat.

Push and pull / you can't resist / closed hand / open fist.

Anxiety comes and goes—that's OK. (A stupid smiley face inside the O.)

Ride out the storm. /Sunshine will come / And with it the morn'.

Sometimes I really hated looking at that crap, that stupid psychobabble self-help nonsense taking up my notebook space where something really cool should've been. Hope was now blocking a lot of my creative darkness: *You can do it! Breathe and Accept.*

I would never say it to Glenda or even to Dr. B, but all those mantra affirmations in group, and Glenda's reminders that the nervousness may just be a part of who I am, helped me to make it through the day when my brother got on a plane to Fort Benning to start his new life.

The sun never did make an appearance that day. I tried not to see it as a sign. It was only the third week of eleventh grade, and I had a bunch of promises staring me in the face. I walked around the house and tried to lose myself in the comfort of my early-morning routine. But when I closed my bedroom door, fuck it, I just cried and cried. Crying felt wrong somehow. When you're trying to put depression and anxiety and OCD in perspective, when you've got feelings to sort out so you can really help yourself get better, it's sometimes confusing to just let go. You cry or scream or sleep all day in the library, and what you've been taught is to stop and "group" yourself. There are tons of questions you're supposed to ask. Emotional checkpoints.

Is this emotion helping me to improve my situation?

What do I think is the underlying problem that set me off?

Alison from group told us this story about how the checker at Safeway put all her heavy items into one bag. When her soda and soup cans spilled out from the bottom of the ripped plastic and rolled all over the parking lot, she didn't even try to pick them up.

"I just sat in my car and cried." She also picked at the scabs around her hairline where her trichotillomania had caused her to pull her hair until that itch in her brain stopped. I totally understood. I saw that "comfort connection" right away. Just like how numbers started jumping off the page and came to life whenever I panicked about them. When I let the numbers do their thing, when I rewrote them the way I thought they should be or put my hand over the ones that looked more menacing, I felt safe.

"Those tics and clicks and checks are repetitive motions to get your mind back on track. To comfort yourself," Dr. B said. "It's important that we keep track of the things that might set off those motions or thoughts. That's why it's important to journal or try to really understand what was happening around you when they begin."

Okay, fine. But the night Alison told us about her Tab soda and clam chowder rolling off into the sunset, I blurted out, "God, does there have to be a connection to everything?"

Most everyone nodded like they knew what I meant.

"I'd be totally pissed too if that happened to me; stupid checker should've known better," I said. "But I mean, are there ever times when it's okay to just let loose and pull your hair?" I pointed to Bill, who had to touch everyone's eyebrows. "Or what if Bill here just wants to make his day a little brighter with other people's facial hair? Yes, it's weird or whatever, but it's not like he's going around flashing people."

Bill's hands were folded over his big tummy. When he laughed even his elbow fat jiggled. "Ha! I wouldn't put that past me though."

Barry asked me why I didn't like writing in my journals. "I find it extremely helpful."

"No, no, that's not what I mean," I said. "I journal all the time, but are we going to have to journal and pick apart every damn thing all the time? Forever?"

Dr. B pulled up a chair in the middle of our circle and sat on it backwards. "For right now? Yes, you do." His gaze on me was merciless. "You've got to make your brain understand that yes, with OCD there certainly is a connection to every little thing."

Getting ready for school the morning my brother left, I didn't give a damn about figuring out if this sadness was going to last or if it was caused by something other than my brother or whatever. I just wanted to cry. I wanted to miss my brother without a journal entry.

I walked up and down the halls of the nursing home, getting my clothes ready, filling my backpack. Pretty much everyone else had gone back to bed, except my mother, who stood at the counter with a cigarette. There was also the Bible and some oatmeal.

How many times had I walked up these hallways, sick and hopeless from insomnia, not having anything better to do than to look at the old people in their beds and notice the difference between inhale snoring and exhale snoring. In a few hours all of them would be ready to begin doing the same thing they did every day, in the same exact way they had done it the day before. Sometimes thinking about that scared me more than worrying about OCD—the death of a motionless life. The pain of feeling nothing at all. Had I tried to run from that too? Is that what my brother was doing? Often I wondered if it was the grip of that kind of stagnation that had me feeling so tight since I'd returned from Santa Cruz. I always talked about moving to LA or New York, starving the artist right into myself. But in Santa Cruz it didn't feel like I had really touched that. Coming home I could sort of tell I was a bigger kind of me, but not as big as I had wanted. And now here I was back in the place where it took a new geriatric walker, a child not coming to visit when they say they'll come, a last breath to change the air. My brother was off to start a new life. Kim and Gil were trying to make one. The people in my house were almost done with theirs.

I didn't fit into any of these equations. Even Goat and I were slipping into a strange territory I thought we'd never return from. Though I certainly wasn't honest with him about my OCD or anything involving therapy, the hints I tried to drop didn't seem to get me anywhere. Not like in the seventh grade when he'd laughed and said people who had to count and touch stuff all the time were being taken over by the military.

I guess everything's pretty damn shiny in the beginning. But now we did this back-and-forth thing all the time where it seemed the only thing we had to offer each other was to see who would be the first to make the other person feel bad. I'd go to his house and try to find that easy diversion from myself. But instead of losing and finding myself in the quiet of our alone time, I'd lie on his bed correcting his English homework while he sketched comic book women with torpedo breasts and Anvil thighs.

"This whole page should be done over," I said, clearing away eraser shavings with an irritating sigh/blow combo. "It can't be that hard to understand the difference between *their, there,* and *they're.*"

He rolled his eyes but didn't look up from his sketch pad. "Just leave it, then. I can always get a regular person to take a look at it later."

"Huh? What do you mean, a regular person?"

He was silent for a while, running his finger over a line of chalk pastels, turning down his eyebrows in that obvious way people try to look interested in anything that's not the person in front of them. "I mean someone who isn't a professional writer."

"Whatever," I said quickly. "But it's not rocket science, you know, and God, look at all these commas." I giggled. "Do you just throw these in there because you like the way they look all curly and—"

He stood up from his spot on the floor and grabbed his paper from my hands. "Why did you even come back! Why didn't you just keep your ass at the beach with your beloved poets?"

These were the other wave-and-retreat times. Just as Glenda and Dr. Benette had always told me about my OCD and anxiety getting better, then acting up all over again, I was starting to understand this rule applied to so many areas of my life. Especially where other people were involved. In group I had to force myself to confront my fears. Exposure therapy meant that you had to make yourself walk on that balcony or drive in the rain or resist the urge to touch doorknobs with only your left pinky. Some days I could do these things with little or no effort. One day I couldn't wait to stand in front of the circle of folding chairs and read an entry from my journal that started with, "Yay for me! I didn't buy any baby wipes this week." But there were still many times when the only thing I had to offer in my counseling sessions was the embarrassing fact that I had not been able to hold myself back from hiding all the knives at my cousin's house the last time I spent the night. Yesterday I was certain I wouldn't get up at 3 A.M. and commit a felony. Today? I'll just stay awake all night—you know, just to be safe.

That's the kind of uncertainty I'm talking about.

While I laced up the black Converse Lisa had given to me before I left her place in Santa Cruz, Roxy called and begged me to write a poem for her English class. She'd been up late trying out her new Lee Press-On nails and ended up not finishing her homework.

"Oh my God." she said. "I'm such a *total* goober. There's no way I can miss another homework assignment for this class."

It was kind of bizarre to hear someone be so concerned about their homework. I'd danced bare-chested with a girl who had to worry about what she was going to do with the fetus inside her womb. But I was like Roxy a long time ago, when making 100 percent on every spelling test and getting my stories published in the school paper meant all sorts of salvation. In the fifth grade, Andrew Smythe's history project for our California Missions exhibit won first prize for most creative use of sugar cubes. I cried for two hours while demolishing the San Juan Bautista I had carved entirely out of Ivory soap. For a month the carpet in my room smelled like bath time. I hardly ever cared about stuff like that anymore.

"Make it a sad poem," Roxy said. "The weather's good for it today."

But on the bus when I attempted Sylvia Plath it was just too hard. I tried to put a variation on some of my favorite lines: *Death . . . death . . . death like baby's breath. Sorrow for tomorrow . . . Cry, cry, why bother to try.* The words just wouldn't come. How totally insane it was to have to force myself to write something dark. I pressed my feet into the seat in front of me and rested my notebook on my knees. In the wind on the yellow hills, patches of headless dandelions shook loose their tiny sepia spines. Just a few more weeks and fall would be here. The time when I could write and think and breathe—and not think. The witches would come. They would bring so many words.

I finished the poem in math class, then gave it to Roxy at her locker. She fondled a dark plum strand of her spiral curls while she read. Then she got suspicious. "Umm . . . this sounds like a sappy love song. Where are the graveyards? There's not even one suicide attempt in here?"

I shrugged. "Yeah, well, maybe I've been hanging around you too long."

"Oh, you're so cute. But are you sure this isn't your innermost secrets thoughts for little Goaty Goat?"

"Whatever," I said, leaning against her locker. "Goaty Goat?" Seriously, I don't think I could ever share something like that with Goat. He was always accusing me of not completely embracing the dark side. For the first time in a long time I wrote something that made someone feel good. I wanted to enjoy that without feeling guilty. The poem ended up getting Roxy an A. I remember the word *serendipity* was in there somewhere and how we laughed about that because she had no idea what that meant. I had to get out my dictionary.

Later that year, with the plagiarized help of me, she ended up acing the entire class. She said if she hadn't made a descent grade we could've figured out a way to make that happen. "You're good at persuading English teachers, huh?"

A joke that would stay with us always—at neighborhood barbe-cues or wrapped in beach towels in front of the mighty Pacific, our baby sons babbling brilliantly in our laps while we giggled about my shameful disgust, then how easy it was for the both of us to stop being ashamed so I could get on with the business of longing for a time when I'd do just about anything to get away from myself.

A few weeks after my brother left, Kim pulled up in her Camaro to pick me up from the Saturday matinee of *The Princess Bride*.

"Get in, goofball," she said. I was supposed to go to Dad and Sar-ah's house for dinner, but there was an emergency with one of Sarah's grown-up kids who somehow came down with a lot of emergencies when it was time for my dad to come and get me.

"So how about we just stop at Denny's for some burgers?" But first we pulled into a 7-Eleven because she said she had to make an impor-tant phone call. From the car it looked like she was crying into her hand. Her mouth said, "Oh my God."

Maybe there really was an emergency. When she got back to the car, her face was streaked with tears. She gripped the steering wheel and put her arm around me. "Guess what?" she said. "You're going to be an auntie."

I couldn't think of anything to say except how great and exciting motherhood was going to be. But everything in that car—my sister's bitchin' Camaro since she was fifteen—felt shifted.

As we drove through the midday traffic of South San Jose I listened to my sister's ideas about baby names and stretch marks. I tried to imagine what life would be like with a new little member of the family. The thought of having a baby niece or nephew was surreal and inspirational. Someone I didn't know would soon have every second of my sister's attention. That was okay. You shouldn't be jealous about stuff like that.

"God, this is so weird." I wanted to say so much more, but that's what came out.

"You're going to be an awesome auntie," my sister said.

I smiled and nodded. I wondered if I could pull it off. What exactly did I have to offer a kid besides advice on how to do so many things wrong? And with what I had been told (with what I knew) about OCD and anxiety never going away, what if I did something to screw up this happy time for my family? What if I even hurt the baby? I started worrying about that constantly. Something might go wrong with the little life in my sister's stomach.

I even told the Wednesday night group about it: "Yes, but how do I know for sure that I'm not going to like, punch her in the belly or push her down a flight of stairs or something?"

Bill said, "That sounds exactly like me when my wife gave birth to our son. I always worried that I might get up in the middle of the night and smother the baby. I couldn't even drive with just the baby and myself in the car without having to pull over every so often and do some breathing exercises."

"This is a really common thing with OCDers or anyone who has a lot of anxiety," Dr. B said. "A new little one in the family heightens the feeling that you have to be in control of everything and responsible for everyone."

Amy the hypochondriac had tears in her eyes. "Oh my God, I completely understand," she said, "I never told anyone this before, but I used to think about putting my newborn in the microwave."

Sometimes it was really unbelievable, the stuff I heard at group.

I learned that for every irrational thought, it helps to say it out loud or write it down and replace it with a positive counterthought. At home I took a piece of paper and wrote: *What if I hurt the baby?* Next to it I wrote: *I won't hurt the baby.* But that didn't seem to help at all. At the next private meeting with Dr. B I showed him my paper and said, "I know what I'm supposed to be doing, but seriously, all I can think about is my sister coming home from the hospital with this beautiful new baby and then the next thought is me being carted off to prison while my sister is left childless and hates me forever."

He told me that just writing down *I won't hurt the baby* wasn't enough. "You know that exercise where you write down the feelings you expect to come from anxiety and how—"

"Expect and Accept," I said. "Yeah, my old therapist was all over that exercise."

"Because it works."

I shrugged. God, is this what it's going to be like forever? Every damn event that happens in life, I'll have to pull it apart like when you're trying to separate colors in a pack of Play-Doh. Pay someone a hundred bucks an hour to help me dissect all the crap that swirls around in my mind. That day in the car when Kim told me about the baby on its way, I think I must have said three or four times, "I'm going to be a good auntie. I'm going to be a good auntie." Now I was told to go home and write about all the reasons why I thought I *wouldn't* make a good auntie, underline the one that seemed the most significant (called the "hot thought"), then write down three reasons why I believe the hot thought is stuck in my head. My journal entry went something like this:

What if I hurt Kim while she's pregnant?

When the baby comes, what if I do what Bill said and try to smother it?

I'm going to suck at being an auntie. I don't know a thing about what an aunt's supposed to do.

What if I try to stick it in the microwave?

I could only think of one reason why my hot thought was the one I underlined:

Because I've sucked at being a sister and a daughter.

Kim kept saying it was going to be such a great experience for me, and how she just knew I'd love having a niece or nephew. "If it's a girl I hope she's as smart and funny as you," she said.

"Right," I said, sniggering. "You forgot, totally loving and caring person."

"But you are," my sister answered. "You've always been a good person."

Pregnancy was making rainbows all over the damn place. So much of me wanted to believe her. I seriously don't think I'd ever heard anyone tell me that I was a good person before. I wanted to be good. I wanted to be normal. I wanted to be someone who didn't provoke chest pains in her mother, someone who could go to a party without making sure she had a paper bag to hyperventilate in or checking to see where the easiest exits were.

And just like Glenda was always saying, Dr. B told me and everyone at group, "You really have to think about the idea that OCD tendencies are something that may not leave you for good. Yes, journaling gets old; yes, dissecting every feeling gets old, but fifteen minutes a day with a pen or tape recorder is a small price to pay for the benefits of learning about yourself."

Kim and I had stopped at a garage sale before going to Denny's that afternoon. We sifted through baby clothes and I watched my sister, her mascara smudged from happy tears, the way every word between us was the most important word in the world. It was exciting and fun to look at all the little onesies and knitted caps, but for one second I let myself hold the moment in my head and think, Why you? Why do you get these happy times without having to feel like a complete crazy person? Am I ever going to have that?

My sister picked up a ceramic angel and paid the garage sale lady fifty cents.

"Oh, that's kind of pretty," I said. It looked like Mary praying, sending God a wish list.

The garage sale lady said, "Her wings used to light up and change different glittery colors. Here, let me take her for a second. I don't think the light works on her anymore." She took the statue into her garage and brought it back. "How about just taking it," she said. "I plugged her in and she definitely doesn't work."

My sister asked me what I thought. "Is she too worn down? Maybe it's just something in the wiring that can be fixed."

I looked at the defective Mary and her wings that would never sparkle. "No, she's all right," I said. "Forget about fixing her. She'd be pretty just sitting on a shelf." I turned her around in my hand. Even at different angles she wasn't all that bad.

part three

I wanted to know if you would ever be interested in building your own house?

—BJÖRK, *INTERVIEW* MAGAZINE

16

i like the drugs
and the drugs like me

I do not fail to recognize that god is in touch with my mom.
Even if he's crossed me off his call sheet.
—ELIZABETH CRANE, "YEAR-AT-A-GLANCE"

In two weeks the new owners will come to the rest home and take over my grandmother's business. Today we'll finish packing the things we need to take. Yesterday we threw my mother's ashes in the Saratoga River, the same river she was baptized in only three years ago. My sister was with her that day. Both of them had raised their arms while Glenda read passages about salvation. I was most likely in fourth-period history when they were all sharing God. Or in the nurse's office trying to sleep. Whatever I was doing or trying not to be, I wasn't there when Glenda baptized my mother, when she told her to hold her breath, her hand supporting the back and shoulders of her friend as she went under the water. I was only there to see the remains of my mother's body submerged in fragments of clear water and busted chalk. I had always wondered if there was a color to our entirety. In a small cardboard box it's gray. In a river it's white, then clouds, then nothing. The Polaroid of my mother and sister on the afternoon of her baptism shows my mom in a yellow muumuu, Kim in a white tank top with the Aqua Net still clinging to her curled bangs. There's a fuzzy white oblong shape above my mother's head.

"My angel," she had said.

Later I would wonder: if that was true, where the hell was this winged miracle two days after Christmas when the doctor told us her lungs were so full of blood and fluid she'd be lucky if she made it through the night?

It was the start of fall in 1989 when the doctors diagnosed my mother with a rare and sudden case of eosinophilia myalgia, a disease caused by the toxins from a genetically engineered herbal supplement she'd been taking to help her sleep. By the end of October her muscles were "like jelly." In November she sat up in her hospital bed with her hair all done up, her rouge too dark. The oxygen tubes in her nose had made her lips so dry that every time she smiled she'd touch her mouth with a bruised and bandaged finger. Me, Kim, Grammie, and Gil brought her a Thanksgiving dinner on my grandmother's good dinner plates. She ate a little mashed potatoes, mostly picked, so grateful for the pattern of yellow roses. She fell asleep before I opened my birthday present. A silver and turquoise watch she had wrapped herself in *AWESOME 18!* gift wrap. Some of the tape was the fabric kind, like on the IV that was now fastened to her jugular because every other vein had had enough. At her bedside was a mauve plastic mug with a sticker on it: HAPPY HOLIDAYS FROM ALL THE STAFF AT ALEXIAN BROTHERS HOSPITAL.

For months Glenda babbled on about "everything's perfect in the time it happens, all we can do is hold on to our faith. . . ." Bullshit like that. By the time Christmas rolled around there was nothing anyone could do but hold my mother's hand and pretend the ice in a cup of Sprite she couldn't even drink was something of importance. I decided the mysterious white shape in the photograph at her baptismal had been a trick of the camera. Angels are lies.

"You know, it was cold like this when Glenda baptized me and Mom," Kim said. She held a packing-tape dispenser in her hand and used her foot to stabilize the lid of the box labeled *Kitchen Stuff*. "The air was just the same as it is now. It was so damn cold in that river."

"It's cold today, Mommy," my niece said. "Maybe it's Christmas again." She jumped around and pressed a stuffed alien with a nose like a guiro shaker against her little body. "Here, Mommy. Look at Alf. Alf thinks it's Christmas. Tell Alf it's Christmas."

I picked up little Bethany and kissed the magic of her baby fat. "We just had Christmas, remember?"

"There was Christmas at the hospital," she said. "Does *Grandmama* come home after Christmas?"

Kim pressed the tape dispenser onto the creases of the box. "That water was like little icicles. I don't ever remember being so cold." When she snapped the tape against the teeth of the blade it made a sound like a spine twisting.

"Bethany, why don't you come here?" I said. "Let Auntie give you a snack." I poured Froot Loops into a Dixie cup and filled my niece's bottle with orange juice. Then I fixed the old people a little dish of ice cream. We had tried to get as many of the residents as we could out of the house while we packed up my grandmother's stuff before the new owners took over. Having them watch us remove furniture and pictures that had been around some of them for six years would have been too distressing. When the decision had been made to sell the nursing home, just after my mother died, we had a big meeting to let the residents know a lot was going to change. Most of them didn't really care one way or the other. Many were already gone. Marisol had been moved to an Alzheimer's facility, then passed away a month later from congestive heart failure. She died in the very same hospital on the very same day my sister gave birth to my niece. Everyone was too excited to care about the symbolism. I saw my grandmother in the elevator and asked her why she was going to the fifth floor when maternity was on the third.

"I need to pick up some papers for Marisol's son," she said. "She died last night."

So calm. Her and her end-of-life business.

She would not act very differently upon learning that her only child had passed away.

Evelyn with the Glasses was still at the home; so was Mr. Gray. Captain had to be moved to a facility that could handle his immobility. His habit of calling me "whore" had progressed to telling everyone to "fuck off" whenever it was time to put on his prosthetic legs.

About ten times a week Glenda said, "Oh my God, oh honey, you are too young to lose your mother."

I guess. But eighteen really felt no different from fifteen, from ten, from whenever I started not feeling like a kid. Actually I'd been more like an adult for the past few months since I moved into my own apartment. A real adult, whatever that was supposed to mean. When the doctor told us our mother was gone, I felt like the only thing to do was to be gone too. Since Kim now managed a scummy apartment complex on the ghetto east side of San Jose, the best I could think of was to sign a six-month lease. Everyone said I should live at the nursing home and eventually run it as my own business. Over the past year, my grandmother's diabetic problems had become too much for her to take care of her health and maintain her business. She'd been in and out of the hospital with kidney and heart problems and missed all her mandatory classes to renew her business license. When she received a letter from the county saying she had to take a complete physical, she decided it was time to quit. "The only time I get outta here is to cart myself off to the emergency room," she said, then admitted she couldn't wait to get back into playing cards and betting on horses. "Hell, you're never too sick for blackjack. You can be half in, half out of the grave and still manage to find a ride to a casino."

After she'd spent a month on dialysis, instead of recovering at home like she was supposed to, we got a postcard from Reno with a funny drawing of a cactus she turned into Cactus Man with a comic bubble escaping from its little Cactus Man mouth: "A hug from Grammie and Cactus Man."

On the phone my brother said, "It seems to me like she's just trying to pass her responsibilities onto us."

Funny. That's exactly what my sister and I thought about my brother the night we called him to tell him that our mother might not make it. He had screamed into the phone, "Don't lay any guilt trips on me. I can't just pick up and run to her bedside! I have to go through the Red Cross and all their paperwork to get an emergency leave of absence."

Most of our phone calls with my brother now ended with Kim in tears. "I'm sick of being everyone's mother." She said this all the time now. She said no one cared how she felt. Bryan said she was selfish. I said they were both big babies. How quickly the air between the children of a dead mother becomes a space of new resentment. At least we had the good sense to know we could never be business partners.

Kim and I put bubble wrap around our grandmother's plants. "I really feel like this is a huge weight off of us, don't you?"

I shrugged. "What do you mean?"

"I mean this place was always a little depressing to me."

Even though I agreed with a nod, I didn't feel that way. After all, it was while living here among the soft minds of people who didn't have a choice that I started the process of seeing my own mind as my own choice. In this house, with its piss-scented bedrooms, my grandmother's greasy cooking, and me so afflicted—orphaned, almost—everything opened. That's the rule of healing. It was in this house, in my awesome purple bedroom with my Madonna poster and all my books, where I poured myself into spiraling/journaling out of control; where I stayed up all night reading things about OCD and anxiety, learning how other people are just as worried as I am about spontaneous fires breaking out in the bedrooms of their loved ones. This is the place where they wheeled away Mr. Pacheco's dead body, where the allure of death grew into a breathing beast, a thing with eyes, ignorant of its beautiful revolt. In the little yellow room down the hallway, Marisol introduced me to Pablo Neruda and cold medicine. Those weren't depressing things, not for me, anyway. Maybe Kim meant the balance rails attached to the walls of the hallways or the day my grandmother called an ambulance to come get my mother because she was in the bathroom clutching at her clothes and her skin was so white and at first it was hard to tell if she was crying or suffocating.

In the weeks that followed the sale of the nursing home I did a lot of Nyquil napping. Sometimes I skimmed through college course booklets, mostly for fun. I felt like the ease of doing nothing was all I could handle. Kim and I split the remainder of my mother's tranquilizers. We cried while we did it. Despicable. Happy. Then one night I called Theresa and begged her to pick me up because I was dying.

"You have to take me to the hospital," I cried into the phone. "I need to go to the emergency room. I can't feel my arms."

She and her boyfriend were moving to Texas the next day. I didn't care about how selfish I was being when I asked her to drop everything and pick me up; all I knew was I had just taken four Halcion. My heart was the size of a football (you don't have to see these things to know these things). The muscles in my shoulders, all the way down to my hands, felt like electrocution. I needed to find the comfort I had always found with a stethoscope and the reassurance that it wasn't me who was about to die. The muse that only the word *maybe* can bring.

"Where's your dad?" Theresa asked. "I can take you and everything, just calm down, but he's closer. Maybe you should call him."

But I had already tried that. Sarah was sick with a flu bug and the auto shop hadn't finished installing the new stereo in their new car and didn't I think it was time to stand on my own two feet? It was getting to that point with my sister too. Since our mother died our roles had become so blurred. For all those times she had to act as my stand-in mom, hold her breath until she could run her own life, be her own woman, now it was as if she was pushing me away with each exhale.

After an EKG and the denial of my plea for something—*please, just give me something*—to help me stop shaking, the ER doctor asked me how many times I'd been seen for this sort of thing. He clamped down the metal cover to my chart—hard. "You've been in here a few times now. Isn't that right?"

"I don't know," I answered. I was so sweaty. "God, what could be causing my arms to tingle like this?"

Without even looking at me, without even checking to see if my blood oxygen was normal, if my thyroid needed testing, if my liver enzymes were up, if my urine protein was okay, the doctor said, "I think it's the same thing that's been bringing you in here all the other times. Just stress." And when he told me I needed to be on medication, I felt like I was the only patient in the hospital—possibly the only patient in any hospital ever—since the beginning of hospital time.

I remember this girl in Dr. Benette's group who was just starting Prozac and said she had dreams where she was eating her own face. Roxy said that was a cool story but sounded very made up. "I totally don't know anything about Prozac and stuff, but she's talking like someone on acid."

The night I took my first dose of antidepressant medication, I reminded myself of that, convinced myself I was not turning my life into a paragraph from a Hunter S. Thompson story. I was also put on a drug called Buspar, a slow-acting antianxiety medication that works on your central nervous system so you're not lit up all the time. Almost right away those pills helped my mind to stop flashing neon. It hushed long enough to let me cry about not having a mother anymore and would later help me cry about all those times I couldn't cry at all. By the end of just two weeks on the Buspar I was literally seeing the words *feel this*. I even checked out two books on turn-of-the-century psychical and paranormal research and actually read both of them back to back. Slow was excellent for concentration but it worried me a little.

I called Glenda and asked her if this feeling of being okay was okay. "Well, I know Prozac is helping a lot of people," she said. "I know it takes a while, something like a month to kick in, but antianxiety medi-cation, I don't know. You have to be careful there, Traci. Your mom liked Valium an awful lot."

I read as much as I could from those pharmacy pamphlets they give you when you start a new medication. I figured when the time came to feel super, I'd be ready.

That's not exactly how it happened.

There really wasn't a beginning of any kind of special feeling; it was more like a slow end to all those feelings that made me think in terms of the word *special. Separate. Sadder than you.* The first place I felt different was in my spine. I don't know another way to explain it. My back became full of something gelatinous and flowing. The opposite of glass. I didn't feel like I had to jump up and run away. The oscillating place just above my tailbone was gone. Even when I cried. Even when I screamed. I didn't cast fire. For a while it was upsetting not to feel that anymore, that familiar part of me that caused my brother to call me Spaz and made a running dialogue in my mind like toxic water. Erratic was leaving. Imbalance was waving good-bye.

From all the stuff I learned on the subject of mood-altering drugs, I found out that when antidepressants start working it's common for people to miss their hyperemotional life—the crazy, depressed, anx-ious way they've been living. When the drugs start kicking in, the familiar becomes unfamiliar. Then you get sad over not being sad. I felt like I was losing an important part of myself. Who was I sup-posed to be if I couldn't be upset about everything all the time? From such an early age, being me meant being annoyed, scratchy some-how. Sounds were too high, the ground wasn't stable—even when I tried, it was hard to conjure a memory where something wasn't wrong. I said this to the doctor when I went back for a refill. He asked me about the times I was in therapy and if that was something I wanted to continue.

"I don't know what I want to do," I told him. "I lost my mother not long ago and my family's just—everything's a little crazy right now."

"I can give you a couple of samples as refills," he said. "But I'm required by law to recommend that you start seeing a psychiatrist to keep you on a maintenance program."

"I don't think I can do that," I said. "The minute I turned eighteen my father couldn't get me off his health insurance fast enough." I got teary at that part and felt stupid when the doctor handed me a Kleenex.

He asked me if I was going to school.

"Not really. I just finished my GED so I could graduate. I don't have any money to get back into therapy."

The doctor gave me hotline numbers and a list of group meetings all over the Bay Area. Some cost as much as $150 a session. Only the ones on the side of town where every drive-through restaurant had bulletproof glass were free. One of the groups had a special late-night service for people who felt like they wanted to jump off the Golden Gate Bridge. I actually called that group. I wanted to hear what the voice was like on the other end of the line. Who was the person who talked people out of tossing themselves into the cold Pacific Ocean? Although the woman sounded as warm as someone who's reading from a script can be, if I wasn't interested in hurling my body into the foggy sky of San Francisco, it was clear she had other calls to take. She did, however, put me on a mailing list with the National Mental Health Association. From their agency I got tons of information, including a brochure with jovial little drawings of the human brain and Mr. Neurotransmitter (suspiciously sketched to resemble an ovary). I learned words like *serotonin* and *dopamine* and how the cognitive systems of people with many mental illnesses have a tendency to overlook the production of these things. I read and journaled until I felt like I completely understood how the medication worked. These weren't make-the-world-go-away pills. The plan was this: help my brain do what it was meant to do all along—produce serotonin and take it to Mr. Neurotransmitter. It was strange to think that I could've been born like this—*mentally ill.* One brochure talked about accepting medication like a diabetic takes insulin. *You wouldn't ask someone with unstable blood sugar to stop their injections or suddenly dive headfirst into a piece of German chocolate cake.* I liked that.

But even with the changes I felt approaching, since the death of my mother I'd had such a hard time keeping myself organized when it came to being on my own. You have to do a lot of grown-up stuff when you become a grown-up. I knew there was going to be a check coming soon from the sale of the nursing home—my grandmother put the money for all three of us kids into a trust so it could be divided evenly (later I would figure out that my inability to focus and understand numbers would make the words *distribute evenly* mean something entirely different for my share of the money).

I used the anticipated check to ignore my bills. When I first moved into Kim's apartments, I was practically running a day care out of my roach-infested one bedroom. I watched six kids, sometimes for mothers who paid me in food stamps or IOUs. Twice my brother sent me fifty bucks. My dad—never. For a few months a guy moved in with me who was kind of a boyfriend, though more so on the days before my gas was due to be shut off. I tried to tell my dad that I wanted to be in a better apartment, that I didn't want to rely on a man I didn't even love to pay my bills.

He said he had no idea what I wanted from him.

"I need some help to move," I said. "Like a first and last month's rent on a place that's a little more affordable." All resulting in me having a complete meltdown, crying and carrying on, screaming he had never been there for me, never helped my mother with child support, you did this and you did that. . . . Some of it was true, some just the dangling threads of a baby's blanket.

In between her gambling escapades and trying to get her health in check, my grandmother would give me a few hundred dollars coupled with an hour lecture on people having to take responsibility for their own lives. "You gotta get a stable roommate in here or something, Traci. You've gotta find a way to support yourself."

So one day I just went for it and asked a bunch of strangers for money. I'm talking about a real pity party, with chips and drinks. In a creepy, third-person voice, and taking direction from those televangelists my mother was so in love with, I made invitations on index cards with crayons and stickers of Kirk Cameron. I passed them around my apartment complex:

> Dear friends: Traci needs her medication. Her mother is dead. Her boyfriend has had enough of her and her father is a jackass. These medications are over a hundred dollars a month. In the interest of good mental health, please come to her party and donate as much as you can.

A whole bunch of people showed up. Everyone loved the beer and chicken strips. The old man who lived above my sister brought an econo-size bottle of Advil. Not a single person gave any money. I should have written on the invitation: *I'm not joking, either.*

Just as the party was winding down, I was standing on my balcony smoking when I caught sight of my sister in her bathrobe striding across the lawn.

"You must be some kind of an idiot." She was holding one of my invitations. "Did you think I wouldn't find out about this or what?"

The information that came with the boxes of Buspar strongly cautioned against mixing alcohol with the drug. The night of my party I overlooked that warning. "Unless you're here to make a contribution," I told my sister, "please refrain from your sarcastic tone."

She didn't believe that I needed money for my medication. She thought I was peddling to shop for furniture.

"Well, here they are." I swayed a little and shoved an orange box in her face. "Call me a liar now." Then I bowed like friends from China. "Ahhh sooo . . . Big retarded sister to apologize to little retarded sister?"

She tossed the box on the old suitcase I used as a coffee table, "These look like samples to me."

"They are. That's all I can afford now. I go to the free clinic and make up stories so they'll give me free samples."

"Make up stories?"

I slumped into my purple beanbag. "Yep. That's the best way. The Prozac is easier to get than the Buspar," I said. "I had to tell the doctor I had post-traumatic stress disorder from doing volunteer work in the Persian Gulf."

"Are you serious?" she asked. "Well, maybe you should think about going into the military. At least it would be something for you to do."

I told her as soon as I got my check from the nursing home I was going to enroll at West Valley College.

"That's something, I guess." She picked up a plastic tumbler and sniffed it. "It's a start to getting your act together."

The next day that act would include trying not talk like a woman sedated in front of the student loan officer.

"And you work how many jobs?" Angela Spitz was the name on the financial aid door. That had to be a sign, I thought—a test for me to pay attention and keep straight, to not act mental.

"I'm just babysitting right now, Miss Spitz," I said.

She told me to call her Angela and said she liked my Blond Ambition World Tour T-shirt. She also told me not to be surprised if my Pell grant paperwork got held up due to me scoring an embarrassing 200 on the SATs. "That's about as low as you can go," she said.

And you've got the gayest last name I've ever heard. Why don't you stop worrying about my SAT scores and change your last name? "My mother had no life insurance," I blurted out—nothing to do with anything. "And my father has a sweet little life with a sweet little wife."

If it was hard for me to accept the diagnosis as a mental patient, I sure as hell was doing a good job of acting like one. At first I wasn't going to hate Angela Spitz and her lavender-tinted glasses or the fact that she was about sixty and had a mouthful of braces and the point of that is so nonexistent there isn't even a way to describe how pointless it is, but then she suggested that I pay for my first semester on my own.

"I can get you started on applying for some other programs, but I don't know if any of them will pan out in time for spring classes."

While I half listened to her suggestions and questions—could I possibly be more than three-quarters Native American? Was my father disabled from a war injury? Some war? Any war?—I thought about the possibility of me paying for one semester on my own, but it made me nauseous, swirly. I wondered how many antianxiety pills I had left at home and how many packages of ramen noodles I could buy with two dollars.

17

---

we hate it when our friends become successful

I pretended to myself that my loneliness was special.
—DAVID FOSTER WALLACE, "GOOD OLD NEON"

The lameness of my life made me feel like I wanted to kill myself. The drugs, I think, prevented that from actually happening. But no matter how much potential came with each dose or what number was printed after the word *refill*, there still wasn't any money for school. I called my dad and hinted that maybe he could help me out with classes and books and stuff.

"I'd love to see what you've got going on." Then he took me to Kentucky Fried Chicken for dinner. That was it.

Roxy said I shouldn't be flipping out about the upcoming spring semester. "How expensive can junior college be, for crying out loud? It's not like you're going to Harvard or anything like that."

Right—telling me this while we're in Target buying pens and notebooks for when she starts the travel agency school her parents just shelled out three thousand dollars for.

One night I said to Glenda, "Everything seems like a complete and total waste of time." We were on the little cement balcony of my apartment, drinking instant coffee by the lights of the search helicopter. I had the physician's desk reference opened on the TV tray beside me; Glenda had her cigarettes and Psalms. We both had a secret prayer that everyone would hold off on the shooting until we went back inside.

"Nothing we do is a waste of time," she said. "Everything leads up to the people we're becoming."

"Yeah?" I said, blowing into my cup of expired Nescafé from the ninety-nine-cent store. "So what if we have no idea about the person we're supposed to be?"

Her answer was a smile and a long drag from her smoke.

"I just feel so hopeless," I said.

"You're not off your medication, are you?"

"No, I wouldn't really say I'm off it, but I'm having a hard time figuring out the bus schedule and getting downtown to the doctor's."

Glenda pressed her lips together and shook her head. "Do you ever ask your sister if she can drive you to your appointments?"

"Not really." Actually I had, a few times, and what I got was a reminder about being almost twenty years old and having no idea of the challenges of being a working mom. "You taking the bus shouldn't be a problem," Kim said. "What you really need to do is forget about the antidepressants for a while and let me show you how to smoke pot."

Glenda said she didn't have any control over how the buses ran. "But maybe I can help you get into a program where you can receive at least one of your medications for free."

All I had to do to qualify for each refill—only two weeks' worth of pills—was get myself to the old immigration services building that didn't even have a sign on it anymore and seemed to have disappeared from all public transportation maps (unless you happen to be sitting next to a prostitute on the bus who advises you to use the alley behind the Amor Caliente Playhouse), then sit in a waiting room that smelled like oily hair for six hours so I could speak to a social worker for five minutes while she assessed all my psychotic needs. You had to be careful though. Not enough sob in your story and they could end up taking you off the program entirely; too much and there'd be seventy-two hours of soft walls with no telephone privileges. The check from the sale of the nursing home still hadn't come. I was too embarrassed to keep asking Kim about it. When she and I were in my grandmother's attorney's office, and the estate agent said she would send us a breakdown of fees and disbursements, my sister pointed to me and sniggered, "You're going to have to *really* break it down for this one. Put a column of numbers in front of her and she starts hyperventilating."

Whatever. But I did end up losing all the paperwork on account of who the hell would try to squeeze something like ten pages of legal-size documents onto three regular-size pieces of paper by photocopying it into the smallest font size possible, then marking all kinds of zeros and blank spots with highlighter pens that don't even match? Sign here, sign there, never mind the uneven number of *sign here* stickers and that one *sign here* was actually handwritten and totally smeared. Why not just mark all the *sign here* places with the same damn stickers? I don't know what happened between mailing back my paperwork and *sign here*, but I do remember sitting in Mr. Chau Donuts next to the post office trying to concoct a story of never receiving my paperwork in the first place. It was difficult to come up with anything believable, because I hadn't had any Buspar for four days and was all buzzy about trying to organize my thoughts. I kept eating jelly donuts until something sounded believable, but then a red blobby *S* fell onto my napkin, which made me think of dollar signs, which made me wonder how I was going to prevent my cable from being turned off and how fitting if they turned it off tonight when this new show called *Melrose Place* was coming on because it totally looked like something I could get very used to.

By the end of the week I was crying on the phone to Glenda. "I just got a letter about not qualifying for my student loan because that stu-

pid woman wrote something in my paperwork about the money I'm
supposed to get from the sale of the nursing home."

It had begun to thunder outside. I seriously thought the weather
was about me. "Well, what did you tell her?" Glenda asked. "How
would she just know that you're getting some money?"

Snot dripped from my nose. My life was one of those lives where
you have to weigh the importance of Kleenex over hot dogs. "I guess I
mentioned it, but it was just like, from us talking or whatever. I didn't
say, 'Oh, I'm getting a big ol' chunk of change.' She asked me if I was
expecting any money from the sale of any kind of property. I mean,
what a stupid question—"

"Traci, calm down now," Glenda said. "I wish you would've let me
come there with you. She's got to disclose information like that. You
can't lie to the government when you're trying to get their money."

"I know, but I was—and plus she was kind of making fun of me
about my SAT scores and then she was all—"

"No. No. There's nothing you can do about it now," Glenda said.
"Look, let's make a breakfast date tomorrow. I've been thinking about
trying to see if we can qualify you for disability."

"What do you mean, disability?" I asked. "I'm not a cripple."

But during our Denver omelets at Bob's Big Boy, Glenda made some
really good points. "If you qualified for more government programs,"
she said, "it would be easier to get money for school. I've helped fill
out lots of applications for people who suffer from anxiety disorders."

I took a slow, unfulfilling bite. The eggs tasted off. It was the first
time I heard the word *suffer* in the same sentence as *anxiety disorder*. I
never once thought that word: *suffer*. That word made me think of the
Vietnam vets in Santa Cruz, pushing their wheelchairs with just one
arm; the picture of our dusty sponsor child from when I was little; that
goddamn HAPPY HOLIDAYS mug by my mother's bed in the ICU.

Glenda went on. "If you could get on disability, maybe you would
qualify for a special-education program."

"Whoa, hold on. What do you mean, special education?" I thought about the Dig It kids from Mr. Delgado's class. I rubbed my chin as if saliva were dripping from it.

"You'd have to visit an education psychologist," Glenda said. "But I can help you with the rest. Look, obsessive-compulsive disorder is a real disease; you're taking medications for a bona fide anxiety disorder."

My head was like the eggs in the omelet.

"I don't know," I said. Outside, the late-winter storm that had come in during the night exaggerated everything. From my place in the restaurant booth I watched the windmills on the miniature Dutch houses across the street at Golfland. The rain fell sideways. Metallic and literal. In my mind I jumped up and declared, "No! I'm not a disability girl!" I wanted Glenda to remind me how far I'd come from the seven-year-old spaz who obsessed over cross-contamination from the lunch meat in the refrigerator. Of course I needed the money. Of course not having to choose between groceries and textbooks would've been ideal, but filing for disability? It just seemed so degrading. Beneath me. People who received money from programs like that did things like keep forty cats in a studio apartment or wear latex gloves to make a phone call.

I guess I thought the way to really convince myself I was brave enough to apply for state benefits was to tell my sister about it. Her advice to not do something usually helped me get right in there and go for it.

"You're going to watch six children in that tiny apartment? That's insane." "Why would you want a futon instead of a regular bed? They're supposed to be awful for your back." "I have no idea why you keep choosing boyfriends who are just as unmotivated about their futures as you are."

I waited in my sister's office while she showed an apartment to a new tenant, inhaling the smells of her Charlie cologne and cigarettes on a shelf. Behind her desk were pictures of Gil and Bethany and my mother.

The photograph of the complex grounds on the wall had the sky colored in to look extra blue, the grass all fake emeralds. The only times I came into the office were to make a half payment on my rent or see if there were any vacant apartments I could clean for twenty dollars. When I first moved in, I imagined living in the same building as my sister, her bringing Bethany to my place when she needed a break, insisting I come to dinner on the nights she attempted my mother's turkey noodle soup. None of that happened. Not once. Her apartment was full of my mother's furniture and *her* family's stuff. It almost seemed as if she'd been relieved of her duties as the sister who was nine years older than me. Not once after my mother's death was I ever asked how I felt about it, or even if I would like to take some of her things.

"Mom's oil painting of Noah's Ark," I said, pointing to a picture above my sister's kitchen table. "I'd really like to have that."

But all Kim did was shrug and brush her bangs from her face, because very busy people have no time to worry about nineteen-year-old sisters and the charity they expect. Ever since I could remember, I'd been telling people to leave me alone and let me do things my way, that I could handle myself and didn't need to be spoon-fed directions and rules. Now here was my chance, and I wasn't sure what to do with it.

My apartment was to remain a stucco dot on that colored-in photo.

When I told my sister of my plan to get on government assistance, she asked me what disease I would use for disability.

"What do you mean, *use*?" I asked.

"I mean, you're not disabled." She opened file cabinets and made movements around her office that were so different than when she was just a sister. "So I'm not sure why you're trying to get government benefits if you're not even sick."

"To go to school," I said.

"Uh-huh. But the thing is, Traci, you need to work like a regular person. School costs money. You don't have any."

"Okay, so are you even listening to what I'm trying to tell you?" I asked. "Glenda said I could—"

"Glenda said. Glenda said—" She pressed buttons on the fax machine. "Glenda's not God, you know."

Someone came in needing a spare key. A single mom I'd seen at the swimming pool a few times. Denise, Debbie? She was always so hectic and out of breath.

"You know, you should really get a spare made," Kim told her. "Don't you think it's irresponsible to keep locking yourself out?"

It was wrong for me to be there with that poor woman and my sister above us all. She opened the cabinet in a way that suggested her life hadn't quite turned out the way she had expected either, and there just wasn't enough pity to spare.

It was almost February when the check from the nursing home finally arrived. I bought some furniture from Kmart, and despite my not having a driver's license due to how heavily I started breathing during the written exam and the line to the bathroom at the DMV being filled with people who looked contagious, I purchased my first car. A very used Fiat—red, mixed with primer and purple stick-on window tints; paint bubbles as thick as a hooker's breath. The guy who sold it to me threw in one of those heavy-duty upholstery staplers so I could keep up with the floating pieces of fabric on the interior roof. The engine sputtered and gagged and I had to teach myself how to drive a stick, convince myself that downshifting was only counting backwards and not real math and probably safer than driving around town in second gear.

"Do we share parking spaces or will I get my own?" Grammie asked. We were moving her stuff into my apartment. "I want my own. It's better that way, don't wanna be parkin' next to someone who can peek in my window and see all my eight-tracks." The plan was my grandmother would stay with me while recovering from the surgery she'd had to repair ripped tendons on the bottom of her feet. Seeing all that old furniture in my tiny space made me feel like a drugged genie in a defective bottle. Her antique dresser with the marks where I had stuck all that tape when I was afraid about my grandfather's horrible statues, all her medical stuff, her dishes with the little circles of faded yellow flowers. Newspapers and moving vans would pass through years of different houses in different places; the dish set wouldn't stay together: four cups in a garage sale I didn't authorize, a platter of sweet potato pie in the house of a neighbor without family—the strays to pop up if a drowsy kid needed a clean cereal bowl. Whenever Roxy found one she'd say, "God, I totally remember these dishes from the nursing home." Never would I mention that my mother ate her last meal in the hospital on one of these dishes, or how I held the plate longer than usual before putting the aluminum foil back on, searching her sad attempts at eating the mashed potatoes for whatever it is we leave behind as we make our last memories.

My grandmother had already given me the money for almost two months' rent. That right there cut off the privilege to use the word *crowded* or bring up the death of daughters. Money makes room for a lot of dishes. While I could breathe a little, I went ahead and signed up for a bunch of classes that would in no way provide any skills for the future use of gainful employment: Comparative Poetry, Drama, and Celtic Mythology. I was so happy the day I bought my school supplies, I splurged on Sizzler for me and my grandmother and had to bring my shopping bag into the restaurant. I organized my new backpack right there in the booth, like when I was ten and had just had my ears pierced and the idea of walking around with my own tube of Neosporin in a little silver makeup bag was as important as a new planet.

"What I'd really like to do," I told my grandmother, "is teach poetry, maybe do a little screenwriting work on the side—maybe move to LA and work on a comedy."

Grammie said she wasn't sure about the whole screenplay business. "Don't you have to know somebody to break into something like that?"

"No," I answered sharply. "That's not what it's like at all."

"You type so fast," she said. "I was a-thinkin' you should go to secretarial school."

I laughed and sniffed my box of pencils. "I'm so sure, Grammie. It's nineteen ninety, they don't even have secretarial schools anymore. I know I won't have any trouble finding a job where I can write or teach some kind of writing." Even as I said these words—so much confidence in my voice, defiance through my all-you-can-eat shrimp—something about it didn't seem real, steady enough. It felt like another one of my screenplays sent to the wrong address.

One night I came home with a first-place award for a short story I wrote about a soldier who passes away slowly and full of shrapnel after a Tet Offensive in Vietnam. To celebrate, Grammie took me to see *Steel Magnolias,* but we had to leave the theater during the graveyard scene when Sally Field's character breaks down about the untimely death of her daughter.

I had never seen my grandmother cry before that night.

"No one can understand this pain," she said in the car. It scared me a little, her face so red and her eyes squeezed shut. "I didn't think it would be like this."

I handed her a wad of napkins from the glove compartment. As awful as it was—the mother of my mother, weeping for the loss of her only child—the release in a moment like that is somehow stronger than the burden. On the last night before her death, my mother's ICU room was filled with doctors and nurses in surgical masks. They needed to push a drainage tube into the side of her body and empty her lungs. Everyone heard my mother try to scream the word *Mom.* I watched my grammie at the nurses' station desk. Her strong, square fingers clutched her walking cane. She closed her eyes when she said, "Nurse, how long do you think this will take?" Those colorless words terrified me, the nothingness over my grandmother's face. Now she was letting me cry with her, both of us talking in easy, strange whispers.

It was Sunday when I finally opened the letter from the disability folks. The thing had sat for nearly a week under a stack of unpaid bills on my kitchen counter. I'd mistaken the blue envelope for a cable shut-off notice. There were also a bunch of my mother's credit card notices that had come to my grandmother. She said we needed to write *deceased* on them and send them all back. That wasn't going to happen. Sooner or later I guess the credit brass from Mervyns would just have to figure out on their own that my mother was never coming back to their Early Bird Christmas sale and that the two of us would never again wait in her car with Thanksgiving smells still in our hair while KLOK Radio played a Helen Reddy Christmas album: *Deceased.* That one word in black ink across white envelopes would have all those things in it.

When I went to throw that crap away I noticed the Great Seal of California on a letter addressed to me. The State had spoken. They said I wasn't crazy enough to get their money. My own voice was a condescending teacher in my head when it said, *See how stupid you were to try?* All my life I had been fighting to be normal, and now when I needed to be not-normal, they wouldn't go for it. I fished around in the pantry for something to eat and pretended I didn't care. I fixed a platter of stale tortilla chips and salsa and brought it to Grammie who waited on the sofa so we could watch Bob Saget introduce video clips of people falling down in a funny way. I drank a Fresca and tried to concentrate on grandparents blowing false teeth into birthday cakes, confused ponies bucking children from their backs.

I said, "Whatever. That's not even funny." I said it until I was asked why.

"I thought you loved this show?"

"Uh-huh. I'm going to the gas station for a Slurpee. Do you want anything? A Diet Coke or something?"

Grammie waved her hand and laughed. "Hell, you think one baby a-throwin' up in their daddy's face would be enough. Honey, come on and put a few pillows under my feet." Like everything the past year, my grandmother's foot surgery had turned into complications and seriousness. The doctors had come very close to amputating. "You wanna go ahead and get me some glycerin suppositories and a case of Diet Rite?"

"I didn't say I was going to the store now. I'm just going to the gas station. There aren't any suppositories there."

She bent over the heaviness of her middle and rubbed her calves. "Well, you go ahead and do what you want. I'm just telling you I've been real constipated all week."

"I think we need to walk a little more," I said. "You're supposed to be counting three hundred steps a day."

On the TV Bob Saget was also sitting on a sofa. He looked worried but in good spirits about something. You couldn't see his calves. If he wanted to rub them he could probably get away with it.

"I lost my pedometer," Grammie said. "You keep moving my stuff around."

"Fine, I'll go," I said. "I'm taking your car because I don't have any gas."

"No, not tonight. Gil still hasn't looked at it."

"But I have to anyway," I said. "You're blocking me."

She made a halfway move to get up, then an uneven sound from her throat like when you're disappointed in a lot of different things all at the same time.

I slammed the door shut and walked to the store for the fucking suppositories. Then I started to cry, weep really. I thought about the kids from school who graduated with decent GPAs and went on to do something with their lives because they didn't have to down a bottle of NyQuil just to stop the numbers in algebra from coming to life and killing them. *We regret to inform you that your application has been denied.* I thought about next fall, when I wouldn't have the money to pay for my rent or medication. I'd have to work. Actual work. Not babysitting. A real job where I could get some health benefits and use the word *colleague.*

In front of the store where they sold suppositories and Diet Rite, someone was getting arrested. A black kid sat in handcuffs on the curb. The police always move so slowly when they're getting information. Everyone waits and waits.

––––––––––––––––

Out of spite and the misery of not being able to take another Saturday night at home with my grandmother and her healing heels, I decided I would go to Goat's last art exhibit before he was scheduled to leave for his yearlong tour in Europe. At first I had totally ignored the invitation and acted kind of bitchy on the phone to him.

"A formal invitation?" I said. "Why didn't you just call like you usually do and say 'Get your ass to my show'?"

He said they had all been mailed via his manager. *His manager.* His person who took care of all that stuff.

"Oh, you mean like dealing with the little folks?" I asked. Heat rushed into my cheeks. I should've never called.

"What's the matter with you? Did I do something wrong?"

"Nothing's wrong," I answered. "I just think it's weird that I'm supposed to send this invitation back to some person I don't even know. Your manager or whatever."

There was a pause of him working out a way to hang up on me. From the bedroom my grandmother asked where the hell I'd hidden her Epsom salts. "Damn foot spa is all clogged up! We need to run some vinegar through it!"

"Look," Goat said, "dearie, sweetie, honey pie, I don't give a shit if you send back the invitation; all I want really want is for you to show up, okay?"

"Well, of course I'm going to be there," I answered. "The last brouhaha before you become a super-famous world-renowned *arteest.*"

From the hobbling sounds in the kitchen I knew my grandmother was needing to be noticed. I pulled the phone outside to the balcony where I could ignore her in better light.

"So you're okay to get here then?" Goat asked.

"Sure. I have my own car now. A super-def ride."

"Because the last time, you were late to my exhibit, then gave some shit story about the light rail being out of service or you felt sick or something. Remember?"

Of course I remembered. It was a week after my mother died. I'd spent a whole day with some Benadryl and vodka. I thought it was clever though—as high as I was when I finally made it to the show I was still able to make up a pretty creative story about trains not running. "Promise you'll be there," Goat said.

"Look, I said I will, so I will."

Then, just before he hung up, Goat advised me to stop being so cranky and get a life. It was hard to tell if he was kidding.

Maybe it was the anti-everything medication that helped me feel excited about eye shadow and hair gel the night of Goat's exhibit. I hadn't worn makeup all summer and it felt good to spend an hour on myself in the bathroom while my grandmother napped. I was like a real girl, almost. A few hours before driving up the 101 into the city I took an extra Buspar to make sure there'd be enough calm in my system to make it through the night. I brought along a cassette tape Glenda let me borrow: *Scared, Just Like Me.* A James Earl Jones–ish voice of warmth and reason saying things like, "There's no need to be ashamed when we feel panicky." "Accept the anxiety and let it pass." "Appreciate how far you've come." Whenever I started feeling nervous I breathed in and out to the count of ten and every so often glanced down at my trusty paper bag on the passenger's seat. I tried very hard not to notice three white cars in the left lane and three *P*s in the license plate ahead of me and that three *P*s could stand for three pale cars instead of three white cars. The sky had been wondering about different shades of gray

all afternoon. By the time I saw the big white letters in the hillside—
SOUTH SAN FRANCISCO THE INDUSTRIAL CITY—the decision had been
made: ash and stillness. Earthquake weather. I focused on James Earl
Jones. He said I needed to do the work if I wanted to improve my life,
but Goat's voice was also in my ears, telling me to get one.

Over the past eight months or so it certainly seemed everyone else
around me was right on the mark with their secret to success. Goat was
selling his art, Roxy had just landed a job at a swank Los Gatos travel
agency (of course she had to call and tell me they were sending her
and another girl to Hawaii to rate hotels); even my grandmother who
could barely walk was all excited about taking gambling trips when
she got better.

Normal people planned.

I breathed into paper bags.

The first thing I saw when I walked into the studio was Goat. He
stood in the foyer with a beer in his hand greeting his guests. I hadn't
seen him in almost a year. He'd cut his hair short and dyed it bright red.
He wore a black zoot suit with a gold chain dangling from his pocket,
not a speck of dirt on his red Doc Martens. We hugged—me harder
than him. He said, "What the hell! You're here?" then made one of
his usual smart remarks about why I had colored my hair so dark. "I
liked you better when you were blond. Now I'm going to have to start
thinking just to be around you." Then he set to work showing me his
paintings.

"Does that one look familiar?" He led me up to an enlarged black-
and-white photograph of a brick wall in our old neighborhood. One of
the first things he had ever spray painted.

"Oh, wow," I said, squinting at the title plaque: *Early Graffiti—1984.*
"God, when you think about it, it wasn't really that long ago. Does it
feel that far away to you?"

He stood behind me and hugged my shoulders. "So much of that time feels far away," he whispered. "I should really walk around the room now and see if anyone's interested in spending money on this shit."

For the rest of the night I sat in the corner smoking cigarettes. Can you believe that? Me smoking? Whenever Roxy saw me with a cigarette she said, "Oh my God, you remind me so much of your mother."

I never thought that. When I looked at a cigarette in my hands I never saw her smooth skin and thick oval nails. My hands were still full of scars and little white dots where I had scrubbed and scratched and picked, trying to get me off me.

I sucked on my Marlboro Light and watched Goat make his way around the room and his new life. He was so cool. I used to be cool. I knew every Devo song by heart and could accurately predict which videos would make the top-three cut on MTV's weekly countdown. I wrote crap (sometimes good crap) and sent my stuff to addresses that didn't exist, but at least I'd tried to get someone to see something in me other than just a girl with a bunch of scabs up and down her arms and legs. I hadn't done that in a while. Since my grandmother moved in I'd grown very used to blaring soap operas in the middle of the afternoon and cigarette nights of canned laughter. I put as much effort in looking through the want ads as I did doing homework.

When school let out in June I planned my days around the shows I now called Me and Grammie's Stories.

"Hey, loner, you going to join the party or what?" It was hours later when Goat sat next to me on a chaise lounge in the corner of the studio. The extra Buspar made me feel thick and swirly.

"Oh, man, I'm so sorry," I said. "I'm a little out of it." A rain like snapping fingers began to fall outside.

Goat leaned back and put his arm around me. "Well, you can't just hide out all night." He was almost breathless, so happy and excited, little dots of sweat on his freckled nose. I remembered how he smelled when we were after-school hot and would lie on his bed listening to the bird sounds coming from his mother's old refrigerator.

"I forgot to tell you how pretty you look tonight."

I had in fact felt pretty earlier, with my eyes all done up like gothic smoke and a vintage velvety dress with a black silk shawl I borrowed from Glenda. Just for the occasion, I'd bought a pair of black-and-silver witch/pilgrim/streetwalker shoes from the Goodwill. "Those look like they belong to some sort of a costume," Grammie said.

"It's a costumey kind of a night," I answered, and left the house feeling smart. Antique. But isn't it funny how envy toward everything you don't have and will never have distracts you from liking what you are?

"You're so lucky," I said to Goat. "You'll have an awesome time in Europe. I wish I could go."

He rubbed his hands together and cocked an eyebrow. "Yep, especially when I get to Amsterdam."

"Right. I'm so sure," I said, and relaxed a little into his arm. Like back then.

He told me to come with him. "Why not? You'd blend right in with your paleness," he said.

"Yeah, no problem," I answered. "I'll just dash off to Europe with you."

"Don't you think it would be fun? You can write, hang out. Whatever."

I shrugged. If only he knew how well I had the hanging-out part down, but I let him go on because it was something I really needed— the idea of me away from here. I even let myself wonder if I'd be able to get my pills through customs. Did they have a lot of OCD in the Old World? What if I died on the airplane? Did the airlines use special coroners to remove the bodies from their flights or did they just call a regular guy? Goat made a remark about so and so was going to give him a million/billion/trillion deutsche marks for one of his industrial pieces. I tried to look interested, but a whole new set of worries

surged through me, the real here-and-now problems: the rain I had
to drive in to get back to San Jose; the two hundred dollars I had left
in my bank account; my grandmother who needed me. It took me
about twenty minutes of circling the on ramp before I got the nerve
to merge onto the freeway. I had to stop and breathe into my bag and
count and rewind the parts of my tape where it talked about being
easy on yourself and to keep reminding yourself that you're doing the
best you can do. I stuck a Benadryl under my tongue. Everything on
that ridiculous tape I agreed with, all except the part about doing the
best I could do. That sounded like something you tell yourself when
it's time to go to bed and you're trying to empty your mind.

"It's called ESL," I said to Grammie as I rubbed diabetic foot cream
into her diabetic feet. "English as a second language. You know, for
kids and adults who need help with basic English skills?"

"So would you have to learn how to speak Mexican to be a teacher's
assistant?" she asked.

"Oh God, Grammie, come on. There's no such language as Mexican." The scars from her surgery felt like a beaded necklace under my
thumbs. "Besides, I'm taking the test for the international school program. The program sends five applicants to Berlin to participate as
teacher's assistants before you can get work at a school here."

"So why the hell do you want to go to Germany to learn English?"
Grammie asked.

"Grammie! It's to learn the skills that German or French or whatever kids need help with when they come to the States. Here, put your
feet on the towel a second."

"Yeah, the French, they don't got no manners. Now you have to make
sure there's no clumps of leftover cream or it'll make the scars itch."

I dumped the gray water from her foot spa into the bathtub and
said it was mostly for the travel. From the bathroom I yelled, "Goat's

going to be there! If I get accepted into the program, how cool would that be to travel around for free?"

I didn't think I would be able to, but I got in just under the wire of the summer deadline to turn in my application. There had been no time to study, but on the written exam I scored a very excellent 92 percent. The enthusiasm from that was a huge push to write the essay about why I thought I would make the best candidate for a teacher's aide. When Mr. Stansky, the English professor in charge of the program, handed me back my essay he said it was one of the best he'd read so far. "It's a gorgeous story, Traci. Some great stuff about your mother, but it's important to stay in the thousand-word count." He pointed out the spots where he'd made some marks. "You really need to go over my corrections tonight and bring this back to me tomorrow. I've got to get these to the final judges in Berlin by next week."

Berlin in a week. Maybe I'd be saying that pretty soon. "Thank you," I said. "Really, Mr. Stansky, thank you so, so much for helping me."

Poor Mr. Stansky, he was the skinniest person I had ever seen. Everyone thought for sure he had AIDS. Plus, his jaw was always set tight, like he'd just heard some bad news and was trying to work out how to deal with it. It was never my method to tell someone to smile, but that day, even with the heat of late August and Mr. Stansky's probably poisoned insides, I couldn't help myself: "You should smile more," I said. "Stop taking everything so serious." Then I threw in a cheesy line I journaled whenever I felt a panic attack coming on: "Nothing is a real emergency."

He flashed a confused smile. "Oh, wait, before you run off—" He shuffled through the papers on his desk. "Emergency, emergency . . . that reminds me. Ah, here it is. You've left a few blank spots on one of the questionnaires." He handed me a paper, one side written in English, the other in German. Both sides wanted to know if I had ever been insane.

"What's this?" I said. "They can't ask these types of questions."

Next to yes or no boxes about tuberculosis and measles was point-blank: *Have you ever been under the care of a psychiatric physician or are you currently under such care or receiving prescribed medications for a diagnosis as a result of a psychiatric evaluation?*

"This is illegal." I pointed to what I was talking about.

Mr. Stansky nodded. "Here in the States, yeah. But the sponsoring university for the program is in Berlin. The laws are totally different over there. I think if you're working around minor children they can ask anything they want."

Mr. Stansky's phone rang. Before he picked it up, he said I didn't have anything to worry about. "It's not like you're psychotic or anything."

I stood there while he waved me away and smiled, his bony hand barely attached to his glassy wrist. "Anything else?" he whispered.

"No," I said quickly, but I didn't really feel the words come from my body. I folded my papers and walked outside under the unsanitary fingernails of a horrible sun.

When I got home, I tossed my application and the essay into the trash.

18

big-girl baggage

A minute, in this situation, is an era.
—CHIP KIDD, *THE CHEESE MONKEYS*

By the beginning of October I had eleven dollars left in my bank account. Then I drove my grandmother to McDonald's and the bus depot. The magic number changed to three. Grammie and I sat on the benches of the Greyhound station smoking, waiting for the senior party bus bound for Palm Springs.

Three dollars.

I said, "I hope I have enough gas to get home," and meant it to sound as pathetic as I could. Jesus Christ, three dollars, that's zero, almost.

"I went ahead and left you a hundred-dollar bill under the phone book in the kitchen," Grammie said. "But promise me you'll have a job when I get back."

Dewy garlic from the hills in the south snapped through the wind.

"Thanks so much, Grammie," I said and for a moment allowed the hope of autumn: the intimate gravity of brakes on a school bus, how nothing can stop a new backpack. "Don't worry about me," I said. "I'm getting things together."

She looked at me the way a person does when the look requires a head shake to go with it. "Honey, I want you to *make* yourself get things together."

"Come on, just—please, okay? Everything's going to be fine."

"Just promise me you'll try," she said. "You just gotta keep trying."

I said I would. "Cross my heart and hope to try."

"Hey, Traci. You've got your cash register short by seven whole dollars," the supervisor of Swanson's Cleaners said, "it's the third time this has happened. How can you manage this three days in a row?"

That was me trying.

"Seven dollars? Really?" My manager was the owner's son, Kipp. "That's not a real name," I told him once, "it's a gymnastic move, a way to mount the parallel bars." Plus Kipp had no business having that name because double consonants kind of require that you're cool or slightly interesting.

The only thing Kipp did was hover behind me all day in a stiff white dress shirt and body odor like a sick person in bed.

"I need you to get all the receipt copies from last week and bring them to my office before you go to lunch." He pulled at the pencil behind his ear. I never once witnessed him use that pencil for anything. "Damn," he said breathlessly. "Now I'm going to have to backtrack all the way from Monday. I should have you do this."

Here are two things you may not notice if you have double consonants at the end of your name and you're not using them properly. A) There is no office at your parents' dry cleaners. There's a card table in the back where your employees sit and read and smoke when they're supposed to be working, but no office. B) Sure, you can go ahead and ask me to fix a seven-dollar cash mistake. I will certainly try, because even though at three dollars and eighty cents an hour with no approved overtime (meaning the overtime still has to be worked, just not approved for my paycheck) combined with my nighttime nanny job, which leaves me with about fourteen hours' sleep for the entire week, I would be more than happy to see where that seven dollars went off to, but I cannot guarantee my mind will be any clearer than it was yesterday when I made the very same addition/subtraction/career mistake.

The only comfort I had in my position as a special-needs cash register person was in the routine I'd developed for my whole fifteen-minute lunch break. Every day I ordered a sausage and sauerkraut sandwich from the European deli next door, then I'd grab my Tom Robbins novel or a copy of *Fate* magazine from my car and sit in the cool shade of the strip mall sidewalk. Repeatedly, I was told not to do this. "Like a homeless squatter," was the way Kipp had put it, and a power action word about me having to anticipate the needs of the customers. *Proactive*, maybe? But from my view on the cement, in between the deli and the dry cleaner, I could see that my lunchtime seating choice wasn't hurting business at all. People still came rushing in from their Mercedes and Audis to spend twenty dollars for nothing more to be done to their Ann Klein skirts than a spritz of salt water and an oversize iron.

My alone time on the sidewalk meant a lot to me for reasons other than bratwurst. It was the site of my latest near-death experience. Three weeks ago I answered the ad in the *PennySaver* for Outgoing Person with Excellent Customer Service Skills and Front Counter Know-How. Everything started off fine: I had my references in check (Roxy, lying about owning a dress boutique and how great I was as a salesgirl) and a solid story about how my driver's license was in the process of being mailed back to me from when I visited my parents in New York City because I had left my purse in the offices of Random House, where I worked as assistant editor in the Young Adult department. When the day of my interview arrived, I wasn't feeling all that nervous. I wore a new pair of black jeans, kind of dressy looking, and even did up my hair with a set of new-to-me steam rollers Kim had found in an abandoned apartment.

Things were okay until I pulled into the parking lot of the dry cleaners.

Right away my chest felt like someone was pushing through my ribs. I couldn't catch my breath. When I reached for my paper bag in my glove compartment, one of Goat's postcards fell onto the passenger seat. A picture of the Eiffel Tower tweaked to look like a gigantic penis with a can-can girl lifting up her skirt over the words *What's up?* Looking at that made everything worse. My throat was like a tight cry stuck in a place where you have to remain quiet. After I breathed into my bag, I put my head down on the steering wheel and repeated to myself, *There are no emergencies.* My arms tingled. I tried to slow my mind so I could find the underlying cause of my anxiety: Goat was gone. My mother was gone. My brother was gone. Theresa was gone. And now I could add to that list my grandmother, who had decided to make Palm Springs her permanent home. During a second gambling trip, she called me and said she had completely fallen in love with an assisted living apartment complex and most likely wouldn't be coming back to San Jose.

"Most likely?" I asked. "Are you trying to say you're just not coming back at all?"

"You should see the furniture in this place," was her answer. "It's like living in a resort."

It was an interesting feeling in my stomach that day on the phone with my grandmother when she said I could keep or toss anything she had left in my apartment. The excitement of another uproot that wasn't mine, the barbed wire glow of being on my own again. But during that terrible panic attack in my car, all I could see was, *Now you are so alone.* I looked at my hands on the steering wheel. The color flushed out of them. I felt feverish. *There are no emergencies.* Some people in the parking lot started talking. Why? What the hell do you need to stand around and discuss in a parking lot? When I found my way to the shade of the sidewalk, I tried to think of all those times Glenda said anxiety attacks would come and go, rise and fall, you just had to ride them out. Under the big awning between the dry cleaners and the deli, I sat down and calmed myself. I didn't reach for a Benadryl or wonder how many Buspar I had at home. I rode through the panic and told myself that was the only thing I could do. When I stood up, I caught my reflection in the windows. Very pale, but not dead. Kipp, before I started hating him, even waved to me through the glass of the dry cleaners. Something was waiting for me. That afternoon, on the sidewalk, under the safety of that awning and my own words, I grabbed it, held it to me. On the ride home from the interview I was bigger than my skin. Okay, so it wasn't going to be the greatest of jobs, not a career or anything, but I had made it through the interview. I didn't run off in my ugly car and drive twenty miles an hour in the slow lane with my hazards on just in case I had to pull over and faint. For a moment I was the early version of my mother.

The day I got fired, I went home and started packing suitcases. One old red Samsonite full of sweaters, a blue duffel bag just right for a notebook and thesaurus, a yellow vinyl makeup bag with plenty of compartments for Vicks and Tylenol. Before I picked up my final check I stopped at the Emporium and set my sights on a teal leather carry-on with a mini padlock.

"I want you to know I'm not feeling comfortable about paying you at all," Kipp said. He handed me my last check along with a letter of termination wishing me luck in all my future endeavors but to please never use Swanson's Cleaners as a business reference. He stood over me. Both hands on his hips. I felt sorry for the way he smelled.

"I really want to apologize, Kipp. I feel like I didn't tell you how sorry I am that I ruined the equipment." That's because I hadn't—apologized for destroying a three-thousand-dollar computerized embroidery machine on my last day of work. A policeman had come in with three handkerchiefs and captain's shirts. He requested a speed order for embroided initials and rank stripes. I was the only one working that day. I had to call Kipp and interrupt a car-shopping moment with his parents. "What should I tell him?" I asked. "Should I wait for Miguel to come back from a delivery?"

I was told to take the order. "Traci, you seriously can't figure out how to work that machine?"

I seriously couldn't. By the time I had finished the officer's order I'd managed to sew two buttonholes into one of the sleeves, misspell *Mackenzie*, and no matter what button I pressed or how many times I plugged in/unplugged the machine, I couldn't get the preset image of Mickey Mouse off the printing screen. When Miguel came back I told him I was sick and drove home. I could only guess that when he realized the blinking blue CODE ERROR had something to do with the uniform shirt stuck in the *feeder*, I was already back in my apartment packing suitcases. When I had all of my suitcases the way I wanted, I walked to the drugstore for vodka and Benadryl.

Kim said the suitcases looked like something an unstable person would do.

"I kind of like it," I said. "Gives the place an anything-can-happen kind of feel." I'd also started putting things in plastic garbage bags with masking tape labels: *Books A–F, Bathroom Stuff*. The one with my grandma's pill cups and Neosporin bore the simple label *Need*.

"I see," Kim said. She opened the red Samsonite and made a face at my sweaters. My grandmother had sent me a card with a picture of her getting ready to pull down the handle to a slot machine. In the card she called me Honey Bunny. *Here's some money, Honey Bunny.*

Kim read the card. "What money?" she asked.

I hadn't paid my rent yet and here it was almost the end of the month.

"Grammie just sent me a little something to take care of my medicine for this month." And next month and probably the month after that. The little something was a thousand dollars.

"Enough for the rent?" Kim asked. She sat on my futon slowly like it was dirty or something. "I don't want to have to kick you out of here."

"What? Kick me out, Miss Manager?" I said. "I bet you'd just love that."

"You know, I came over here because I went to the cleaners today to take you out to lunch and they told me you didn't work there anymore."

"Right, like you really wanted to take me out to lunch. I'm sure you were just noseying around. You couldn't wait to get over here and tell me this, huh?"

"I need the rent, Traci. You're not exempt from paying rent and bills just like everyone else."

I walked into the kitchen and started sweeping. "Of course I know I'm not exempt." I wanted to remind her that up until last month, when she went to some stupid property management convention, she had pronounced *exempt* as *expent* at least a dozen times. Instead I told her I was probably going to move out and made up a story about how me and Roxy had been looking at condos.

"Uh-huh, you and Roxy?"

I knew she didn't believe me. "Well, before you can think about living the high life with your friends—"

"What do you mean, 'living the high life'? What a stupid thing to say. I'm talking about me and Roxy getting a place together." I felt like I was going to start crying, so I asked her to leave.

"No," she said. She lit up a cigarette. "I can't leave without your rent."

"Well, I don't have it."

"Where's the money Grammie sent you?"

I leaned my broom against the wall and took a deep breath. "I know a way you can get the money." My cheeks shook a little, my lips went numb. "Why don't you sell Mom's furniture?"

My sister had made one cleaning/packing trip to my mother's house after she died. "If you don't come to help pack everything," she told me, "you aren't getting a damn thing out of that house."

I didn't come. She had meant what she said.

As she got up to leave she warned me not to give her any more shit. "I'm not going to put up with your damn crying or your lunatic lies."

"What lies?" I asked. "You're the liar. Your life is sad because you don't want me well."

It was Glenda who had shared that observation with me a few months back when I told her I was so sick of being treated like I was in the way of my big sister's life. "It may just be that you have to step aside," she had said. "People get used to the roles they play in life. You've just always been the crazy one—" She put her arm around me. I'd been crying about not being invited to Kim's apartment to see *Ghost* on video, even though she knew how much I loved Patrick Swayze and I'd been complaining that every time I tried to rent the movie it wasn't available. "I really think she does want you to get better, Traci, it's just everything is out of place right now. You may have to spend a lot of years proving to everyone that you're no longer the one who needs all the help and attention."

But I wasn't sure I wanted that. Not entirely. I mean, of course I knew I needed to take control of where I was going in my life but I also didn't want to be tossed out to sea without any chance of making it back to where my sister had been waiting for me.

"Just leave me the hell alone," I said to Kim. "You can't come in here telling me how to run my life."

She crushed out her cigarette in an ashtray I just cleaned. "Well, someone needs to tell you how to run your life, because you sure aren't running it."

I picked up the letter from the international school program. It had come the week before to let me know that since they had not received all my paperwork I was no longer considered a candidate for the program. "Oh yeah? Well, what does that say?" I pointed to the return address. I knew she wouldn't read what was inside. There were apartments to manage, a daughter and a husband to take care of. "You didn't even know I applied for a teacher's assistant position in Germany," I said. "I'm going to travel with Goat."

"Oh my God, you really must be losing it." She tossed the envelope into my open suitcase. "So you're telling me that Goat's traveling around Europe? Doing what, spray painting? The guy's a flake and a thug. Did you check the return address on his letters, you sure they aren't coming from San Quentin?"

I slammed down the lid. Her fingers moved just in time. "I'm so sick of you! What the hell do you know about art or my life or anything? You collect Precious Moments figurines and Beanie Babies, for Christ's sake. I want you to get the hell out of my face and my apartment!"

"Yeah, fine, because it's not going to be your apartment for long if you can't figure out a way to pay your rent."

As she took off down the walkway I yelled from the porch, "And don't bother to help me pack. I know it's too much for you to help me with anything!"

She turned around. "Help you? Are you kidding? All everyone ever does is help you and you do nothing to help yourself."

That was the night my sister called me a crazy bitch. It's a funny thing when you finally hear the words you know someone has been thinking for so long, when they claw through the spaces you have prepared for them, like wounded children coming home from a long war. *Crazy bitch.*

That was also the night the janitor showed up at my front door.

"Fred? Isn't it kind of late?" I asked. "I thought we weren't fumigating until next week." I was totally spent from the earlier fight with Kim. When I was screaming from my porch I'd seen the teenage girl who lived next door sitting outside on her balcony talking on the phone. After "crazy bitch" and me with a retaliation as mature as, "I know you are but what am I," the girl ducked back inside her apartment and watched from the sliding glass door. For the rest of the evening I could think of nothing else but the phrase *white trash*. I guess that's what had made it so easy for me to open my door to the maintenance guy. Even though my apartment was all the way in the back of the complex near the parking lot. Even though it was almost nine o'clock at night. This was how stupid I'd become.

"Oh, I'm not here to fumigate," Fred said. "I've got something to talk to you about. Can I come in?"

Fred was a strange guy with bugged eyes and a past that probably included a lot of all-you-can-drink nights at the bowling alley.

"Sure," I said. "Come on in."

Right off I could see his eyes following my path of suitcases. Dominos in a perfect circle. Crime scene stuff. I hadn't thought of that until I saw how nervous his smile turned. "You going on a trip?" he asked. There was something machinelike in his hands.

"I think so," I answered. "So what's up?"

"I uh—well . . ." He shuffled his feet, then pressed my new purple backpack with the tip of his sneaker. It tipped a bit so that all my new shampoo fell forward to the lip of the opening. I had purchased forty travel-size bottles of Head & Shoulders. The sea green and white logos matched so well with the purple I decided that pack would only be used if I suddenly came down with a raging case of dandruff. Otherwise, it was very nice to look at. "I want you to know I took two years of psychology at community college," he said.

"Uh-huh."

"And I learned a lot during those two years."

"What school?" I asked. Had he been drinking? What the hell was he talking about? Fred once asked me to the movies. I said no thanks because, aside from a sort of obvious list, he had an "I just tried meth and love it!" look that had become so popular in our marginal area of San Jose: dry, grayish skin, an inappropriate loud voice/laugh/cough, a Victory Outreach T-shirt. "Well, what I meant to say," Fred continued, "is that I went to automotive tech school in Brisbane, but I enjoyed taking psychology classes for fun when I wasn't working."

"Fred?"

"Yeah?"

"What are you doing here?" I asked. "Do you want to talk about school or what?"

He looked at the machine part in his hand. "No," he said slowly. "But I do want to talk. You've been—Well, I mean, we're kind of worried—Kim thinks you may need someone to talk to. She told me about the troubles you're having."

I stepped in front of him and opened my door. "Fred, I was just on my way out, okay?"

He touched his thin brown hair with the machine thing, as if rubbing it over his brain would help him think. "I know a few things about people with problems, Traci," he said. "From school, you know, and if you need someone to talk to—Your sister said you may need someone to talk to. . . ."

"Fred, thanks and all, but I don't really give a rat's ass what my sister thinks."

It was a shock that my phone still worked. I hadn't really paid any bills in almost two months. But there it was, the empty soup can echo of waiting for my sister to answer her phone. When she did I hung up and started to cry. I wanted to scream at her and ask her what the hell was she thinking, telling Fred all my personal problems? Who did she think she was? I wrapped a roll of paper towels around my hand and buried my face in it. I hated myself when I cried, it was ugly. I hated the truth of OCD and depression and anxiety.

That night I packed and unpacked. I folded sweaters and counted how many sweaters I folded and how many socks needed to be rolled to equal the number of sweaters. I color-coordinated everything. I opened each bottle of dandruff shampoo, then wiped the inside of each cap with a dishrag before I refastened them. I put on Nirvana and walked around with one of the suitcases in my hand. I did a funny John Cleese strut and said, "Good day to you, sir." Then I wondered about my blue towel. Had I packed it? My brand-new blue towel. I had to make sure it was still folded in the hall closet, because if I used it, and since it was the exact same color as the water in the apartment complex swimming pool, it would mean that my beautiful little niece could wander into the swim area and drown. I started pulling things out of my suitcases; if I found it packed and it was smooshed too tight, she might suffocate in her sleep. I started sweating.

I thought about Fred who cleaned the fuzz from the laundry room dryers and suggested that Vanilla Ice's *Cool as Ice* would be "way killer" for a movie date. What was wrong with my stupid sister? How could she blab all those things about me to Fred? Where was that goddamn fucking blue towel?

By the time I found it in the red Samsonite, I was ready to start hyperventilating. But I found it right on top. Safe. Still three folds and rounded edges. I stuck my hand through each fold. Lungs. Enough space for air. Bethany wouldn't drown. I'd been out of Buspar for a while now, but I had a little NyQuil and some leftover vodka to get me through the tingling sensation that had started in my arms.

When I felt faded enough not to cry, I called my brother, who was now stationed in Hawaii, but the number I had was wrong. It rang up a barbecue restaurant. I called Kim and tried not to sound too NyQuilly. "Do you have a number for our brother?" I asked.

"I do," she said. "And so do you. I've given it to you three times. Where's your phone book?"

I looked around. "Um. I don't—I guess it got packed."

She sighed impatiently. "Look, I don't want to fight with you, but I really can't talk right now. Me and Gil rented a movie."

"That's shounds some funs."

"Huh?"

I rubbed my face, hit my brow with the base of my palm. "Oh, okay be right there!" I yelled like someone was at my door, "Roxy's coming now. I'll say this tomorrow." I hung up before I let loose any more foamy messes. Then I called the number for people who want to jump off the Golden Gate Bridge.

"How close are you to the bridge?" the woman asked me.

"It doesn't seem very close to me at all," I said. "I'm in my living room with the suitcases, actually. You know what you could say? You could say I'm not close to anything. This response would be accurate."

That night I lay on my futon in my clothes and cried for dead women. I wanted the ghost of my mother to stand in the middle of my ugly apartment, in the hallway where I had accidentally broken a huge mirror while cleaning it but had yet to pick up the glass because I was afraid to touch it. I wanted her to pick up the pieces for me, to stay in the vision above my head like a sky pulse or angel on a Polaroid.

"Tell me what to do, Mom." But she wouldn't talk. I wondered if my grammie ever asked her own dead mother the same thing. *What do I do*? Never once did I ever ask my grandmother, "Hey Grammie, would Great-grandma Ruby answer you if you talked to her?" I had so many opportunities for that kind of caring. But no. I wanted those stories of Crazy Ruby and her sick mind. I wanted to hear about brand-new televisions being thrown out a two-story window and how she died on the floor before anyone could come to lock her away. I wanted lit eyeballs and children getting dropped on hot griddles and needles and opium.

More tragedy, please. Let me stay awake in those darkest-before-dawn hours, and when the sun comes up—oh, sorry, I'll be asleep. Sunlight can kill you anyway. Take the babies to the healers, the smart ones don't have parents or a way out.

We like that.

I pressed my face into my bleach-stained pillowcase. I wanted to scream but could only cry in that tired, thick way when your esophagus is filled with chemicals and yourself.

Look how interesting you are now. Put this in a poem. Pills and stories to doctors. Friends I was so jealous of I couldn't even see straight. Panic if I did. Panic if I didn't. When you really look at it, when it's staring you in your stupid puffy face and won't go away, Pathetic isn't pretty at all.

It was well after noon when I awoke the next day. The air was like the mouth of an old man. The sun shone hard all over the apartment. I'm not sure how the sheets came off my window or how the AC got turned off. My eyes were so swollen and my mouth was so dry I had to stop and wonder if maybe I'd brushed my teeth with Ajax during the night. When I got up to walk around, I felt dizzier than I had ever felt before, but I managed to wash my face, which brought about a twinge of hope for a bowl of Golden Grahams and an episode of *ThunderCats*. But when I went to turn on the television, my cable had been shut off. I called the bank to check my balance from the thousand dollars Grammie sent me. Seven hundred and sixty-two. During my shower I tried to imagine myself walking into Kim's office, giving her at least half of the money I owed, but somewhere between spraying my bedsheets with Lysol and wondering why my *Brady Bunch* videos were all lined up by the front door, I knew it would never happen.

Roxy had left four messages on my answering machine about going dancing or cruising up to Santa Cruz in the new car her parents had given her for her twenty-first birthday. I called her back and told her about my night.

"Fred?" she asked laughing. "Fred the maintenance guy, are you serious? Isn't he like a hundred and eighty-six or something? Is that the one who was all obsessed about taking you to see MC Hammer?"

My own laughter made my sinuses feel like they were going to split open. "Vanilla Ice," I said. Then I told her I didn't feel much like going to a club due to the headaches from so much crying.

"Up all night crying about what?" she asked.

"I don't know," I said. "I guess my grandmother, like she was so nonchalant when she called to tell me about her starting a new life."

"Is that what she said, she was going to start a new life?"

Not really. I mean, she had worded it a little different, but wasn't that what everyone was doing these days—starting things? There was

such a disgusting irony in me trying to get better. The medication—
when I could afford it—was definitely making a difference, a slow and
steady relief from hyper everything. But that was all I had going on.
Other than being less and less of a spaz, I hadn't really achieved much.

I heard at one of Dr. Benette's groups that when you begin to feel
better, when the OCD doesn't have a grip on you, don't expect the
world to beat a path to your door and present all these terrific opportunities just because you've stopped folding yourself into wall corners
whenever you spot someone with uneven kneesocks. You still have to
make your own future. Exactly how to get that future, though, I don't
think that was ever mentioned in group.

"Come on now," Roxy said. "Don't get all stupid about your grandma
leaving to whore it up in Palm Springs."

We both laughed. She gave me these completely gross scenarios
about old people in hot climates. She said, "Flopping in the desert" and
I just about vomited from laughing so hard.

"Come over tonight when you get off work," I said. "I found all my
Brady Bunch tapes. We can make fun of Greg's nipples when he's in
that surf contest in Hawaii."

"Yeah, totally," she answered. "I have to hang up now or I'll get into
trouble for making personal calls."

"That's cool. I'll see you tonight then." But before we said good-bye
I asked her to look something up for me. "Hey, how much would a
one-way ticket to Germany cost?" I asked. "And is there a way to make
sure you don't reserve a seat next to someone who's coughing?"

19

sign of the first clear word

But is there a deadline inside him for when he must finish,
a day, like Noah, when the rains began? When the boat,
finished or not, begins to rise from the cradle?
—NICK FLYNN. *ANOTHER BULLSHIT NIGHT IN SUCK CITY*

You don't always have to stay where the problems are to fix them. Even when you're the problem. When you've been one way for so long, sometimes you have to go where there is room to find another way. Yes, people will say you're doing the cowardly thing, that escaping the mess of your life is never the answer because we never escape ourselves. But isn't everything crystal clear from the distance of a future that isn't yours?

I wanted to leave. I had to make something begin.

Once when I was eight, full of worries and bronchitis, my grandmother took us out to dinner at the Pilot Room in the Red Baron Hotel near the airport. It was my mother's thirty-seventh birthday. I had just started unplugging appliances; a set alarm clock meant I didn't love my mother enough to care whether she exploded in her sleep from faulty wiring and my selfishness. Coffeepots had just started threatening entire existences. Night after night I awoke from dreaming about flames with lots of screaming and me being responsible for it all because I didn't do my checking. Somehow I got it into my head that I should seriously start thinking about suicide. I wondered what it would be like if I put a stop to all this nonsense in a hurry. Like a snap of fingers, a crack of a knuckle, I could be gone. Blank. No more fiery itches in my brain. How would that be for running away and making things right?

That night at the restaurant I decided jumping off the roof of the hotel was the fastest way to get to that. Bryan was supposed to be watching me after I'd begged him to take me to the outside observation deck so I could look at the planes. But I managed to escape toward the back of the balcony where an Employees Only stairwell led up to a small patch of roof. I loved the sound of the airplane engines, like monsters waking up from boring dreams. I watched the steam from the oven pipes in the kitchen below me as it poured into the night sky. It was all so close to God. When you really think about it, the possibility of an airplane is a strange thing. Something to make you sadder than you've ever been in your entire life—something to carry you away from all that sadness. I watched the wheels as they tucked away inside their metal napping place. A plane, I thought, does more than one person can ever do in their entire lives.

I heard whispering. "Traci, please come on. Get back downstairs. You're going to get me busted." My brother had lost me. That made me feel kind of bad. I thought, if I decided not to jump, if I decided to just stay with sleepless nights of crying over stove burners, maybe I could get used to it, maybe, if I waited long enough, I would eventually end up feeling like I felt on the roof of that restaurant. I could melt into myself with steam and jet fuel and gravel and my name being whispered into the darkness. *Traci, please come on.* I balanced myself against the rail-

ing and tried to feel what it would be like to jump, to float through the
world like a limp doll whose expression never changes.

The night Roxy drove me to the airport, I pointed to the edge of
that balcony when we passed the Red Baron Hotel. I told her that story.

"Insane," she said. She was all nasally. We'd both been crying practically all the way to the airport. "I'm glad you didn't jump, but still,
you're nuts."

She parked her car and together we lugged my suitcases to the
Southwest terminal. I stood in line for my boarding pass and a ticket
for my connecting flight in San Francisco. Lufthansa: depart SFO 1:35
A.M. arrive BER 1:48 P.M. Both of us promised we would cool it on the
crying once we were in the airport. "It's so stupid when people make a
big scene," I said, and she agreed. But while sitting in the boarding area
trying to focus on a *People* magazine, we both sobbed like someone
just died.

"Look, lady," I said, "you tell Sprinkles his mama has finally cracked,
but she still loves him." My cat had been living with Roxy ever since
I moved into my apartment. Of course it broke my heart, made me
physically ill to the point of throwing up, that I had to give my best
friend away to my other best friend. But there was no way I could
swing the pet deposit.

Roxy laughed. "Oh, he doesn't give a damn about anything anymore. Did I tell you my mom makes him scrambled eggs once a week?
Supposed to be good for his heart or something."

"Well, you just make sure to take all that crap I boxed up in my
apartment to the Goodwill. I can't leave those boxes in there or Kim
will hold my security deposit." I had a feeling she was going to do
that anyway. My sister wasn't happy at all about my leaving for Berlin. Funny how that was the only time she offered to drive me to the
county hospital so I could be assessed by a doctor. After four waiting-
room hours of listening to my sister tell me I was making a huge mistake, I was deemed by the psychiatrist on call to be rational and of
sound mind. Kim tried to get into the conversation by telling the doc-

tor it was her opinion I needed further evaluation. Not unlike what she had done with Dr. Schmidt when she and my mother whispered tales about what I'd been writing in my journals. I had felt so helpless then, so full of anger over something I couldn't control. Now I was armed with an airline ticket, my prescriptions and refills, plus a little Valium for the plane ride. My sister made a drug reference about Elvis and I just didn't give a damn. I knew how much better I was with my pills. Why couldn't she just take her pot and her assumptions and leave me the hell alone? Even the shrink who evaluated me told her to back off after she compared me to the King in front of him.

"Mrs. Johnston," he said to her, "I can see that you're concerned about your sister and that's great, but I've read everything in her file. This is a twenty-year-old woman who is making a decision to move. People have a right to make decisions they feel will help them to be happy."

The doctor's words lit me up with a frightening truth, like when a drunk finally finds their car keys at a party. I tried not to let the heaviness in the car cancel out that frightening excitement. I asked my sister, "What do you want from me?" I sometimes really wondered if my sister wanted me to get well. Or was it like Glenda had said, my sister was too invested in me being the crazy one?

She just shrugged. There was a long silence until she said, "I want you to think about your decisions. You never—it's just—you never really think things through."

There was so much I wanted to say but I figured, what's the point? "I don't think things through?" I asked, trying to keep my voice calm. *Don't cry, dammit.* Why did she have to do this now? The only thing I ever *do* is think. Didn't she know that by now? It was my thinking, my scary and twisted way of it, that was the reason for OCD. My thinking had been sick. My thinking needed medicine. I had to get my head into a place where I could control it.

It was so damn frustrating when the people I loved didn't get that.

Everyone hears what they want to hear. They see what they want to see. When you say you're too nervous to drive on the freeway and would it be okay if someone came to pick you up, they hear a lazy girl who is too stupid to read a map. When you can't make it to the birthday party because you've been wearing gloves for the past week due to the opening of flu season with a CDC report of twenty-four Beijing influenza viruses in your immediate area, all they see is an inconsiderate girl who doesn't care about her friends. I guess in the same way I wasn't quite myself when I first started feeling better, maybe the people around me just weren't sure what to think when they saw me trying to get it all together. No one wanted me to take medication. No one wanted me to leave. Someone in group used to say we are all easier to love when we're down. I think there's some truth in that.

Both my brother and my dad said the first thing I should do in a foreign country was find out where the police station was and learn the number to emergency services. "And always know where you are," Bryan said. "When we do fieldwork the sergeant has to remind his men of two things: where they are and where they're supposed to be. Dammit, Spaz, do you think you're doing the right thing?"

"Yes, I do," I said. "And of course I will know where I am and where I'm supposed to be." I promised this because knowing where I was had never been the problem: wasn't I usually on the edge of something? Of spazzing out, of fading away? That part was easy. The red arrow in the middle of my map had pointed to this gray area of insanity for a very long time. Now the place where I was supposed to be—well, that's what I was trying to find out.

When I told my grandmother I was leaving, I hadn't expected her to react by crying. "I'm just afraid I'll never see you again. Oh, Traci, are you sure you've thought this through?"

I wanted to say, *You mean like how you thought it through when you just decided on a whim to stay in Palm Springs*? But I didn't. She was crying so hard. Though I wouldn't realize it until much later, I think it was my grandmother's ability to escape that gave me the courage to leave California. Her rising above the insanity of her own childhood with a very ill mother, two failed marriages, then the pain of losing her only child. Her running away to Palm Springs showed me that anyone can change a situation they're not happy with. But many years and places to run to would have to pass before I could understand anything of what my family went through helping me to grow up. I would have to be sick and heal many, many times before I would even begin to understand how difficult, how utterly wearisome it must have been for my family to manage the responsibility of looking out for me while trudging through the exhaustion of being around me. It takes a long time to figure out you can still love someone and be tired of them at the same time.

Twelve hours in my coach-class window seat. Not once did I feel like I was going to fall apart. I'd taken a Valium in the car and half a Dramamine in the bag-check line. I worried that I might need more, but worried more about getting all babbly and wet-sanded when I got to Berlin. I kept asking myself do I feel okay? I did. I had my paper bag, and when Roxy booked my ticket, she told me exactly how far the bathroom was from my seat. Up until the very last minute, I doubted my ability to go through with the whole thing, but when the time came, I didn't freak out. I got on that plane.

I also didn't sleep. The entire trip, even with all the downers in my system, I was alert enough to read the newspaper and my old booklets from when I first started learning about OCD. I wrote in my journal. I thought a lot about my mother. A few days before I left, Sarah and my dad took me out to dinner. My dad said I was to provide him with every single number where I could be reached, first and last names of everyone I stayed with. "I mean it, goddammit. If I get a phone call in the middle of the night saying they found your dead body floating in the Rhine or something . . ."

Sarah told him to shut up. "Ted, my God, how morbid." She pushed my hair back from my shoulders and gathered it into a ponytail. "Leave her alone, she'll be okay."

On the plane, when I thought of that moment, I imagined it was my mother touching my hair, telling me to ignore everyone and do what I needed to do to help myself. I pretended my mom was in the sky, watching me through the black and purple clouds. When the stewardess and the drink cart came by, I asked for some red wine and didn't even get carded. With my little plastic cup and a copy of *Der Tagesspiegel*, I felt like I was halfway to a place where I could change, where I would be so much more than just my gray Santa Cruz sweatshirt and a paper bag in my purse. I barely drank the wine. It tasted like NyQuil. Instead I wrote poems.

Before I bought my ticket Goat had made arrangements for me to stay with some women artists he'd been working with since his arrival in Berlin. "One of them totally reminds me of your mom," he said. I didn't ask, "In what way?" Lately, when I thought of my mother my memories were layered in so many different facets. Maybe this was the beginning of me seeing her with all those complexities a woman will feel about her mother in her lifetime: through the angry eyes of a spoiled child who demanded too much attention. The steely rebellion of a teenager who hated herself for hating everything.

For me, that's where it would stop.

I would never know what my mother thought of me as I became a young woman finding my way out of my head and into a mind I could somewhat manage. Later still would come the gratitude toward all the secret hardships a parent must endure and the steadfast patience required to raise a difficult child. It would take me having my own children, experiencing my own push and pull of those little souls, before I could fully grasp the bittersweetness of being a grown-up woman, of knowing the kind of love and contempt that is born from the uneasy union of what a woman wants to be and what a mother has to be.

Goat said he wouldn't be the one to meet me when my plane landed. He was hosting an exhibit in Amsterdam. Though I had visions of me in a taxi and a map folded in a gloved hand like Sophia Loren or Lauren Bacall, he insisted on sending one of the girls I'd be staying with.

"Ingrid's the only one I know with a car," he said. "There's no way you can miss her, she's like fourteen feet tall and her chest—oh, you'll know it when you see her."

I could tell by his voice he was deep into a "thing" with Ingrid. That was fine. I wasn't going to Europe to be with Goat. I was going to see what would happen.

The girl who towered above everyone just outside the doors of customs had to be my ride. The first thing I noticed was her bright white hair, her bangs cut all thick and curled under like Betty Page, but the top was short and spiked out, kind of like how I wore mine in the tenth grade. When the crowd spaced a bit and she held up a welcome sign with my name on it—yeah, that had to be Ingrid all right. I stepped onto a moving sidewalk, trying not to look too awkward as I kept one hand on the rail and both eyes on Ingrid. The airport was so hot. I still felt a little dreamy from tranquilizers and altitude. Goat said one of the things I would notice when I got here was the number of turtlenecks and black overcoats. He wasn't kidding. Time and again I would wonder if pastels had long been outlawed by some fascist fashion police. Most everyone smoked, too; they lit up cigarettes right in the terminal and walked with them. When I waved to Ingrid she waved back with her cigarette and her sign. When the conveyor-belt sidewalk ended and the spaces between us shrank, I noticed the sign had big drawings surrounding my name, detailed sketches of foreign cartoon characters no American would even care about. A lot of work had gone into making my welcome sign. There were blue and purple swirls of paint, some weird glittery lightning bolt darting out of a unicorn's ass and my name spelled all wrong. Where there was supposed to be an *i*, a fancy green and black *y* had taken its place. It wouldn't have been out of character at all for me to mention this. New country/friends/life notwithstanding—I don't know why really, but it had always bothered me so much when anyone misspelled my name. Like when a therapist who was supposed to know you so intimately has to be reminded over and over again how you choose to spell your own name, or when a stepmother who maybe you never let in enough to really know you at all stops caring if *Traci* is right or not.

As I walked toward Ingrid, I decided I wouldn't say anything about the *y*. I just breathed deep and kept on. I guess when someone is holding up a sign with your name on it, that's really the only thing you can do.

a conversation with
traci foust about ocd

You describe your earliest symptoms of OCD as starting at age seven. Is that typical? Is OCD more common in girls or boys?

According to the National Institute of Mental Health, the mean onset age of OCD is nine. Girls are twice as likely as boys to develop symptoms. I think my behaviors started just before I turned eight. My fascination with making sure food was properly wrapped and worrying about germs on the kitchen counter are pretty common in kids who are showing symptoms but can't yet voice the idea that something isn't right.

So you think most kids who are beginning to show signs of OCD are aware that there's a problem?

Maybe not at first, but for me, I used my friends and family as a gauge. I didn't see anyone in my house pull out strands of their hair if the bologna wasn't sealed. When I went to a friend's it only took a few minutes to see that washing your hands with Ajax wasn't something "regular" people did.

Is there anything that sparks OCD? Is it an underlying symptom of something else, like post-traumatic stress disorder (PTSD)?

Not usually, no. Post-traumatic stress disorder can certainly trigger many of the same physical manifestations as OCD, such as the over-whelming feelings of guilt and worry that someone will die or become ill because you didn't touch the light switches twenty times each before going to bed. But OCD falls in the same class as generalized anxiety disorder, meaning there really doesn't have to be just one incident that you can pinpoint and say, "That's when it began." However, the repetitive motions or "checks and tics," such as when I had to snap my fingers after saying the word *God*, or how some OCD sufferers have to click their tongues, touch objects repetitively, or cough after certain words; those behaviors fall under the same body symptoms as Tourette's syndrome, and can best be described as a sort of soothing mechanism when high anxiety approaches. The brain experiences a sensory overload and the body uses motion to calm itself. Like a baby rocking back and forth or a cat purring.

With a topic as sensitive and personal as mental health, was there a time, when writing the book, that you worried about revealing too much?

Of course. Especially when it came time to reveal parts of myself that I had once felt so ashamed of. Such as the times I drank NyQuil and took antihistamines—doing those things to quiet the voice in my head seemed like such a cop-out. Writing about getting on prescription medication was difficult as well. There's such a stigma attached to that sort of thing.

On that note, tell us how it feels to have so many people know you take "drugs."

First off, it's important to understand about how the "drugs" work. (I don't mind calling my medication *drugs* because, come on, that's what they are.) But something that gets me a little hot and bothered—that I run into quite a bit—is the idea that antidepressants are addictive. *They're not.* They are non-narcotics and don't stimulate the same receptors of the brain as, say, an opiate-based drug would, or a tranquilizer. Without going into a whole science lesson, let me give you a scenario that a doctor gave me (I use this one all the time, so I put it in the book): Someone with diabetes has a sick pancreas, in that this organ cannot properly produce or maintain the amount of insulin needed to keep blood sugar levels normal. When a diabetic injects insulin they are simply putting into their bodies what their pancreas should be taking care of. With that in mind, think of antidepressants as helping the neurotransmitters in the brain to properly carry serotonin back and forth to one another. Without the appropriate distribution of serotonin between neurotransmitters, the body cannot regulate the "good-mood hormone" called dopamine. When an antidepressant is introduced to the brain, it takes two to six weeks for your body to adjust. It's not like you take a pill and hooray! Happy sunshine days! Not at all. But if a pill like that ever comes out, I'm telling you, I'll be the first one on the list for the clinical trial.

You mentioned the stigma attached to being on medication. How do you deal with that now?

I have learned that when it comes to the matter of my health, of taking care of my sanity, the last thing I can worry about is what other people think. When I was in group therapy, as I mentioned in the book, I met so many people from all different walks of life, all different social classes. Most of them had just started their medication and had the fear of being "found out." But they were all there to get better. *We* were all there to get better. There just comes a time when you have to say screw it, I need to get my life in control, who cares what everyone thinks? Hell, who cares what *anyone* thinks?

Do you ever wonder if starting the medication at an earlier age would've changed things for you? Maybe things would have been easier if you'd had that kind of help early on.

In the eighties, when serotonin medication (SSRI = selective serotonin reuptake inhibitor) was just making its way out of the lab, there were no studies of side effects in patients under eighteen years of age, so who knows. It's difficult, actually, to try and think what my life would've been like had I not hit those peaks and valleys and just muddled through it with cognitive therapy. There's got to be a certain amount of crap you have to go through in order to look back and see how far you've come. So I guess I'm saying, no, I wouldn't change anything.

Cognitive therapy, or "talk" therapy. How does that differ from just taking medication and how did it help you?

Well, for one, and I think the biggest reason, is that talking out what was going on in my head made me feel like I wasn't alone. Sure, there were times when I felt as if I wasn't getting much from therapy. I think anyone who spends eighty bucks an hour to sit on a sofa and talk questions whether or not they're doing the right thing, but for the most part I can't imagine getting help for anxiety and depression without having someone listen to what I was going through. Sitting in front of someone who didn't know me was scary at first, but I just wanted so much to get better, I had to keep telling myself that this person, eighty bucks an hour or not, was truly there for my benefit.

What parts of OCD and depression linger in your life today?

In reality I have to say that most of my irrational thoughts are still there. They're just not active. I think most people with OCD are aware of "something" under the surface. You just have to know that it takes work—hard work—to keep them down. I wanted to do the work. I wanted to get better. Of course there were many days when it was so damn exhausting to talk out my feelings or write in my journal or repeat another stupid affirmation, but more than anything else I wanted to get better. I've gone through school, got married, I have four sons, I've traveled to so many exciting places, and I truly believe I made this happen because I have continually stayed on my medication and have kept up with cognitive therapy.

What do you mean exactly by your OCD being under the surface?

Just as I had found out in my early stages of therapy about anxiety problems always being there, how so many people with OCD always felt something wasn't right, it really helped me to accept that the core of OCD (having a personality that is prone to anxiety) may always be there. Rising above the stigma of mental illness (which is a fancy way of saying people are ignorant and you just have to deal with their crap) means that you have to say, Okay, I'm getting better, I can see that I'm getting better, I'm going to school, I'm holding down a job and raising a family—but I always have to remember that my brain is hardwired to be hypersensitive. This doesn't mean I'm weak or weird. It only means I have to do a little more work than someone without OCD would have to do to keep their thoughts in balance. I can go for months (and I have many times) without a single symptom, then something might cause me a little extra worry—the swine flu hoopla in 2009–10 is a good example here: there were several weeks when I couldn't use a public restroom or stand in a queue without feeling like I was going to break out into an anxiety attack. Then I'd go home, pull out my notebook I keep for these occasions, and write down the same affirmations I've been writing down since my first time in group.

Do you have any favorite affirmations?

Well, believe me, each and every one of them helps. Even the really corny ones like *I am safe in myself* and *there are no emergencies.* These were the ones I would carry around on sticky notes in my wallet and even write on my hand. But I think my favorite ones are those that end in *who cares?* Like, *I have a little more anxiety today than yesterday—WHO CARES!* Or, *if I have to leave the party because I'm getting anxious—WHO CARES!* We did this exercise in group where someone would stand up and the group leader would say things to this person like, "What would happen if you made a fool of yourself in front of everyone?" Then the whole crowd would shout, "Who cares!" And that's the kind of stuff that you have to drill into your brain. I've spent half my life working myself up into a panic because I was always so afraid what other people were going to think or do. You cannot imagine how freeing it is to let go of that.

What advice would you give to someone who is struggling with obsessive-compulsive disorder?

Ask questions and listen. Read and find out everything and I mean *everything* you can about what is happening to you. Never stop the journey into yourself, because it is on the path to educating yourself that you will see you are not alone. There are so many great resources to help you get hooked up with other people who are suffering. Utilize everything you can possibly imagine. When you know you're not alone, it takes off so much of the pressure. Surround yourself with people who are willing to listen. They don't necessarily have to understand, but talking about what you're going through is the key to listening to yourself. People with OCD and anxiety have a constant running "what if" dialogue in their heads. If you can use your mouth as an outlet, you get some of those irrational thoughts out of your mind. Also, don't blame anyone for what you think and feel. No one is in charge of your mind and your emotions except you.

When you look back on who you were then (in the book) and who you are now, what are some of the greatest differences/similarities?

Well, I think this kind of goes back to not blaming others for what is going on inside your head. I think the greatest difference between Then Me and Now Me would definitely be that when I was younger I was pretty angry. Not really understanding what was going on with my mind, like so many young people, OCD or not, I internalized everything. I blamed people for the way I was feeling because it's so hard when you have little life experience to embrace the idea that we are all responsible for the way we feel. Today I totally get that the only one who can make me better is me. Another thing I think is important—which took me a little longer to get—is that I could not use OCD and depression as a scapegoat to treat people badly or push them away. I see this often in people when a mental illness has really affected their personality. I saw this in me. And so much of it was about shame. When I didn't know how to properly handle myself I turned my guilt and shame into anger against other people. *Big* mistake. Because I'll tell you what, even though I made a choice that I was going to be the one responsible for my own healing, if I hadn't had the support and love of my friends and family I don't think I would have made much progress. In fact, I *know* I wouldn't have.

author's note

Dearest Reader:

Even with all the advancements in the practice of mental health medicine, there are still those in the general public, AKA: people who aren't big readers and/or thinkers, who enjoy sticking labels on folks who reach out for help with anxiety or depression issues. If you are thinking about improving your life and the lives of those who love you by seeking help for your problems, congratulations—you are living proof that we are, as many studies and health professionals suggest, on the higher end of the creative and IQ spectrum than those who claim to be "normal." Also, you should know this: On the journey to healing yourself, no matter whether you choose pharmaceutical and psychiatric care, alternative medicine (or a combination of both), get ready to hear this phrase slipping often from the mouths of those who may mean well but really have no idea of what they are talking about: "I'm glad I could fix my anxiety/depression on my own and that I never had to rely on any doctor or pill to help me." While this is admirable in a don't-ask-don't-tell / 1950s happy housewife sort of setting, I can almost guarantee that these sturdy people did *not* suffer from a clinical mental health illness. (That, or they figure anything Dr. Jack Daniel's can't cure isn't worth having.) In almost all cases, as with most people who are sick, help is needed in the process to get well. Never be afraid or ashamed to admit the fact that you need to talk to someone who can help you to help yourself. Don't let anyone sway you from reaching out to medical professionals (or anyone you feel comfortable with). Don't let anyone tell you that asking for help is weak or against God or that psychiatrists are all involved in some sort of pharmaceutical conspiracy plan or that it's disgraceful if you're not handling things all on your own. If you think you need help, please get it. Do whatever it takes to make yourself well. Don't let anyone or anything stand in the way of being the best person you can possibly be. You have a right to feel good and find happiness. Following are websites, books, or other resources to help you reach out for help with anxiety and depression. I have used all of these myself at one point or another, and I am always adding new resources to my self-help list because I truly believe that nothing gets taken care of by wishing it away. Read. Research. Talk and listen. But most important, love yourself for the smart, awesome, weird, and wonderful creature that you are.

Traci

resources

Midwest Center—Lucinda Bassett's program, Attacking Anxiety and Depression Workshop. www.stresscenter.com. I have used this and highly recommend it, especially if you have driving issues or live in an area where resources are limited or hard to get to.

The Anxiety & Phobia Workbook (third edition), Edmund J. Bourne, Ph.D. (New Harbinger Publications). A very detailed and useful book explaining several techniques of journaling your way out of anxiety and many phobias common with OCD. I still use lots of the writing exercises in this book.

Planetocd.com—Online chat rooms can be a tremendous source of strength and support. As with any chat site, please be smart and never give out your personal information.

The National Institute of Mental Health www.nimh.nih.gov—An enormous amount of information, including the latest developments from the Americans with Disability Act concerning mental health and advocacy programs.

OCD and OCD related disorders/Stanford School of Medicine ocd .stanford.edu. Easy-to-read articles on the latest treatments and research for obsessive compulsive and anxiety disorders from the department of psychiatry at Stanford School of Medicine. (This site offers open invitations for research volunteers.)*

Don't Panic: Taking Control of Anxiety Attacks, R. Reid Wilson, Ph.D. (Harper Paperbacks). Lots of relatable stories of others who have suffered and overcome panic attacks and OCD related behaviors.

From Panic to Power: Proven Techniques to Calm Your Anxieties, Conquer Your Fears, and Put You in Control of Your Life, Lucinda Bassett (Harper Paperbacks). I still refer to this book to help me when I'm in high anxiety phases. In a completely down-to-earth voice with heartbreaking and heart *healing* candidness, Lucinda tells her own story of suffering from panic attacks and how she conquered her debilitating phobias.

---

* Volunteering as part of a drug research study is a good way to begin the process of starting medication, especially for those who cannot afford medical care. Almost every major university in the country offers these programs, in most cases with closely monitored psychiatric consultations.

acknowledgments

There are so many people to thank, so many people who have made this journey as heavenly and hellish as the road into oneself should be. Laney Becker, you saw the story under the jokes and encouraged me to tell it. You kept me grounded and reminded me that nothing works without the work: Thank you, my pretty pit bull with dimples, for your patience and perfection. To my smart and funny editor, Abby Zidle, and the creative forces at Simon and Schuster: Thank you for your genius and letting me curse so much. My forever gratitude to the strong women who raised me: For my grandmother and her art of weaving beautiful words. You taught me how to listen—and tell everything again. To my sister, the ride of learning and loving is never smooth, but I am proud to have taken it with you. And for my beautiful mother who I know would be proud to read this book, I hope this shows you I was listening a little. To my brother and father who taught me that you really can make anything funny, and to Sandy for always asking to read my horrible poems. My deepest thank-you to Jens Ochlich for letting me grow as a writer and always encouraging me. To Elizabeth Jones and Renee Tompkins for being the first fans of all the stuff I forced you to read. Thank you to Thorn Sully for your hard work and for making me feel like a true artist, and to Marcella Maggio for your tireless efforts to get things done on the business end while making sure I stayed together. I love and respect you. Thank you to my mentors of talent: To Kerry and Eve, Kat Kessler, Rachel and Kyria, to Jack P., David O., J. Traig, Dave E. To K.C., your words and music changed me forever—I see you in my dreams. To Gerald Hedlund, Russ Shore, David Boyne, Kyle and Ed Coonce. To everyone in my writers' group for supporting me and "beating the crap" out of my stuff when I asked you to. To Derek, Becca, Adam, and everyone at Two Spoons, and to Sharron French for being there on such short notice. So many thanks go to Andrew Ervin, who read my zombie story and asked if I had anything I could send to him. You changed my life, Drew. To Wayne V., your support for this book (and for that awful time) means more than you'll ever know. To Julie Weinstein and Ann Bancroft for keeping me sane with our weekly chats of how much we love and hate what we do. Ginny Hitchcock, you encouraged me to change my life and find happiness in the woman I could be. I adore you, Crazy Cat Lady. Debbie Martin in MoTown, you gave me back my spirituality and showed me that truth is to be sought, not found. For Jenny Hardy, who kept my life together while I had (many) mini nervous breakdowns in my room. My aching arms and neck thank Asher and his healing hands, there is no chance I could have done this without you. A big always and forever thank-you to Tino, I prefer to think of us flying. To Lunisa, I will remember you with only love. To my soul sister Tina, you are such a part of who I am. Sonia Badilla, Tony still loves us, man. Thank you to my sons, for giving me my writing space and, hardly ever, complaining when we practically had to move in to the bookstore. I love you guys more than you will ever know. Thank you to Lucinda B., Dr. Palmer, Carole and Holly, and everyone at the Crossroads Center for encouraging me to heal myself (that and the meds). Thank you to Sharon Fincher for being an example of a true modern and strong woman.

One big thank-you to Mrs. G. at Bernal who believed in my writing and all the teachers/tutors who saw the good student underneath the class clown. Oh, and for the teacher who said I was too wrapped up in my own head to learn, as much as I loved detention in your class, I think being a published author rocks just a little harder than stapling your ditto packets. Finally, thank you a million times with my deepest love and gratitude to the un-sour Kraut who said, "Let me handle everything so you can do what you were meant to do." You are the reason this book (and the happiest part of my life so far) has come to be.